TOWARD A SOLUTION

Toward a Solution

By

ISRAEL GOLDSTEIN, M.A., D.H.L.

Essay Index Reprint Series

 BOOKS FOR LIBRARIES PRESS
FREEPORT, NEW YORK

First Published 1940
Reprinted 1970

INTERNATIONAL STANDARD BOOK NUMBER:
0-8369-1877-0

LIBRARY OF CONGRESS CATALOG CARD NUMBER:
79-128248

To

BERT, AVRAM AND VIVIAN

Contents

Toward a Solution

Contents

Studies in Backgrounds

In Memoriam

Foreword

FORTUNATE IS the man who knows with certainty whither he is headed and is sure that he is on the right road to his chosen goal. For such a man the problems of life are much simpler, though often more trying, than for most men. Tempting detours will not divert him. Obstacles will deter him only as long as it takes to overcome them. Stumbling blocks he will endeavor to convert into stepping stones. Whatever hardships he may have to endure, one peril which besets most men he will always be spared,—the peril of confusion.

It is a lot not granted to many in the confusing age in which we live. The more modern the age, the more complex its issues and its values become. It usually requires a crisis to clarify issues, sift out incidentals from determinants, and fix the hierarchy of values. Such a crisis now confronts us.

The issues of our civilization are becoming much simplified and clarified by the impact of Nazism, Fascism and Communism. In the process of meeting the impact, the resistance tends to be as concentrated as the attack itself. We are therefore becoming more conscious, more cognizant and more sensitive than we have been in a long time regarding our way of life and the goal toward which it is meant to lead.

Actually, the crisis has not as yet come sufficiently nigh to us here to compel a reorganization of our thinking. It is more the apprehension of a crisis than the crisis itself which we feel. Nevertheless it is enough to sharpen our perceptions.

The "we" herein referred to includes the American Jew who has been for a score of years both observer and participant in the civic and cultural engagements of the American community at the same time that he has felt, pondered and endeavored to solve the problems of his Jewish people. His task has been doubly difficult. Added to the complex of the problems of the age in which he lives have been the special problems attached to the Jew as Jew, his relation to his environment, his resistance to his modern persecutors, and his struggle for survival as a distinctive people.

Problems are more easily posed than solved. Yet the statement of the problem and its analysis, are indispensable steps toward its solution.

Toward a solution of our manifold problems as American Jews, the series of discussions comprising this volume are offered. They represent an attempt, however halting and inadequate, not only to state and analyze some of the fundamental problems, but also to ponder ends and to suggest means for attaining them. Several aspects of Jewish and general American life are included, —the place of Religion in the social order, the content of Democracy, the problem of Jewish-Christian relations, the role of the Synagogue in Jewish life and the relation of Palestine and Zionism to the solution of the Jewish problem.

The themes, instead of being treated as separate units, permeate the volume as a whole. The memorial tributes which are included have been selected both because of personal sentiment and because of their relevancy to the guiding themes. In addition several studies in backgrounds are presented as material helpful toward a more thorough understanding of some of the problems under consideration. Though relevant to the general purpose of the volume, these may be found of interest by those readers particularly who do not mind the prosaic stolidity of facts.

While the material deals mainly with Jewish themes, the larger issues of our time are implicitly if not explicitly contained. In the climate affecting Jewish life, there is more than a little barometric portent for the general climate affecting the life of the larger society. The spiritual kinship between Judaism and Christianity which is affirmed equally by those who love Democracy and by those who hate it, the utilization of anti-Semitism as a spearhead of attack by the sworn foes of Democracy, and the proven congeniality between the weal of Jewish life and the vitality of democratic institutions, constitute ample warrant for the observation that the focusing of attention upon the Jewish scene is not without consequence for the larger issues of our time. Indeed, the conditions and the problems of the Jewish people are in varying degrees the product, token, mirror, barometer, and touchstone of world conditions and problems.

If the contents of the volume seem to be weighted on the side of Palestine and Zionism, it is because of the deeply felt conviction that therein lies the center of gravity of the solution to the Jewish problem, a conviction which derives renewed cogency from the events and currents of our time.

The volume has been undertaken at the urging of friends who wished to see the writer's score of years in the Rabbinate marked by the publication of a representative number of his addresses and studies which would reflect his interests, views and public activities. There is an essential difference between the written and the spoken word, a difference both of style and of content. In deference to the circumstance which brought about the publication of the volume, the character of the spoken word has been retained as far as possible, even though it be at the expense of full-bodied development of ideas. The objective has been the idea rather than its amplification.

It is hoped that even those discussions which refer to dated events and situations may still hold some guidance and value today. Much as the settings may change, motivations and objectives are constants amid the variables, especially in the life of a people as shifting in its settings and as permanent in its ideals as ours.

If the material offered herein will suggest a few worthwhile aims and a hint of the proper directives as to the road toward a solution of some of the problems which perplex us, it will be to the writer, reward enough.

One parting thought attends the manuscript before it leaves the writer's hand. So rapidly and drastically is the world's political configuration changing before our eyes, and so potent is the threat to the form and content of our civilization, that one may be considered to be risking obsolescence in setting down in permanent type those discussions whose political and ideological premises may possibly be forced out of currency by the time the printed page is off the press.

It would be a cardinal sin against the spirit of any quest of worthwhile goals to halt the quest because hostile forces are seeking to impose different goals. On the contrary, the zest should grow with the peril. Life in our Democracy, if it is to have vital meaning and driving force, must be lived on the grand assumption, rooted in a deep faith, that the evil, destructive forces afflicting our civilization will meet the doom which they deserve.

ISRAEL GOLDSTEIN.

November 1, 1940.

The Price of Peace and Freedom

Substance of addresses delivered at the New York World's Fair, before the Federation of Jewish Women's Organizations, Temple of Religion, June 6, 1940, and at the celebration of "I Am an American" Day sponsored by the National Conference of Christians and Jews, Court of Peace, October 15, 1940.

The Price of Peace and Freedom

PEACE AND FREEDOM represent the "summum bonum" in the life of a people, the highest good toward which a commonwealth should direct its aim. Therefore, the extent to which these boons are attained is the yardstick by which the success of any form of government can be measured.

When we espouse Democracy as the best form of government, it is not an arbitrary insistence upon Democracy merely because our fathers thought it to be the best. Americans least of all are tradition-bound. Readily, nay eagerly, we change styles of dress, housing, locomotion, and communication; surely we should not continue a form of government merely because our fathers adopted it.

If we espouse Democracy today, it is because we today, viewing the world of our time and the conditions of our time, and observing the other forms of government which are being tried, have come to our own conclusions that Democracy is the best form of government for the reason that it offers the surest guarantees for the attainment of those goals which are the highest good of society, namely Peace and Freedom.

Obviously, if war and regimentation are set up as the highest good, as the Nazis and Fascists proclaim, then Democracy would be the most undesirable form of government. Therefore our proposition is vindicated by its converse as well as by its direct application.

There is the danger, however, lest these concepts of Peace and

Freedom be little more than high-sounding words, so far as most Americans are concerned. The difference between empty phrases and precious principles can be measured by the price men are willing to pay. It is important, therefore, to identify the concepts of Peace and Freedom in terms of what they have cost us in the past and the cost we must be ready to bear for their preservation today.

It is an old law of human nature that those things are dear to us for which we pay dearly. What is acquired at a small price is usually cheaply regarded. Is not the mother's love for the child in direct proportion to the pain and the sacrifice which the child has cost?

If the ideals of Peace and Freedom have meant more to our forebears in American history than they mean to us, it is because they have been called upon more than we to pay a price for these boons. To the generation which fashioned the Constitution and the Bill of Rights, Peace and Freedom meant much because they cost them much in comfort, blood, life itself. To the generation of the Civil War, Peace and Freedom meant much because they cost them much in comfort, blood, life itself. Our generation has not known crises comparable to those. The World War in which we entered in 1917 did not shake the American people to its foundations. It was not our struggle in the same sense as the Revolutionary War and the Civil War were our struggles.

For reasons which are quite understandable, therefore, the ideals of Peace and Freedom may not have been up to this point as vital to us as they were to our forebears.

We are, however, at a point now where the American people are beginning to realize that the threat to this continent by the anti-democratic forces of war and tyranny is not as remote as it seemed a year ago. As that awareness dawns upon us, the ideals of Peace and Freedom naturally begin to take on more vital meaning, a vitality of meaning in proportion to the danger by which they are periled from within and from without.

It is apparent now that we can no longer take our Peace and Freedom for granted as easy blessings which fall like the gentle dew. It is becoming clearer every day that these are boons which must be safeguarded lest they disappear and for the maintenance of which a price must be paid. Are we ready to pay the price? What is the price of Freedom?

The first price of Freedom is self-discipline. A sensible parent would not permit a child the freedom to do as it pleased. He would postpone that gift until the child has been trained and has achieved at least a modicum of self-discipline. No American citizen deserves freedom of speech or action until he has himself well in hand as a human being.

Another price which has to be paid for Freedom is consideration for the rights of others. As the English political philosopher, Hobbes, once put it, it is the underlying premise implicit in the social contract, that the citizen has obligations as well as rights. The principle has been recently stated in a more homespun manner by someone who said, "My freedom to swing my arm ends where the other fellow's nose begins."

A third requisite, perhaps it should be listed first, is the primacy of our national interests versus the national interests of any other nation. In a well-ordered world there would be no conflict between our interests and the interests of any other nation. Certainly that is true of the United States more than of any other people because of the vast expanse and the untold resources of our continent. But, viewing the kind of world in which we are living today, conflicts between us and other nations are not beyond the realm of possibility. Therefore, it is relevant to affirm the principle of the primacy of our national interests.

If the Communist in our midst admits, or if it can be established beyond the peradventure of a doubt, that in case of a conflict between the United States and Soviet Russia, he would give his prior allegiance to Soviet Russia, he is not entitled to the prerogatives of freedom here. If the Nazi in our midst admits, or if it can be established beyond the peradventure of a doubt, that in case of a conflict between the United States and Nazi Germany, he would give his prior allegiance to Germany, he is not entitled to the prerogatives of freedom here. The "fifth column" is not entitled to anything at the hands of American democracy except contempt and expulsion.

What is the price of Peace? What should we be ready to pay for that boon?

The answer which comes first to mind is,—adequate national defense. True enough, but how many of us realize what cost it will entail to every man and woman, whether they pay taxes directly, or indirectly through rent and other items in the cost of living? We must be prepared for substantial sacrifices, especially those of us who are fortunate enough to be able to carry the burden of taxation. We should be more than willing. We should be grateful if we are among those who are able to carry the burden.

Our national defenses will require more than money. They will require manpower. Universal military service is a new strange concept for peacetime America. Yet it is the inevitable corollary of the proposition that we are not quarantined from the danger of war and invasion. If we accept the premise that the danger of war is not remote, that the two oceans do not render us immune to attack, and that countries to the south of us may be used by an enemy as a springboard of attack, there is no alternative but universal conscription for training and service in our manifold defense program as a necessary part of our national self-protection.

Certain safeguards, however, must be provided in order to remove misgivings which properly agitate many of the youth. The selection of men for the various types of training must be broad and democratic, ensuring that wealth will not be used to win exemptions. The wage scale for those who will be conscripted should be made more commensurate with an adequate minimum standard of living than the scale being now proposed. The youth of America would feel reassured if the government's demands upon material resources would be no less rigorous than those upon human life. Wisely and democratically administered, the conscription of our manpower and of our economic wealth to the extent that it may be deemed necessary, may toughen the fiber of our democracy.

Equally important for our national defense, perhaps even more important than military defenses, is national unity. America must beware of those who are using the slogan of unity as a cloak behind which they are actually promoting the very opposite of national unity. The caution which is needed today is against any effort to stir up suspicion and ill-will between American and American on the basis of race or creed. There may be legitimate differences between men and groups on the basis of economic interests or on the basis of political party interests, but there cannot be any legitimate differences between men and groups on the basis of racial or religious distinctions. Those who are exploiting such differences have ulterior ends in mind which are disastrous to the cause of national unity. By this time, the "Trojan horse" technique in Hitler's program of world conquest has become all too transparent. Anti-Semitism has been the favorite and the most successful of "Trojan horses". Let America be on guard against this technique for the disruption of its national unity.

Peace means more than the absence of war. The Hebrew word "Shalom" is much more descriptive of what Peace really connotes. It means integrity and well-being, balance and harmony. It is a broad subject with ramifications extending into the whole problem of economic justice, employment, housing and all the other indispensables of decent livelihood. Men will fight to defend what they have at stake, the things that give their lives content and value. A nation in which a large portion of the citizenry is underprivileged, is built upon a structural fault which may not successfully withstand the strain of unusual stress.

Just as Peace means more than the absence of war, Freedom

means more than the absence of tyranny. The freedom of the artist has worthwhile meaning only if it leads to creative self-expression which enriches not only his own life, but the life of the community as a whole. The freedom of the citizen too should lead to creative self-expression, enriching not only his own life, but the life of the community.

What is this self which Americans should express? What place should the diverse cultures constituting America have in the national self-expression? How is Religion related to all these considerations? These and other questions germane to the theme, can only be hinted at here. The posing of the questions points to the duty of seeking the realities behind phrases.

The value of our democratic way of life must be so convincing to the majority of the people that they would consider it to be worth defending at all costs, worth every sacrifice.

In intellectual as well as in lay quarters there is a good deal of discussion about the ideological challenge of the Nazi-Fascist forces. The amazement at their military successes is paralleled by an awe of the philosophy which they have harnessed to their war chariots.

The situation can bear sober analysis. It would be profitable to determine whether it is the Nazi-Fascist ideology which is responsible for their military successes or whether their achievements may be accounted for by other factors which are not necessarily related to the set of ideas and standards which they have dinned into the ears of their own people and of the world. We must be on guard against becoming "conditioned" by two sets of phenomena which may exist co-ordinately without being actually and essentially interdependent as cause and effect.

What is the secret of Nazi Germany's successful aggressions? It is a genius for organization and efficiency coupled with daring and foresight, propelled by the psychological dynamic of a persecution complex labeled "Versailles," which has been cultivated in the minds of the German people by their Nazi leaders.

On the other hand, the people of England and France lacked a corresponding dynamic because they had emerged the victors from the last war, and their leaders were no match for the Germans in the capacity for organization and efficiency, daring and foresight. Even if they had possessed these qualities potentially, their actual situation or the way they felt about it was not such as to demand and evoke these qualities.

Moreover, long before 1933 or 1919, the Germans were credited with extraordinary talents of organization and efficiency. It should not be forgotten that they came near to winning the last war, and only the entry of the United States on the side of the Allies turned the tide. That was not Hitler's Germany but the Kaiser's Germany whose political and religious philosophy, on the whole, though there were exceptions, represented the conventional views of Western Europe at that period.

Let it also be remembered that in England and France since 1933 there were voices which sounded warnings against Hitler, which pointed out the dangerous potentials of his policy, opposed "appeasement," when he marched into the Rhineland, then into Austria, cautioned against accepting at face value his protestations and his promises, and urged strong rearmament to meet the menace in the offing. Those warning voices were unheeded by the ruling parties which, according to the most charitable view of the situation, were timid, vaccilating and short-sighted. That is the best that can be said for the men in positions of authority during those years. There is reason to believe, however, that some of these leaders were taken in by Hitler's pose as the arch enemy of Communism and truckled to him in the hope that he would turn Germany's might upon Communist Russia. The majority of the English and French peoples were apparently satisfied with their leaders and their policies. Otherwise, being citizens of a democracy, they could have turned them out of office. The mood of the people as of the leaders was one of complacency and appeasement, due to a variety of factors including the psychological aftermath of a victorious war.

Churchill was one of the protesting voices. It is no accident that he was singled out as the target of Hitler's special wrath. He foresaw and forewarned, but was not heeded. What would have happened if in the years between 1933 and 1939, Churchill had been the Prime Minister of England heading a Cabinet composed of Eden, Attlee, Morrison, Greenwood, Duff-Cooper, Bevin, and other kindred spirits? The aggressions upon Ethiopia, Austria, Spain and Czechoslovakia, rehearsals and preludes for the war of 1939, would probably never have materialized. In any event, England, and correspondingly France under similar circumstances, would be infinitely better prepared today to cope with Nazi Germany.

What would have happened if General Gamelin's strategy would have been more daring, or if the Maginot line had been extended farther toward Belgium, or if Germany's "fifth column" in France had been ferreted out more searchingly? The story would probably have been a different one.

Is it to be assumed that these faults are inherent in Democracy?

Even today, ten thousand airplanes might spell the difference between defeat and victory for the democracies, or between nearby victory and ultimate victory after a prolonged conflict. If the issue of the struggle can be reduced to a matter of ten thousand additional airplanes and to a problem of efficiency and organization, daring and foresight, what happens to the thesis regarding Nazi ideology? Are anti-Semitism, anti-Christianity, anti-culture, anti-labor, and the degradation of woman's position, the new and "revolutionary" recipes for national strength? Spain was at the height of its glory four centuries ago. Would it have been logical to draw the inference then that the Inquisition was the formula for national success?

Nazi ideology is a technique which did indeed serve a useful purpose. Inside Germany, it has proved to be a useful technique in preparing for the war which was to avenge the defeat of 1919. Outside Germany, the anti-Communist slogan was the technique for screening the real aim, which was expansion and conquest, while the race cult was used to good advantage, economically and psychologically inside Germany, and as a means of holding the allegiance of German nuclei outside Germany. When it became necessary to safeguard the eastern borders, the anti-Communist slogan was dropped, and Hitler and Stalin became friends. Conceivably the "Aryan" cult may also be "soft-pedaled" if necessity should dictate it.

To mistake an expedient for a philosophy is to accept the Nazis at their word. To credit the Nazi set of doctrines with cosmic potency, as if they were the universal formulas for national success, is to permit ourselves to be "conditioned" by a specious chain of cause and effect. We may be expected to be somewhat more discerning.

The question is, can efficiency and organization, daring and foresight, which are necessary for self-defense, exist in a democracy side by side with freedom? The answer which suggests itself is two-fold. Daring and foresight is an attribute of men, not of systems of government. Efficiency and organization, it must be admitted, may be more readily achieved in a regimented, totalitarianized state, but they can be achieved in a democracy when a patriotic people, led by daring and farseeing leaders and capable of making sacrifices, are ready of their own free will and through their democratically elected legislators to yield some of their liberties in order to retain the bulk of them.

Much is being said about the danger of losing our freedom in the process of defending it. The converse of the proposition, however, needs also to be recognized, namely, that in the face of Nazi ambitions of world hegemony there is the danger of losing our present form of government, if not our sovereignty,—and with it our freedom altogether, if we arbitrarily refuse to yield a fraction of our prerogatives in order to safeguard the general area of our liberties.

What is to be the guiding formula? Obviously, as much freedom as is consistent with the main task. Who is to define the amount and determine the consistency? There can be no arbitrary definition. Every proposal to curtail any of the prerogatives of a free Democracy must be vigilantly scrutinized. We must be realistic enough, however, to distinguish between freedom as a whole and freedom in a particular detail. There is a hierarchy of values. For the sake of safeguarding the topmost values, those in the lower scale may have to be temporarily yielded. Otherwise, by arbitrary, undiscriminating rigidity, we are in danger of losing the power to defend our liberties as a whole. To urge such a policy would be a counsel of unwitting naïveté or malicious treachery.

To what conclusion does the analysis lead? Only in one respect, namely, national efficiency and organization, is a democracy at a disadvantage in competition with a regimented totalitarian dictatorship. It is a disadvantage which can, however, be overcome, when there is daring and farsighted leadership, and a patriotic citizenry willing to make the necessary sacrifices.

On the other hand, looking at the problem again from the standpoint of national self-defense, there are advantages inherent in a democracy which more than make up for the admitted disadvantage. Chief of these, is the spiritual fiber which freedom cultivates. It is more than an intangible asset. It is as important as armaments. It determines the staying quality, the morale of a people in a long conflict. It decides who is to win the last battle.

The discussion which has been ventured is of more than academic interest or vicarious interest. It touches vitally the immediate and ultimate welfare of the American people.

Nothing that has happened abroad should weaken our faith in Democracy. The disasters which have befallen England and France thus far in the war are explainable by factors which are not inherent in the essence of Democracy. We here in the United States can and must learn from the mistakes of our sister democracies. Fortunately we still have time in which to put those lessons into practice.

Once the ideology of Nazism is understood for what it is, and not for what it purports to be, it loses completely whatever impressiveness it may exercise upon those who stand in awe of it. Then, divested of its pretentiousness, it appears in its naked ugliness, the hypostasis of all the demonic forces lurking in the lowest recesses of human nature. It is not the first time, nor is it to be the last, when the beast in man strains for domination. The only thing new about it is its self-exaltation into the intellectual plane of philosophical formulations. Attila went about his ruthless business without pose or pretense. Hitler has dressed up his beast, with the help of Nietzsche, in modern clothes. The Nazi-Fascist ideology is a convenient utilitarian device for those whose program is conquest, expansion, war.

For us Americans the democratic way of life is not a device made to order for the purpose of expansion, conquest and war. It is our ennobling heritage which has been tested in a century and a half of national policy, through war and peace, and has not been found wanting.

The history of the United States is the most exciting of all national annals. Ours was a New World in more than one sense. It was a newly discovered continent. It was colonized by men and women who by their coming to the new shores broke with their own past and with many of the traditions of the old society. They and their offspring were psychologically as well as physically free to re-evaluate the social and political conventions of the Old World. They kept what they deemed worthwhile and rejected what they considered obsolete.

In the American Revolution the New World consciousness came into its own, politically. Making due allowances for economic motivations and configurations, it still cannot be gainsaid that the American Revolution was a momentous spiritual adventure comparable to the noblest and most ennobling experiences of the human race. It was the second time in history that a new nation was founded in a set of ideals. The first was the nation of Israel.

This republic of ours was founded with a purpose and a mission, consisting both of protest and affirmation. These were not an afterthought or a post facto rationalization, but an initial propelling motivation.

In the world of stress and challenge in which we live, when the ideas and ideals of Democracy are ridiculed and repudiated in foreign lands and spurned by some who dwell within our own shores, they derive new cogency from the menace of the anti-democratic forces. They are not dead letters but living flaming truths for our time.

We need to recapture the spiritual excitement, the dynamics of idealism, which moved the founders of this nation. Our shining armor has tarnished with the passage of a century and a half, but only the surface has become dulled. With little effort it can be made bright again. We need only to be reminded. The metal is sound, and uncorroded.

We are being told that the new order which threatens to dominate Europe today is a "revolution." No one can predict how far it will go or how long it will endure. Sooner or later it must collapse, because it shackles the mind and chains the spirit of man. Against that kind of "revolution" we Americans set our way of life conceived in a revolution which was marked by the unshackling of fetters which chained the human spirit.

As soon as we become sufficiently aware of what we have at stake in the present world crisis we shall realize that no sacrifice is too high a price to pay for our Peace and Freedom.

Lincoln's Guidance for Our Time

Address to a Negro Congregation, delivered at the St. James Presbyterian Church, New York, February 13, 1938.

Lincoln's Guidance for Our Time

Today when the American people honors the noblest son whom the American soil and the American nation have reared, every group seeks to identify itself as closely as possible with the subject and the theme. The Jew feels a special sense of kinship.

When Abraham Lincoln lived, the Jewish population in the United States was small compared to its numbers today. There were less Jews in the whole country than there are today in the Bronx alone. Yet, among that small group Lincoln found a few of his earliest and staunchest friends, and many of his later and most enthusiastic supporters.

Abraham Kohn, a Chicago merchant, president of the local Synagogue, presented Lincoln upon his election, with a silk flag, which he had made with his own hands, and which bore in its folds, in Hebrew characters, the verses from the first chapter of the Book of Joshua, ending with the words: "Be strong and of good courage, for the Lord thy God is with thee wheresoever thou goest!" In the great national issues which shook this nation to its foundations, the Jews of America were preponderantly on the side of Lincoln. A Baltimore Rabbi was driven from the city because he dared to lift his voice in denunciation of slavery.

Since the death of the great Emancipator, as year after year on the anniversary of his birth the American people paid a tribute to his memory, there came forth from scores of Jewish pulpits and platforms, Jewish appreciations of Lincoln which were more than formal eulogies. The utterances revealed understanding aglow with love, and reverence touched with passion. America's foremost student on the subject of Lincoln as well as foremost collector of Lincolniana, was a Jew, Emanuel Hertz, a New York lawyer, brother of the Chief Rabbi of England. One of the best essays on Lincoln written in the English language was written by the former head of the Jewish Theological Seminary of America, the late Professor Solomon Schechter, who fell in love with the subject long before he came to these shores.

The interest of Jews in Lincoln is not a casual or accidental circumstance. It is an affinity between the soul of the Jew and the soul of one who breathed ideals which the Jew has been taught to cherish above all things on earth.

Our own history as a nation begins with the story of emancipation from the bondage of Egypt. Our first Commandment is, "I am the Lord thy God, who brought thee out of the land of Egypt, out of the house of bondage." The historic memory of our race has been kept ever fresh touching that episode of slavery and emancipation which marked the beginnings of our nationhood. The commandment to observe the Sabbath has for one of its premises, the need for remembering that we who were once slaves, must not now enslave ourselves to work without surcease, and that not only for ourselves but also for those who are employed by us there must be a Sabbath of rest and recreation. Throughout our Bible and our Prayerbook, the days of Egyptian bondage are recalled for the purpose of keeping us ever mindful of our responsibilities as free men, to use our liberty not for base ends but for high purposes, and with a view also to cultivating in ourselves sympathy for the oppressed and the downtrodden.

The life of Lincoln abounds so much in rich human material that the temptation is great to cull episodes from his biography, anecdotes from his rich repertory, and memorable sentences from his masterly utterances. The temptation will be resisted not only because most Americans are probably familiar with the best of these, but especially because it is desirable to dwell upon today rather than upon yesterday, to discuss some of our present problems in the light of what Lincoln means and should mean to us.

If Abraham Lincoln were alive today and could look with his deep discerning eyes upon this generation of American life, what would he think, how would he feel about the fruits of his labors? Would he feel satisfied that the work of his hands has been well established, that the race he emancipated is truly emancipated, and that the nation he taught to break the fetters of bondage, has learned the lesson?

We see millions of the race which Lincoln freed, still held in bondage, not legal bondage, but economic bondage, political bondage, educational bondage and social bondage.

The Fifteenth Amendment to our Constitution guarantees political equality to citizens of all races and creeds. "The right of citizens of the United States to vote shall not be denied or abridged by the United States or by any State on account of race, color, or previous conditions of servitude." Yet there are States in the Union which still disfranchise millions of men and women, getting around the law by means of literacy and property qualifications which in effect are aimed against the Negro.

There are educational institutions, supported in whole or in part by public funds derived from taxes in which not only the property-owner but the rent-payer pays his share, which practice unofficial restrictions, making the road to knowledge and culture ten times harder for the Negro than it need be. In some of our States thousands of Negro children of school age are without any school facilities.

There are courts of law where every man should be guaranteed the right to trial by a jury of his peers, which by technicalities circumvent the purpose of the law and rob the downtrodden of the justice due them.

Worst of all is the record of economic discrimination. It is shameful enough in normal times, condemning members of one race more than any other, to virtual peonage. The plantation system with its share-croppers and tenant farmers is the nearest thing to feudalism that we have on this continent. As for those who are lucky enough to live in happier places, even they, with few exceptions, are almost doomed from birth to the lowest jobs and the most menial labor. Their gifted sons and daughters have to be ten times as gifted as their white-skinned neighbors, in order to receive equal consideration. When times become abnormal, as they have been for the past number of years, the blow falls most heavily upon this denied and underprivileged group. They are the first to lose their jobs, the last to be reinstated.

In the "submerged third of our population," they are the submerged of the submerged. They are the victims of a vicious circle. We deny them decent housing and then we berate them for untidiness. We deny them employment, and then we chide them for lawlessness.

If, in spite of its handicaps this downtrodden and under-privileged group has produced Booker T. Washington, friend of Theodore Roosevelt, W. E. B. Dubois, colleague of philosophers, Major Moton, peer of educators, Roland Hayes, Paul Robeson and Marian Anderson, pre-eminent among singers, Paul Dunbar and Langston Hughes, noted among poets, Harry T. Burleigh, famed among musical composers, Richard B. Harrison, revered among actors, Edward Bannister and Henry Tanner, hailed among painters, Metta Warwick Fuller, acclaimed among sculptors, it is not only a tribute to what has been achieved, but it is also a golden promise of how much more the Negro race might do for American civilization if it were given an equal chance.

We must not close our eyes to social discrimination, but social discrimination, however deplorable, is not as fundamental as other injustices. I cannot compel my neighbor to love me, to fraternize with me, to admit me to his clubs or to his churches. It is regrettable indeed, but it can be borne by a people which has dignity and self-respect, and a bit of a sense of humor. There is more truth than fiction in the story which is related about a Negro who came to the clergyman of a fashionable Church and announced that he wished to become a member of the Congregation. The pastor greeted him kindly, but suggested that possibly he would be happier while worshiping among his own people. The applicant was not to be dissuaded. He said that he was certain that that was the Church he wanted to join. As a final resort, the clergyman advised him to go home and pray for guidance in his decision. A week later the Negro called again. "You were right," he said, "I've decided not to join. I talked it over with God, and He told me, 'Give up the notion, Robert, I've been trying to get into that Church for five years myself.'"

Social discrimination, painful as it is, can be borne. Political disfranchisement, economic oppression and educational discrimination, however, are violations of fundamental human rights. To demand these rights is to demand nothing more than justice. America injures itself when it denies justice to one-tenth of its population. It injures that which is best and highest in its own tradition, the principle of the equality of all races and creeds.

There are nations in Europe today, practicing discrimination, oppression and persecution against racial minorities within their borders, who when some of our spokesmen rebuke them for their uncivilized behavior, scoff at us and say, "What about your treatment of the Negro? Clean your own house first!"

Their rejoinder is on the face of it insincere, for they would persist in their barbarism, regardless of how other countries treat their minorities. Why should our great nation, however, have this blemish against its fair name?

The problem of minorities is the touchstone of American Democracy. The weaker and the more helpless the minority, the more significant is the test. A nation which abuses its minority groups, be they racial or religious minorities, is not a wholesome nation. "Ill fares the land, to hastening ills a prey, where wealth accumulates and men decay."

If Abraham Lincoln were alive today, he would probably say to his fellow Americans, in the simple grandeur of his own phrase and spirit, that the job he began is far from finished. He might write another Emancipation Proclamation, proclaiming the right of every human being not only to equality in law but to equality in fact, to an equal right to earn a livelihood for his family, to educate his children and to take part in the affairs of government.

Minority rights are the responsibility of the majority. It is they who have the power to grant them or to deny them. I pray that the American people may have the spiritual insight to see with the eyes of Lincoln, the compassion to feel with the heart of Lincoln, and the moral force to act with the conscience of Lincoln.

There is also, however, a task which the minority can do for itself, to bring about the betterment of its lot. An ancient Hebrew sage, Rabbi Hillel, who was gentle, patient and wise as was Lincoln, handed down a maxim, "If I do not help myself, how can I expect others to help me, and if I depend only upon myself, what am I?"

A minority group can help itself in large measure. It can strive by self-criticism and self-discipline to raise the level of its conduct and the tone of its living to the highest point possible within the limitations imposed upon it. The better its own quality, the less pretext is offered the unfriendly neighbor to practice his unfriendliness. It can seek to make the fullest use of such limited opportunities as may exist for political suffrage, education and self-improvement.

The members of a minority group, wherever they have the right to vote, can make effective use of that great American weapon of peace, the ballot, in demanding their rights. By intelligent use of the ballot they can elect liberal, progressive and forward-looking officials and reject candidates for public office who evade important issues and screen themselves behind high-sounding but empty slogans. They can give serious thought to the question of whether our economic order altogether cannot be so improved as to avoid the terrible cycles of depression and unemployment which visit their tragedies most heavily upon the minorities and make the atmosphere rife for inter-group irritations and frictions. When there are not enough jobs to go around, and not enough livelihood for all, men become surly; and when men become surly it does not take much to fan sparks of prejudice into flames of persecution. A sound economic order is the best guarantee of peace and goodwill. The ballot can be used to encourage every honest attempt for the improvement of the social order.

The members of a minority group should exercise their right of suffrage with extra care and special discernment. Because they have so much at stake, they must be more than ordinarily wary of the demagogue, especially in times such as these when the chaos throughout the world and our own economic uncertainties are making many of our people gullible to political "fakirs."

Anyone who aims to curb freedom of expression is not to be trusted by minority groups. Anyone who aims to restrain the freedom of workers to organize for collective bargaining, though he may be personally friendly to all races and creeds, represents a point of view which has in it seeds of danger to minorities though they may not be immediately apparent. Anyone who preaches against any minority race or creed is potentially a menace to all minority races and creeds, no matter how much he professes to love all the others.

These are a few self-helps which members of minority groups can exercise, and by exercising can contribute something to the solution of their problems. The time to try the ounce of prevention is when there is still time to do it.

Being a Jew helps me, I believe, to see and understand your problem all the more clearly, for the Jew too is a minority group subject to the hazards which are likely to affect the life of any minority.

It is helpful to review the contemporary scene in the vein both of criticism and self-criticism. The road to progress often leads through thorns of discontent. A chorus of "Hallelujahs" sometimes has the lulling effect of an anodyne. Occasionally, a frank confession is good for the soul. Therefore, as fellow

Americans speaking to one another, a frank avowal has been made that things are not all that they should be in the republic which bears the stamp of Lincoln.

We should be less than honest with ourselves, however, and less than fair to our beloved land, if we did not also avow on this great American day, that if some things are wrong with us there is much more that is right with us.

Where else do a hundred and thirty millions of human beings live under a government which governs with so little force? In what other land is there such freedom to worship in accordance with the dictates of conscience? What other nation is constituted of so many diverse elements bound together by a loyalty not of force but of choice? In what other country are political views so freely expressed, and where else can the Chief Executive of the nation be criticized by the humblest citizen with impunity? Among what other people does the worker, on the whole, enjoy a standard of living, including educational opportunities for his children, comparable to that of the American worker?

The goose-step, the firing squad, and the concentration camp are not normal to our way of living. Lynching is on the decline. The conscience of our nation, as a whole, is revolted by inhuman and subhuman practices.

Our nation, with all its imperfections, is still the greatest republic on the face of the earth.

Because our portion has fallen in these pleasant places, we dare to hope that here in the America of Abraham Lincoln, more than anywhere else, wrongs can be righted and crooked paths can be made straight.

Facing a Bankrupt Age:
Is Man a Failure?

Substance of an address delivered at the Commencement Day Exercises of the Jewish Theological Seminary of America, New York, June 5, 1932.

Facing a Bankrupt Age: Is Man a Failure?

A GENERATION AGO WE faced a world which was sure and confident. It was sure that science held the key to the salvation of the race. It was sure that machines would banish poverty from off the face of the earth, and would make happiness epidemic. It was sure that our economic system was impregnable. Democracies were confident that the democratic government was the only successful form of government and the only form which could endure. The major portion of the civilized world was sure that something good would come out of the World War. Our own America, like a young giant becoming aware of the full strength of his manhood, was in a mood of exuberant optimism. If one sounded a Cassandra note, he was charged with blindness. It was a world sure of itself and sure of its future, Spengler to the contrary notwithstanding.

Today, we face a world oppressed by a sense of bankruptcy and frustration. The faith of the western world in Democracy has wavered, as Nazi and Fascist regimes have marched from victory to victory. Man's machines have proved efficient to the point of Pyrrhic paradox. Truly the human race is in peril of dying of improvements. Our economic system has been found wanting. Climax to the disillusionment, the war to end wars has proved to have been the most futile carnage in history. Its sequel is now ravaging the face of the earth.

What of those who pinned their faith on science and invention as the saviors of mankind? New inventions, adding to the comforts of life and increasing its speed, are no longer hailed with apocalyptic enthusiasm, as it is realized that comfort and speed are not synonymous with happiness. The scientific fraternity has grown less sure of itself. The title of C. E. Ayres' book speaks volumes. It is called, "Science, The False Messiah." One of the keenest of our younger philosophers, Irwin Edman, discussing "The Contemporary and His Soul," avows that science, which only yesterday, "was the god, whose thousand altars were in the laboratory and whose prophets went by the names of chemists, biologists, and physicists . . . has lost its majesty. . . . It has not, nor does it pretend to any commandments. It can discover the formula for a poison gas but can give us no categorical imperative for the ends for which it is to be used."

The catalogue of disillusionment might be easily extended to include our educational systems, our social theories, and the whole gamut of our standardized procedures. We are no longer sure of anything.

Disillusionment is the mother of cynicism. Cynicism is the temper of our day. It has invaded our literature and our stage. A distinguished contemporary American dramatist, Robert Sherwood, in a solemn preface to one of his lightest comedies, "Reunion in Vienna," bares his soul when he says that the writing of comedies is for him an escape mechanism offering an escape from the deep despair which life and the world induce. "Looking about him," he says, "man sees a shell-torn No Man's Land filled with barbed wire entanglements, stench and uncertainty. Before him is black doubt, behind him is nothing but the ghastly wreckage of burned bridges." And, so, to find an escape, he pens comedies.

Cynicism has been known before as a way of life. It is the way of moral defeatism, or to use the modern term, "futilitarianism." There is another way, however, to face life, which is the extreme opposite of cynicism. It is the way of religion, faith in God, faith in man and faith in the future. It is the faith that mankind has been endowed by Providence with a capacity for spiritual development so that though at any particular moment, humanity may seem to be at a standstill or even in a lapse, yet, in the long range view, as measured by the One in whose eyes "a thousand years are but as yesterday," man's progress though slow, halting and oft interrupted, is, in the main, unmistakably forward.

In evaluating the progress of the human race, we need a sense of perspective. Man's culture of speech, writing, art, and social institutions, which make up the context of civilization, spans no more than six to ten thousand years. It is very recent, in comparison with the untold age of the human species.

Someone has said that if a postage stamp were pasted on the top of an Egyptian obelisk, the thickness of the stamp compared to the height of the obelisk, would represent the age of man's civilization compared to the total period of man's existence.

In the light of man's brief experience with civilization, he should not be judged too harshly.

Sometimes it is asked, "Why has man advanced intellectually and scientifically so much more rapidly than morally and spiritually? Why is it that the development of his mind has been so far ahead of the development of his character?"

It is because of an essential difference between the two aspects of life.

The achievements of mind, once established, usually remain. A medical cure once discovered, a scientific principle once proven, a practical invention once introduced, are permanent gains and serve as stepping stones for succeeding achievements. In the moral and spiritual life, however, emotions and instincts play a large part. These are, for the most part, hereditary. Every generation is therefore obliged to start with more or less the same handicaps. Every human is born with more or less the same bundle of instincts and impulses which condition his conduct, and impel him to greed, hatred, exploitation and war. Every generation tries to learn from the mistakes of its forebears and to improve upon the past, but it is inevitably a slow and difficult process.

Considering, therefore, the limitations both of human history and of human nature, it is man's successes rather than his failures which are noteworthy. Has he not during these few thousand years developed a conscience against human slavery, which in the ancient world was a recognized institution? Have not standards of labor improved? Has not woman's position risen? Has not international-mindedness progressed at least to the extent that there is an attempt, however weak and inadequate, to plan, even in the midst of war, a society of nations following the war, which might profit from the mistakes of the past?

These are only the first halting steps in a long road toward the desired goal. The important thing is the direction in which man's face is turned.

If there is no justification for exuberant conceit, neither is there justification for abject despair. If it cannot be said that man has succeeded, neither can it be said that he has failed. He is on the way, headed toward a fuller realization of his God-given possibilities. Only they have the right to be impatient who have faith in human progress.

In the broadest sense, this is Religion's message for our time. Let it be said for Religion, every Religion, that it promises a hopeful view of Man. To believe in God is to believe in a divine urge in Man to rise to ever higher levels.

Those of us who take a hopeful view of human nature feel stirred by these times. We feel that perhaps the terrible ordeals through which the world is passing just now, are the labor pains presaging the coming of a better age. Many have discarded the idea of a personal Messiah, but they dare to hope that the augury of a better day lies not in a man but in Man. We are not affrighted by social and economic changes, however drastic they may be. Rather do we welcome them if they will help to make life more abundant and more secure for the great masses of the people.

Such a faith provides an abiding sanction for the commandments of a moral and ethical life. The non-religious ethicist may cite the standard quotation from the Hebrew prophet, to show that even the prophet demanded nothing more than justice, mercy and humility, but he forgets the first part of that apostrophe, "What doth the Lord require of thee, O Man." Justice, mercy and humility, to the religious man, are divine imperatives. An ethical life, built upon the assurance of a divine sanction, is the one most likely to stand the test of time and of shifting fortune.

"Religion," to use the words of a professor of philosophy, Professor William P. Montague, who, though modern, is also something of a metaphysician, "is the faith, theoretical, practical and emotional, in something in Nature that is making for the values that we cherish." He devotes an entire book, "Belief Unbound," to proving the thesis that there is such a reality in nature which responds to man's highest postulates. That reality is God. The religionist invokes "my God and my Redeemer who lives."

Although the fundamental premise of religion is independent of philosophy or science, and can be neither proved nor disproved by the process of pure reasoning, as Immanuel Kant established more than a century ago, it is nevertheless strengthening to know that the best minds of the age are sympathetic to that premise upon which religion rests, namely, that God is. Sir Arthur Eddington, Sir James Jeans, Professor Whitehead and Professor Millikan, who are among the greatest scientific minds of the age, justify the belief in the reality of God and in the ethical concept of Free Will, as against the materialistic and mechanistic views of the universe. According to Jeans, the universe is the creation of mind, perhaps mind itself, "of course not of your individual mind or minds but of some great universal mind underlying and co-ordinating all minds." Eddington declares that "we are meant to fulfill something in our lives," and that back of the symbols in which reality now finds its logical expression, "lies a spirit in which truth has its shrine, with potentialities of self-fulfillment in its response to beauty and right."

These are cited not because philosophers and physicists can

make converts for God. Faith in God is primarily an intuition and only secondarily a logical deduction. It is well to know, however, and it is moreover our duty to know, that our religion is compatible with the best thought of the age.

It is not dogmatism which is urged. He who presumes to know the nature of the Deity is perhaps as much an atheist as he who denies His existence altogether, for how can the infinity of God be comprehensible to the finite human mind? Jewish tradition has found in the text, "I shall be that which I shall be," the safeguard against the pedantic theologian and the intransigent dogmatist. No religious system is as free from dogmatic impositions or as hospitable to independent formulation regarding the God concept as is Judaism. There is, moreover, an irreducible affirmation of belief, a point beyond which no theistic religion can go, and that is the belief that God is. Needless to say, it is the first affirmation of Judaism.

The Jew who died with the "Shema" on his lips did not die for a metaphor, and the Jew who stands in reverence at the "Kedushah," saying "Holy, holy is the Lord of Hosts, the whole earth is full of His glory," is not saluting a sociological hypothesis.

The Jewish people has endured upheavals and sinking spells quite as precarious as those which afflict the world today, but the Jewish people, as a people, has never turned cynic because it has never lost its faith in God.

Faith creates spiritual resources which no material disaster can destroy and which no economic crisis can crush. While defeatism paralyzes, Faith vitalizes effort and hope. It generates initiative and self-help, sustaining the confidence that under God's Providence, mankind will go forward, not backward.

To some who are sensitively attuned to the still small voice of tomorrow, it seems that there is going to be a reaction against the lack of faith, the sense of bankruptcy and frustration, the cynicism and "futilitarianism" which characterize the temper of the present age.

Joseph Wood Krutch, one of our most thoughtful cynics, in a book on "The Modern Temper," concedes the subtle force of the reaction against materialism and admits that if it should succeed, then the world would undergo another transformation hardly less complete than that which it underwent at the Renaissance, and that Religion might well flourish quite as luxuriantly as it did in former times.

It has been known in the past that disillusionment, the mother of cynicism, has sometimes proved to be the grandmother of faith. Many a great believer has come to God through the tortuous path of skepticism. There have been periods in history which saw the rebirth of religious fervor out of the womb of hopelessness and despair. It may be so again.

In the meantime, the remnant that will resist spiritual prostration will be the saving remnant. To join that company is the high challenge today.

Bar Kappara expounded the question, "What is the succinct text upon which all the essential principles of Judaism may be considered to hinge?" (Berakot, 63a.) We can afford to reiterate the fundamental question which the ancient Rabbi pondered, and to give the same answer, enlarging its original scope, so as to include not only Judaism but the spiritual basis of the whole of humanity.

The first principle upon which all of our work and hope must rest, is the verse from Proverbs, "In all thy ways acknowledge Him, and He will direct thy paths."

A Word of Comfort to
Czechoslovakians

Delivered before United Czechoslovakian Societies, Carnegie Hall, New York, October 1, 1938.

A Word of Comfort to Czechoslovakians

IT IS A PRIVILEGE, though a sad one, to add my voice as an American and as a Jew, to this symposium of sympathy with the victims of physical force.

As an American, I have felt a sense of pride that the father of the Czechoslovakian republic, Thomas Masaryk, had personal as well as spiritual ties with our republic, in the fact that he patterned the chart of his new republic while in this country, and in the fact that his role in the founding of his nation has been compared with the role of George Washington in the founding of the American nation.

As a Jew, I feel a sense of gratitude to Czechoslovakia because of its treatment of its Jewish citizens. The Jewish population there numbers three hundred and fifty thousand. They are represented in every important activity in the life of the republic,—in agriculture, commerce, industry, literature, science. Its best known man of letters is Franz Werfel. The Jews in Czechoslovakia are guaranteed minority rights by the constitution which has been drawn by Thomas Masaryk together with Eduard Benes. Of all the governments in Central and Eastern Europe which promised equal rights to Jewish minorities, the only one which has kept its promise has been Czechoslovakia. It has been free from anti-Semitism because it has been free from Fascism.

The Jews of Czechoslovakia have deep roots in that country. The Jewish community of Prague goes back to the tenth century. The old Synagogues, the old cemeteries, and the relics of the old Ghetto, including the old tower clock with Hebrew numerals, still stand as witnesses of a flourishing Jewish community which endured for thousands of years. Out of that community sprang the quaint legend of the Golem, that huge figure of clay into which the Rabbi of Prague is alleged to have inserted the mystic Name which gave it life, so that it became the mighty defender of persecuted Jewry; then one day when this robot ran amuck, the Rabbi had to withdraw the mystic word that had given it life, and the huge figure became inanimate clay again.

Perhaps the Golem would be an appropriate token of the state of Europe this first day of October, when soulless robots are on the march. October first will be remembered as a day when a valiant little republic fell victim to a Golem civilization.

In the capitals of Europe, there is jubilation that the day which threatened to be the beginning of a world war, witnesses peace instead of war. It is not difficult to understand the jubilation of wives who can have their husbands again, or parents and sons who can have each other again.

What is difficult to understand is the effort to make it appear as a great moral victory. No amount of sophistry or ratiocination can obscure the sad fact that this is not "peace with honor," as Chamberlain and Daladier termed it. It is conceivable that men may have to accept a situation under duress, but let them not defile the word "honor" by calling it "peace with honor." The title "honor" belongs only to one people in Europe today, to the Czechoslovakian people, whose steadfast courage, quiet heroism, and magnificent poise are without parallel. It is a sad commentary that such virtues should be thus rewarded.

One naturally looks for consolation in grief and affliction. The Czechoslovakian people hardly need our consolation. Their leaders have demonstrated by their words and the people by their bearing, that they know how to bear defeat as nobly as they have borne victory. We whose hopes of twenty years ago have been cruelly dashed, we need consolation.

We refuse to believe that this kind of terrible world will long endure. We believe that dictatorships, like the Golem, bear the seed of their own destruction. We believe in the ultimate vindication and triumph of Democracy. If it will not be in our time, it will be in our children's time. And when that day of Democracy's vindication will come, it will see the wrong of October 1, 1938, righted.

In the meantime, we trust that the Czechoslovakian people, consolidating its best and strongest elements, will maintain its integrity, its memories and its hopes.

Perhaps a spokesman of the Jewish people has a special right to utter a word of consolation and hope, seeing that the Jew is the victim of the same forces of reaction and of the same Golem civilization,—we are brothers in sorrow,—and seeing also that the Jewish people has lived to outlive its tormentors of the past.

Twenty-four hundred years ago the Jewish state of Palestine was destroyed by mighty Babylon. Seventy years later Babylon was conquered by Persia, and Judea was restored. Eighteen hundred and sixty-eight years ago the Jewish state was destroyed by Rome, then ruler of the world. The walls of Jerusalem were razed to the ground. The flower of Judea's youth were sold into slavery. The Jewish population was dispersed to the uttermost corners of the world. Jewish hope, however, was not destroyed. We still hope for the day when a Jewish State will arise in Palestine.

A people lives as long as its memories and hopes are alive.

A people that has been seared by sorrow, lashed by waves of misfortune, lacerated by nineteen centuries of affliction, but un-defeated, speaks on this dire October first to the spiritually un-defeated Czechoslovakian nation in the words of an ancient Hebrew prophet, "Comfort ye, Comfort ye my people."

Christian-Jewish Relations

Substance of addresses delivered before the Younger Churchmen, at the Knights of Columbus Club, December 7, 1929, and before the Conference of the Race Relations Commission of the Federal Council of Churches of Christ in America, at the Union Theological Seminary, New York, October 6, 1939.

Christian-Jewish Relations

IF NATIONAL UNITY SPELLS national strength, Christian Jewish relations constitute an important area in our program of national self-defense.

To the professional anti-Semite, there is nothing to say. He who foments inter-group conflicts for economic or political ends, or as a technique on behalf of a foreign enemy in order to break up American unity, need not concern us, except to put us on guard. We are concerned more with the ill-disposed who having no ax to grind may be amenable to reason, and with the well-disposed who are interested in doing something to combat ill-will but are not sure as to what program ought to be pursued.

There are two premises which ought to be recognized in any frank and wholesome approach to the problem of Christian Jewish relations. The first premise is that the responsibility rests chiefly upon the majority group. The second is that it behooves the minority group to do what it can, commensurate with dignity and self-respect, to avoid giving cause for frictions and irritations.

Some of our Christian friends and neighbors are under the impression that Jewish leaders, engrossed with protests against the enemies of the Jewish people, do not sufficiently reprimand their people for their own faults. Rabbis are charged with reluctance to "declare to the house of Jacob its transgressions."

Only those whose knowledge of Jewish life is external and superficial can possibly believe that the Jewish masses are coddled by their teachers. On the contrary, the didactic and mentorial tone has become almost a mannerism in the Jewish pulpit, platform and press. There is no regulation in the Synagogue which restricts the penitential mood to the first ten days of the new year. Nor is there any limit to the agenda of exhortation, and what is more important, of education, in the conduct of life.

When the minority group incurs the ill-will of the majority because of characteristics which are morally, ethically, or even aesthetically reprehensible, the responsibility lies squarely upon its shoulders to correct the evil. The majority group needs to be cautioned, however, against falling into the temptation to damn a group for the sins of an individual. That is why the word "characteristics" is employed in defining the issue.

When, however, the strain or the hostility is caused not by a reprehensible act but by the mere fact that the minority group is religiously, culturally or socially different, the guilt is on the other side. The dislike of the unlike, a phenomenon most observable among the animal herd, may explain ill-will between human groups, but it does not excuse it. Only by camouflage or suicide can the dislike of the unlike be avoided. Hence dignity and self-respect must never be permitted to become the price of harmony.

It is the first principle which needs to be emphasized, though it should seem axiomatic, that the responsibility for harmonious inter-group relations rests chiefly upon the majority group. The achievement of harmonious Christian Jewish relations in this country is primarily therefore a Christian responsibility.

In the fulfillment of his responsibility, the Christian needs first to understand the Jew, and second, to psychoanalyze his own prejudices against the Jew.

Sometimes the Jew is charged with being clannish. It is averred that even when he has the opportunity of free and easy intercourse with the non-Jew, he fails to make the most of the opportunity, and in many cases even sets up a psychological resistance. As a categorical observation, it is, of course, unfounded. Countless instances can be cited of friendships and comradeships between Christians and Jews which are free from the slightest strain or uneasiness.

Insofar as the observation is true, the Christian who is bent upon understanding the Jew, will realize that nineteen centuries of persecution leave a heritage of fear and mistrust which cannot be erased as quickly as desired. He will also come to perceive something of the dilemma which confronts the Jew who desiring to preserve Judaism and perpetuate it through his children, is troubled as to how far fraternization with the non-Jew can proceed without leading to the breaching of the "fences of the Law," and even to intermarriage.

The Christian who tries to understand the Jew will also understand the feeling of the Jew that in seeking to preserve and perpetuate Judaism he is engaged not only in self-preservation, which is a legitimate enough ambition, but also in preserving a culture which by general consent enriches humanity as a whole.

He will understand why the Jew resents Christian proselytizers, and has mistrusted the "Goodwill" movement in its early stages, fearing lest it be motivated by an ulterior purpose. Jews concede that Christianity is an adequate religion and way of life for Christians, but insist that Judaism is adequate for Jews and offers them all that is needed both for the here and the hereafter.

He will understand that so-called Jewish manners and mannerisms are not Jewish but traits carried over from former environments. He will understand that the inclination of the Jew to gravitate toward business and professions is not a racial trait but a sociological aftermath, the result of having been barred from other avenues of livelihood and that, given a chance, as in present-day Palestine, to normalize his life, he can excel in agriculture no less than in business, in handicraft no less than in the professions.

Understanding is the solvent of prejudice. When the Christian understands the Jew he will find it difficult to nurture prejudices against him.

Even more important is it for the Christian to psychoanalyze his prejudices. He will find that he is carrying some second-hand prejudices. One of the most potent of the second-hand prejudices is the traditional malconception of the Jew which has been inherited from the Middle Ages. Rooted in the New Testament story of the crucifixion, which has been taught to countless generations of Christian children, confirmed by nursery rhymes, popular by-words and literary caricatures, and dramatized by the Passion plays, the connotation of the word "Jew" has come to be one of opprobrium. Christians who may never have seen a Jew in person, are prepared by these second-hand impressions to find in the Jew the incarnation of the devil himself.

The most effective cure would be to bring such prejudices out of the unconscious into the conscious state, to psychoanalyze them. For Christians to try to understand their misunderstanding is a long step toward the achievement of Christian Jewish good-will.

The will to good-will requires to be implemented by a program. A three-fold program suggests itself,—education within the Christian churches, encouragement of inter-group contacts in local communities, and utilization of the press, radio and motion picture.

In the Christian churches of the United States, tens of millions of communicants are enrolled. Their contact with their people is periodical and recurrent. Their access to the children through the Sunday and weekday schools is an important formative influence. Within their walls Christian teaching free from anti-Jewish prejudices can be indoctrinated. From their pulpits economic discrimination can be condemned. In their printed literature the message of inter-group fellowship can be urged.

That many of the churches are expressing their responsibility as messengers of better understanding between Christian and Jew, is tribute to their lay and spiritual leaders. The leadership of the Federal Council of Churches of Christ in America and of the National Conference of Christians and Jews has been outstandingly helpful. May their tribe increase.

In local communities civic and religious leaders can promote a consciousness of inter-faith fellowship in a variety of ways. Round Table discussion groups and Brotherhood Day meetings such as have been sponsored by the National Conference of Christians and Jews, have helped to clarify misunderstandings and generate good-will. Popular community courses in Judaism, Protestantism and Christianity have proved helpful. Set occasions for honoring the outstanding citizens of the community provide an opportunity to point to the contributions of Jews and Christians alike. The initiative in these efforts must come from the non-Jews, for it is their privilege and their responsibility as the majority group.

The power of the press, radio and motion picture cannot be over-estimated. A local inter-faith committee in every community, keeping in touch with the local newspaper, radio station and motion picture theater, can exercise a wholesome influence. We in the United States have not begun to make adequate use of our tremendous facilities for the building of the democratic community at its best. Were we to use our available instruments for the creation of public opinion on behalf of the needs of our Democracy, as efficiently, ingeniously and persistently as the Nazis, Fascists and Communists do to promote their aims, we should have little to fear.

Christian and Jew have too much to do together to permit their forces to be divided.

Never in their history did Judaism and Christianity have as compelling a reason to feel closely allied as today. That does not mean that Christians are in danger of becoming converted to Judaism. Judaism is not a proselytizing Faith. Nor does it mean that Jews are in danger of becoming converted to Christianity. Christian leaders should have learned from long experience that converted Jewish souls are both expensive and unreliable, that the proselytizing of the Jew under ordinary circumstances is a fruitless effort. Many a Christian leader has acknowledged that he has enough to do keeping Christians Christian.

The sense of alliance between Judaism and Christianity is based upon mutual respect, and a mutual recognition that they are two great kindred religious traditions, offering a set of values which the world of today needs urgently, desperately, above and beyond anything else. They represent both a protest and an affirmation.

The protest is against the deification of Science.

We have gone through a period when the scientist was exalted as the savior of humanity. Worship and adoration were transferred from the Cathedral and the Synagogue to the chemical laboratory and the research chamber. The herald of the "Messianic age" was the Ph.D. armed with a test-tube in one hand and a microscope in the other. Religion was either disdained or merely tolerated by the pacemakers of our civilization. It was disdained as an opiate for the underprivileged, or it was tolerated as an anodyne for children and a consolation for the dying. Science and invention were held out as the great hope of humanity, the ushers of its salvation.

And we have seen the great disillusionment. It needs no detailed specifications here.

One day in August, 1939, on the eve of the war, as I was visiting a children's shelter outside Paris, the lesson struck me vividly. A group of children were there, who had been taken off the steamship *St. Louis,* the boat which for days wandered about aimlessly between Cuba and Florida, unable to land its refugee cargo, and finally returned to Europe where at last its refugees were distributed between England, France, Belgium and Holland. Here were some of the children separated from their parents, orphaned in fact if not in law, to whom the name of their tragic boat, the *St. Louis,* will always be a nightmare reminiscent of the brutality of the land of their birth, which made them refugees, and of the callousness of other lands, including our own, at whose shores they hovered, which denied them a haven. Yet it occurred to me as I stood before these children of the *St. Louis* cargo, that the name "St. Louis" bore also another connotation. Not far away from this children's shelter was Le Bourget, the airfield where eleven years before an airship called, "Spirit of St. Louis," landed amidst applause of the world, exemplar of the march of science and invention. What a contrast between the "Spirit of St. Louis" of 1928 and the spirit of the *S. S. St. Louis* of 1939, between the glory of Science and the ignominy of human nature!

Science has brought material comforts, but not happiness. It has removed barriers of space but has not brought nations together. It has taught men to master nature, but they have not learned to master hatred and greed. On the contrary, it has created tools of destruction a thousand times more devastating than the simpler tools of a less scientific age. The products of science are now ravaging the face of Europe a thousand times more cruelly than war ever ravaged Europe before.

If ever the message of Religion was needed, its moral inspiration, its exhortation to Faith, its injunctions to Justice and Mercy, its definition of values for the guidance of men and nations, it is needed today.

What, essentially, is Religion's message? Divested of its outer habiliments, its theological doctrines, its organized institutional forms, its ritual and ceremonies, "x-rayed" to its very essence, what is the essential message of Religion? What does it say?

Religion says that the individual is something more than a totalitarianized grain of sand to be kicked and trampled on at the will of a dictator, and that his soul and his personality are inviolable. It says that the individual has rights divinely guaranteed which not even the State or its rulers can trespass. Thus, the prophet Nathan speaking in the name of God, points the accusing finger at King David, "Thou art the man," when the mighty ruler and warrior has sinned, and the prophet Elijah tells King Ahab to his face that the dogs will lick his blood in the streets because he has stolen a vineyard from one of his subjects.

Religion says that the most important and the most sacred relationship in life, more sacred than the relationship between the subject and the State is the eternal triangle of father, mother, and child.

Religion says that morals and ethics are not timely expedients but timeless imperatives, that right and wrong are not devices of ruling classes but standards which no man, however exalted, may upset, and that by these standards nations as well as individuals are weighed and judged, that no nation is so priviliged as to be beyond the bar of eternal justice.

These affirmations of Religion time and again went counter to the programs of the strong and the mighty, and challenged the conquerors of the earth. The spokesmen who spoke in the name of Religion were not popular in high places. Jewish prophets were imprisoned and Christian teachers were persecuted. They were not daunted, and because they were not daunted there was a flame to light up the path for future generations.

Sometimes it happened that Religion itself was distorted out of its original meaning, nay, misused by unscrupulous men who spoke in its name but violated its essence. Sometimes the priests who were meant to tend and minister at its altar, put so many wrappings about it, doctrines, rituals and institutions, that they almost choked the flame. Somehow it survived both its scheming foes and its over-solicitous friends, and it is here today as the Jewish-Christian tradition which is the mentor of the Western World.

Religion, far from being the dull dry regimen which some people consider it to be, who see only some of its form but miss its spark, has actually been the most exciting of human adventures. Far from being an anodyne for children and a soporific for adults, it has been a spur and a challenge.

Today the Nazi and the Communist are bidding menacingly

for the hegemony of our world. We are witnessing a resurgence of that paganism which always had a surface plausibility and attraction. What is needed is the resurgence of Religion, to play again the part it once played, of saving the world from paganism.

This is a broad task incumbent upon Jew and Christian. The present crisis in human affairs has drawn them more closely together than they have been for centuries. Let each seek nourishment in the rich, spiritual matrix of his own religious tradition. Let the Christian repair to his altar, let the Jew repair to his altar, consecrated by the Prophets and Sages, the Psalmists and Saints.

We have too much to do together to permit our forces to be divided. Together we must seek, by the exercise of our living creeds to impress upon our world of chaos and darkness, the primordial command, "Let there be light."

Inter-Religious Fellowship

Based on the responses to celebrations of the Jewish New Year by the Fellowship of Faiths at the Grace Episcopal Church, New York, September 23, 1930, and at the Union Auditorium, September 30, 1935.

Inter-Religious Fellowship

THE PSALMIST HAS said, "Behold, how goodly it is that brethren should dwell together." Tonight has been a spiritual dwelling together for all of us. The God of us all has been here glorified. Everyone here is the better for having shared in this experience of fellowship, better as a man and citizen, better as Christian, Jew, Buddhist or Mohammedan.

The fact that a Protestant Episcopal Church serves as the scene of this meeting, is a happy accident, for one of the first neighborly acts performed by the Jews of New York, going back more than two hundred years, was a contribution from a group of Jews including the Rabbi of the community, toward the building of a steeple on Trinity Church. This meeting is worthy of that "lofty" precedent.

What can be the response of the Jew tonight except an appreciation of your tributes of appreciation?

The broad note of fellowship which has been sounded here, is altogether congenial to the character of the Jewish New Year, for Rosh Hashanah, the Jewish New Year in the Jewish consciousness has always had more than a particularistic significance. It has been endowed with universal themes and broadly human connotations. It is counted as man's birthday, the anniversary of his creation. It impels the Jew to give thought to the problems of mankind and to the large canvas of the human drama.

Jewish lore tells us that when man was created out of the dust, the Creator was careful not to choose the dust from any particular spot on the earth's surface, lest subsequent generations, inhabiting that spot, should boast that they were the original children of God. Therefore, the Creator gathered dust from all the corners of the earth, in order that all men might know that they are His children, equal in His sight. The prayers recited on Rosh Hashanah center around the theme, "May all men be joined into one fellowship, to do Thy will." The ram's horn is blown in the Synagogue on that day, to remind the Jew of the Messianic day when the trumpet call of a new age will be sounded, an age when the words of Israel's prophets touching Universal Brotherhood and Peace will at last be fulfilled.

This is what Rosh Hashanah means to the Jew. That same New Year message is the best response the Jew can make to his neighbor's tribute.

Israel's experience as a neighbor in the midst of other peoples has been as old as recorded history, and as widespread as the face of the earth. In the give and take of civilization and culture, the Jew has given abundantly and received abundantly. A Jewish Queen Esther to Persia and India, Prime Ministers to Mohammedan and Christian governments, a founder to Christianity, and a Bible to mankind, are a few of Israel's spiritual contributions. Its cultural gifts you have graciously referred to. The Jew in turn gratefully acknowledges the influence of India's mystics, of Moslem's physicians and scientists, and of Christianity's Western culture.

An analysis of the age in which we live would reveal that the chief divisive forces of our time have been chauvinistic nationalism, obscurantist religionism, and exploitatory capitalism.

Nationalism as such, which is the unique expression of the personality of an historic group bound together by a community of race, geography, history, language and culture, is not a force for evil but for good. Far from being deleterious to the welfare of society as a whole, it makes for the enrichment of civilization. Nationalism in its proper expression can enhance the welfare of humanity just as family loyalty in its proper expression enhances the welfare of the State. Nationalism becomes a force for evil when the sentiment of patriotism is used to foment hatred against other nations. The ideal of internationalism is premised upon nationalism as its basis. It needs to be a nationalism, however, which unlike its present forms, considers itself subservient to the higher interests of humanity as a whole. Internationalism means not the abolition of nationalism but its education and ennoblement.

Religion as such, which is the faith in a Higher Power as the source of goodness, beauty and truth, and the implementation of that faith by a moral code of human conduct, is the noblest expression of the human spirit. When the free flow of spiritual truth becomes hardened, however, into rigid institutionalism, it becomes an obstruction in the path of mutual understanding and co-operation. Diversity of religious expression is as inevitable and as little to be deplored as diversity of national expression. Religions need never become one so long as they can remain at one.

Capitalism, it must be admitted even by those who advocate its reform or abolition today, has served a useful purpose in the evolution of human progress. It has stimulated invention, encouraged the cultivation of natural resources, reclaimed waste areas, pushed forward the settlement of uninhabited spaces, promoted commerce and industry, created increased employment opportunities, and added to the physical comforts of living so that the modest wage-earner of today enjoys facilities which were not available even to the kings of former centuries. Exploitatory capitalism, however, has subjugated native populations, fomented wars, caused cycles of unemployment, and enabled a few to grow rich on the labor of the many.

Every great World Religion has addressed itself to the need of curing the evils represented by chauvinistic nationalism, obscurantist religionism, and exploitatory capitalism. At this time when narrow nationalism builds up barriers of hatred between people and people it is timely to recall that religion in its pure form, visioning one humanity, has been a force for internationalism.

The sentiments expressed tonight represent the broadest preachments of all the great religions,—Judaism included. Religions, of course, have also their individual themes, the unique and characteristic elements which give them individual and local color.

It can hardly be expected that the peoples of the earth, each coming from its own unique background and experience, should arrive at one uniform system of belief and worship. As long as racial distinctions will mark off human natures and historic backgrounds will cast their shadows over human impulses and emotions, as long as humanity will remain a great differentiated organism, as long as poets will sing, each by the muse of his own inspiration, so long will Churches, Mosques, and Synagogues vary in the character of their respective rituals and modes of worship.

As neighbors we respect the unique and characteristic elements in one another's cultures though we may not entirely understand them because they are the product of unique habits, environments and experiences. In the Fellowship of Faith in which we are met tonight, we are privileged to seek one another across our differences, and to understand one another across our distinctions. Let each Religion and culture maintain its identity and cultivate its own spiritual resources. Liberal-minded men recognize that no race, religion or nation has a monopoly on goodness or truth. If each but be true to its highest law, humanity as a whole would be served best.

Our meeting tonight as neighbors and friends is in the best American tradition. Is it not the test of our democracy that within the broad American constituency, there should be a congenial setting for a variety of religions and diversity of cultural expressions?

America, of all lands, seems providentially ordained to be the great testing ground of this principle. It is the one state whose very character enunciates in unmistakable accents the ideal of racial and religious equality.

Equality is here a guaranteed constitutional right which can be challenged whenever it is infringed upon, but legal guarantees are not enough for the proper functioning of a democracy. A plus element is needed. That plus element is the tone of the dwelling together of men and communities. It is the plus element which transmutes the dry formulae of principles into the richly vivid and vital interpenetration of ideas and affections. This is the area where fellowship and good-will have an important part to play. Fellowship and good-will cannot be legislated by constitutions or by ordinances. They can only spring from the hearts and the minds of the people. They must come freely or not at all.

Therefore, tonight's meeting is significant. It is a meeting of citizens and neighbors who have come of their own free will to make an affirmation of brotherhood, in that sphere which has so often been the scene of dissension, the sphere of religion which at times, alas, has been used as a pretext for hatreds and conflicts. We are here, thank God, to affirm that Religion need not serve as a barrier but can and should be a bond, that we who profess different religious faiths have more in common than we have in difference.

However much we may differ in the terminology, we have in common an outlook upon life which denies the primacy of material factors. We have in common a conviction of the reality of the spiritual forces in the universe. We have in common a devotion to the establishment of social motivations in human conduct. We hold in common a denunciation and renunciation of war as the goal of a nation's life. We hold in common a hopeful view of humanity's future, a belief in the capacity of the human race for spiritual progress. We hold in common a loyalty and a love for America. By these considerations, we are, I believe, bound together. Religion, in its most literal sense, means that which binds men together. Therefore, Religion has been glorified here tonight.

Is it not significant that all the great religious teachers of humanity, in their supreme moments, sounded the universal themes and blessed all men, regardless of race or creed? The texts of the Jewish and Christian Testaments exhorting love of neighbor and good-will toward the stranger are too well known in this company to require repetition. Let us here recall and honor the words of Buddha who said, "All religions are just as good. Just as near a village or a town there are many and various paths, yet they all meet together in the village, just in that way are all the various paths taught by various religions. They are all saving paths which will lead those who act according to them into a state of union with the Divine." It was Mahomet, who spurning those who took a partial view of Paradise, said, "Nay, but he who resigneth himself to God and doth that which is right, he shall have a reward with his Lord."

Would that the understanding and appreciation expressed tonight might translate itself before long into practical fellowship among the rank and file of the people. The Jew knows what it means to suffer racial prejudice, economic discrimination and religious animosity. Shameful violations of the principles we hold in common could be cited as they occur in the business and industrial life of our country. There are sons and daughters of my people who are denied employment without any investigation of their personal merits, for no reason except that they are Jews. There are sons and daughters of my people who are denied admission to educational institutions.

Sometimes these disfranchised and underprivileged of my folk come to me, scoff at good-will meetings and fellowship demonstrations, and even chide me for lending myself to such occasions, where the protestations of good-will are of no consequence. I can only console them with the thought that they must not be impatient in matters affecting deep-rooted and often inherited prejudices.

We are dealing with prejudices which are as old as history. The significant thing is that we are dealing with them at all, that we are trying to eradicate them, that we are making an effort which has never before been attempted as a joint enterprise by representatives of several great world religions. It may take a thousand years before the ideal "Fellowship of Faiths" is fully realized, but it is heartening to feel that we are traveling in that direction.

What has been said and done here tonight is still an exceptional gesture, and an unusual demonstration. May it become a precedent and a prophecy for the time when mutual appreciation will bring all the peoples of the earth into a bond of comity and good-will.

That day will be a universal Rosh Hashanah. It will mark the new era in the fellowship of man.

What Makes Jews Jews?

Address delivered before Congregation
B'nai Jeshurun on Purim (Feast of Lots),
February 17, 1935.

What Makes Jews Jews?

HAMAN IS PROBABLY the first non-Jew in history to call attention to the unique phenomenon of the Diaspora Jew. "There is a unique people scattered abroad and dispersed among the peoples in all the provinces of the kingdom, and their laws are diverse from those of every people." Villain that he was, he sought to use the uniqueness of the Jewish people as an argument to arouse the king's suspicion and ill will. The uniqueness of the Jewish people has, however, continued to perplex the non-Jew and to challenge definition by Jews. Let us make an attempt to define what makes Jews Jews.

Two interesting books, both written by Jews, but very different in content and outlook, may be helpful in our quest of a definition. One is, "Hear Ye Sons," by Irving Fineman, a well-known American novelist. The other is, "My Life as German and Jew," by Jacob Wassermann, the pre-eminent German novelist, who died a few years ago.

Irving Fineman's book gives us an insight into the life of the East European Jew, his manners and mannerisms, customs and beliefs. To the uninitiated these may seem bizarre, but to the understanding they appear quaint and beautiful. His passionate devotion to the Torah, his fine home life, the spiritual quality of his character and the complete adequacy of his Jewish culture for his intellectual and spiritual satisfaction, are appealingly narrated.

Jacob Wassermann's book is a biographical document written

77

many years ago, with a concluding chapter added subsequently. Unlike the narrator of "Hear Ye Sons," Wassermann was reared not in an ingrown Jewish atmosphere, but in an assimilation atmosphere which dominated a large part of German Jewry during the second half of the nineteenth century. Wassermann's great grievance is that though he was molded by German ideas, character and customs, he was not accepted by the German people as an authentic exponent of the German spirit. Everywhere and always he was made to feel that he was not a German, but a Jew.

These two books considered together, present a vivid contrast between the East European Jew and the West European Jew. A study of these two contrasted types may reveal something of an answer to the question, "What makes Jews Jews?"

In arriving at a definition of a type, it is useful to study contrasted species within the same genus. To observe what they have in common despite their differences is helpful in ascertaining the essential characteristics which belong to the genus as such. The same method may be applied in defining what makes Jews Jews. By taking different types of Jews as the field of observation, one may draw conclusions as to the characteristics which Jews as such have in common.

The first denominator which Irving Fineman's Jew and Jacob Wassermann's Jew have in common is that both were born Jews. The accident of birth is the fundamental fact.

The second common denominator is that both chose to remain Jews. They could have renounced Judaism and turned to Christianity as has been done by Jews again and again, under the stress of ambition or of fear. It is often said, "Once a Jew, always a Jew." Hitler's imposition of the Jewish label upon those even whose grandparents had turned to Christianity, is sometimes referred to in order to indicate that being a Jew is not a matter of choice. It is not, however, a realistic view of the situation. There have been numerous cases of Jews who have left the fold, of whom nothing further has been heard. They have succeeded in disappearing as Jews. Remaining a Jew, therefore, is an act of choice, for there is a possible alternative, that of leaving the Jewish fold by an act of renunciation.

The third fact to bear in mind is that both characters were regarded by the outside world as being aliens, as not belonging integrally to the national group in whose midst they had been born and reared. Neither of them was accepted by the non-Jewish world. Though in each case the rejection was different, it was a difference in degree, not in kind. The Jew in "Hear Ye Sons," was out of the Gentile context by mutual consent. He was violently excluded and he was glad to exclude himself. Jacob Wassermann wanted to be a part of the picture, but was not permitted.

We sometimes hear definitions of the Jew which on the surface seem plausible.

It is held by many that the term "Jew" is a religious designation. It used to be the standard declaration of Reform Judaism. This definition is easily refuted when, as sometimes happens, Jews who are indifferent or even hostile to religion but identify themselves as Jews and serve their people, are recognized by the Jewish community and by the non-Jewish community as belonging to the Jewish people.

Others advance the theory that Jewishness is a racial characteristic. Anthropologists, however, reject the theory that there is a Jewish race. Even the lay observer can discern the difference between the Yemenites and the Polish Jew, between the Spanish and Portuguese Jew and the German Jew.

It is sometimes heard that the Jewish designation derives from unique Jewish temperamental and psychological characteristics. Upon investigation these personal traits prove to be as varied as the variety of human equations and as diverse as the conditions in the diverse backgrounds of the individuals or groups respectively.

There are many who call themselves "nationalist" Jews and contend that the Jews are a nation. With reference to the Jews of the Diaspora, they do not employ the term "nation" in the sense in which it is used to describe the nations in which they hold citizenship. Politically their allegiance goes unreservedly to the nation of which they are citizens, and they have demonstrated their readiness to offer life itself in the fulfillment of their allegiance. But they point to other group phenomena which are the earmarks of nationhood. And they look to Palestine as the place where Jews constitute a nation in the political sense as well.

It is evident that under present conditions Jews are not a nation in the political sense, nor a race in the scientific sense, nor a religious sect in the denominational sense.

Each of these proposed theories and definitions has a certain surface plausibility but cannot stand the test of analysis. Each of them, however, contains a relevant observation and all the theories and definitions together do convey something of the total historic reality.

Originally, historically, when the Jewish people had its independent, sovereign existence in Palestine, it was a nation, bound like any other nation by ties of race, religion and geographical kinship, cultural and temperamental characteristics, such as mark any normal nation. As we are today, however, due to our abnormal history as a Diaspora people, some of the historic characteristics have lost much of their validity. There still remain the feelings of religious attachment, cultural community and racial kinship. Some of these feelings may not stand the test of analysis, but they are emotionally real, for they give one Jew a sense of community with other Jews.

It is the sense of community which is the subjective element of the definition. We feel our kinship with the religious mystic in far off Safed and with the atheist Jew on Union Square, with the light-complexioned Jew in Scandinavia, and with the swarthy Jew in Abyssinia, with the Talmudist in Poland, the "halutz" in Palestine and the football star in America. We belong to a great community comprising many, many varieties, and yet bound by a world-wide sense of kinship. We belong to this community by virtue of the facts, first, that we have been born into it, second, that we choose to remain in it, and third, that we feel bound to perpetuate it.

We are thus united by ties which are partly historical and partly psychological. As for the past, we cherish a common history of four thousand years. A distinctive language, culture and religious tradition are our heritage, though individuals among us may be ignorant of it or indifferent to it. As for the present, we feel a racial kinship, though scientifically speaking we are not a homogeneous race; we acknowledge collectively the ties of a common religion, though individuals among us may proclaim themselves atheists. What is most important, we do as a people exercise a common will to live and to survive as a distinctive people though individuals among us may not accept the mandate.

This is as near as we can get to a definition. If it is not near enough to be satisfactory, the difficulty lies in the fact that the Jewish people, by virtue of its peculiar history, is unlike any other people and cannot be satisfactorily measured and defined by the conventional yardsticks.

Herein is the common denominator across the differences between Irving Fineman's "Hear Ye Sons" and Jacob Wassermann's "My Life as German and Jew."

Now that we know what these two types have in common, let us go back to see what they have in difference. The fundamental difference is that one finds his peace of mind and sustenance of soul in Jewish values, and the other tries to find it in non-Jewish values.

Irving Fineman's Jew is not troubled by what the civilization of the outside world thinks of him. He is confident that it is inferior to his own civilization. When one considers the Russian and Polish environment in which "Hear Ye Sons" is set, one can hardly blame that Jew for his attitude. To him the "goy" meant brutality, drunkenness, stupidity. The Jew who held in contempt the civilization of the "goy" knew only its worst aspects from earliest times, the primitive "Moloch" worship, the immoral cult of the Baal worship, the paganism of Greece and Rome, and the fanatical persecutions perpetrated by Christendom. This Jew was not much troubled by what the world thought of him. Looking upon the hostile world as the ineluctable villain in his drama, he resolved that if this enemy cannot be overcome he must at least be circumvented; at any rate he must be prevented from laying his unholy hands upon the inner sanctuary of Jewish life.

Irving Fineman's Jew has peace of mind because he is not troubled by what the world thinks of him. His only problem is to be let alone to cultivate his own resources, to live in his own world. He has not only peace of mind but integrity of soul, because he is himself an authentic and consistent personality who finds complete spiritual satisfaction in his own traditions, his own literature, his own moral code, his own festivals, rites and ceremonies.

The Jew represented by Jacob Wassermann, however, misses both peace of mind and integrity of soul. Emancipated from the "ghetto," living in close contact with the outside world, holding converse with his neighbors, and surrounded by a civilization whose values he cannot deny, much less spurn, he is troubled by the need to work out an adjustment between the Jewish culture, which is his heritage, and the culture of the environment which he respects and admires. He is troubled by what the world thinks of him, because he respects that world, desires its good opinion, and wants to make his intellectual and spiritual contributions to it. Therefore, he is deeply wounded when the world spurns his offering, refuses to accept him as a part of it, and makes him feel that despite everything, he is an alien who does not "belong." That is the psychological problem of the westernized Jew.

Which of these two kinds do we wish to be? Obviously, the choice is not ours. We can no more be the Jew of "Hear Ye Sons" than an airplane can be an oxcart. We may believe that type of Jewish living to be quaint and beautiful, but we cannot model our lives upon it. It is like a museum piece, to be admired but not emulated. Occasionally, in a romantic nostalgic mood, we may long for that pattern, but when we are actually confronted with the choice, we could not choose it. Once having been subjected to the influence of western culture and civilization, we could not deliberately isolate ourselves.

The type of Jew whom Irving Fineman depicts is a disappearing species. He may last a while longer in Poland. In Russia, he is fast disappearing. In Western Europe he is becoming extinct. Even the revival of anti-Semitism under the Nazi impact will not avail to revive the "ghetto" Jew. Driven into a physical "ghetto" he will still resist cultural ghettoization. He will still continue to be a European. The tide of westernization sweeps on and cannot be stopped. It sweeps on despite the attempt which is being made in Germany to isolate the Jew and to excommunicate him. That effort will not endure. Hitlerism is a temporary abberation. Though it may go on for years, it is against the current of modern life and is bound to fail. So the Jew throughout the world will be more and more of the type, not of Irving Fineman's Jew, but of Jacob Wassermann's Jew, subjected to the currents of western civilization, and obliged to find his place in that civilization.

Unfortunately, there disappears with this type some of the fine spiritual values which Jewish life can ill afford to miss.

The problem of the modern Jew is how to make terms with the world in which he must live, and at the same time to maintain his spiritual integrity and his peace of mind. The tragedy of the modern Jew is the tragedy of one who having given up his own traditions in order to take on world civilization, finds that he has made a worse bargain than even Faust made, for Faust at least got his moment of happiness though it proved illusory, while the Jew, spurned by the world he woos, is alas, bereft of his peace of mind and integrity of soul.

That is the essential failure of the "assimilationist" philosophy.

The "assimilation" Jew has been misled by the naïve liberalism of the eighteenth century into believing that he was at last entering into a society free from prejudice and discrimination. Now it has proved to be a false hope.

What is there for us to do, seeing that we cannot go back to the kind of life which Irving Fineman's grandfather lived, and that we must necessarily live in a world which, having broken down the physical "ghetto" walls, still looks upon the Jew as an alien?

It is for us to accept the situation not bitterly and morosely as Jacob Wassermann does, but manfully and self-reverently. If Jacob Wassermann's Judaism had been more positive, if his attitude had been one of espousal rather than toleration, he might have found in his Judaism much to console and compensate him for his disappointments, much to bring him spiritual satisfaction. It is no excuse, as he suggests, that as a child he did not have the right kind of Jewish teacher. He could have found sources of Jewish learning and inspiration after attaining manhood. Theodore Herzl, who though reared in an assimilation environment was reclaimed for Judaism after attaining manhood, could have served as an example to him. Herzl found his spiritual rebirth in Zionism. Wassermann, however, makes a weak apology for having spurned Zionism. Wassermann could have steeped himself more thoroughly in the culture of his people without excluding German culture any more than Herzl excluded western culture. Herzl's experience has been duplicated in thousands of men of intellectual and spiritual gifts who succeeded also in finding themselves as Jews.

There is something everyone of us can do to give more content to the Jew within him, intellectual content and emotional content. It can be cultivated by study and by service. Affiliation with Jewish causes,—the Synagogue, Zionism, philanthropy, offer opportunities to act Jewishly and to serve Jewishly. Intellectual content can be acquired by reading and study. The ignorance of American Jewry in Jewish matters is abysmal. It is doubtful if ever before there has been a Jewish population in any of the lands of the Diaspora as untutored in Jewish culture as is American Jewry. Orthodox, Conservative and Reform Jews are alike in their "am ha-arazuth," "know-nothingness." Even more imperative than gaining intellectual content ourselves, is the duty of giving it to our children. The greatest tragedy of the German Jews is that they have so little now to sustain them. The most unbearable suffering is to suffer without knowing wherefore. It is doubly tragic that a people should "perish without knowledge." The old Socratic formula "know thyself" devolves upon us and upon our children.

What then makes Jews Jews? Is the term "Jew" a racial designation, a religious label, or a national epithet? It is none of these alone.

Being a Jew in the broadest definition means first, the accident of birth; secondly, the act of choice, choosing to remain Jews despite the difficulties; thirdly, the act of cognition, learning to know the history and literature of his people so as to understand its soul and appreciate its place in the world; and finally, the act of transmission, transmitting to the next generation his heritage and the will to carry it on so that the Jewish people may not perish from the earth.

Jewish Youth in a Troubled World

Substance of addresses delivered as President of the Young People's League of the United Synagogue of America, at its National Convention in New York, November 30, 1930; as President of Young Judea, at its National Convention in Long Branch, June 26, 1931; and before the Palestinian "Tzofim" (Scouts), in Jerusalem, July 15, 1932.

Jewish Youth in a Troubled World

J EWISH YOUTH WOULD be more than human if it did not reflect the temper of the age and the people in which it lives. The moods, vagaries and predilections of the youth generally, are naturally mirrored in the Jewish youth.

The youth of the 1920's wore as its hall-marks, cynicism, and self-expressionism.

Cynicism, as an aftermath of the World War, was to have been expected. The mood penetrated down to the age level of the "flapper" and up to the age level of the "rounder." The cycle was not as long-lived as might have been expected from Gilbert K. Chesterton's remark about skepticism, twin brother of cynicism, that it "lasts only two generations." Within a decade the youth began "losing its disillusions." One does not have to be an expert in psychology to know that life cannot flourish upon a diet of withering negations. An intelligent life must be analytic but a beautiful life must also be synthetic. Romance which youth requires for its happiness is not limited to sex attraction. In its broadest sense, it is a quality which touches the whole of life. It is the very opposite of cynicism.

If cynicism was the mood of the youth, freedom of self-expression was their insistent demand. They scarcely paused to consider what kind of "self" they were straining to express. The "self" which found expression in the manners and moods of the post-war youth did not justify the freedom. The first law of self-expression in the best sense of the term is self-discipline. In music and art painstaking training and discipline precede the final stage when the artist feels free to express his talent. Why should it be less so in the art of living?

"L'Allegro," of the 1920's was succeeded by "Il Penseroso" of the 1930's. Youth, depressed by the Great Depression, fell into a more sober and searching mood. Unemployment was the specter that stalked in ten million homes. Mature men and women, skilled workers, experienced hands, the parents and the brothers and sisters of the young people were jobless. What chance did the young people have for jobs? In the economic sphere they were the "unwanted children." The cynicism and the self-expressionism of the 1920's were followed by the bitterness and the radicalism of the 1930's. Youth gave an attentive ear to the heralds of a new social order where jobs and livelihood would be available to all. Conventional Commencement Day orators left them cold. The fear of war as the last resort of a failing economy, gripped them. They resented the readiness of the elder statesmen to gamble with the lives of the youth.

If an American brand of National Socialism had arisen here, led by an American edition of Hitler or Mussolini, exploiting the discontent and relying upon the dynamics of an embittered youth, it would not have been surprising. It was staved off partly by the New Deal and partly by the lessons from abroad, demonstrating the price of National Socialism in terms of human liberty.

The Jewish youth here were not segregated from the influences and the problems of the age and the environment in which they lived. Indeed the edge of the problem was sharper for them than for their non-Jewish contemporaries. The Jew was subject to special disqualifications, which made the burdens of the Jewish youth extraordinarily difficult.

Not only special burdens rested upon the Jewish youth. They had special responsibilities. In addition to all the obligations, educational and patriotic, which devolved upon the youth in relation to society, the city, state and nation, there were special obligations which the Jewish youth were called upon to assume toward Jewish education, Synagogue allegiance, philanthropic service, Zionist affiliation, and all the other factors in the problem of Jewish survival.

The response was meager. In no other land was the Jewish youth on the whole as indifferent in Jewish feeling and as empty of Jewish knowledge. A few cases of effort and interest deserve to be noted. The United Synagogue of America has sponsored a Young People's League since 1921. The Zionist Organization of America sponsored Young Judea as far back as 1909. Junior Hadassah, organized in 1921, Aleph Zadik Aleph, the junior affiliate of B'nai Brith, organized in 1924; Avukah, Masada, Young Poale Zion, Hashomer Hatzair, Hapoel Hamizrachi, Habonim, the youth affiliates of the Orthodox and of the Reform Synagogue organizations, and the junior affiliates of the Charity Federations, held the field. In none of these was the content commensurate with the receptacle. The total number of young people engaged in a conscious endeavor to serve Jewish interests and promote Jewish culture was a meager fraction of the Jewish youth population, far smaller than the proportion of adult Jews similarly engaged. It was a signal of decline in Jewish life.

Only toward the end of the third decade, as anti-Semitism expanded throughout Europe and showed its fangs here in the United States, did the Jewish youth begin to show signs of restless eagerness to do something about the Jewish problem. In greater measure than ever before they have become alert, sensitive, interested, concerned and worried.

Today, therefore, the Jewish youth need to be guided, not chided. They want to resolve their state of agitation into a program of action, but do not know how. They would like to be of help to their people but do not know through what medium they can best serve. They would like to find an antidote for their fears but are at a loss for a formula.

Is there a program to suggest?

One type of program is often suggested, which on the face of it makes a strong appeal, but upon analysis fails to satisfy the requirements of the Jew as a Jew. It is the program of social, economic reconstruction. The argument is that anti-Semitism is a social disease, and that when the social economic order can be cured of its ills, anti-Semitism will disappear. On the face of it this argument has an undeniable appeal to youth impatient for a better world. Why does it fail to satisfy? Firstly, because the reconstruction of the social economic order is a long range operation pending which Jewish life may be destroyed; secondly, because even in a better world Jewish identity may be in danger of melting away under the sun of prosperity; and thirdly, and what is most important, because the Jewish youth of today impelled by a sense of honor and resistance, is seeking for its own peace of soul a more intensive Jewish self-affirmation and greater self-assurance.

While a forward looking social economic program is all to the good, there is needed a more immediate and a more intimate program of Jewish self-expression and of Jewish service. The immediate and intimate program, far from injuring the larger objectives, actually moves in their direction.

Such a program should offer as its motivation, the Jewish Will to Live. It should offer as implementation the renascence of Jewish cultural and spiritual values, something more than philanthropy. It should offer as a medium for affiliation and service, an organized group dedicated to the Jewish Will to Live, and to the renascence of its culture and spirit.

The media which suggest themselves as meeting the definition best are the Synagogue and the Zionist movement. Both need the Jewish youth desperately. The Rabbis spoke for our time as well as for theirs when they said, "The departure of the youth is as disastrous to Israel as the destruction of the Temple." (Midrash Rabbah on Lamentations, 1:15.) The carriers of an ideal, as they grow older are prone to succumb to the inertia and conservatism which usually go with age. Youth are needed to infuse vigor and daring into an ideal.

It is not enough, however, that the elders should desire the participation of the youth. They must be ready to invite youth into the precincts of leadership. In the affairs of many a nation young people in their twenties enjoy full-fledged rights, carry adult responsibilities and exercise influence. Are young people of the same ages less qualified to receive recognition in Jewish affairs? Yet we deal with them patronizingly in most of our Synagogue institutions and we coddle them in most of our Zionist organizations.

When Theodore Herzl founded the Zionist Organization he was a young man in his early thirties. Chaim Weizmann was a youth in his twenties when he already participated fully in Zionist affairs. The great majority of the carriers of modern Zionism in the first decades of the movement were young men. American Zionism needs the ardor of youth more than it needs the dignity of age. Viewing the hard road which faces Zionism, the youth should be welcomed with something more than verbal felicitations, and the youth should take upon itself something more than the acceptance of subsidies. If the youth in American Zionism and in the American Synagogue occupy a position on the periphery instead of at the center, it is partly the fault of the elders who are reluctant to part with power and authority, and partly the fault of the youth who are lacking in boldness.

It remains to be demonstrated that the immediate and intimate program of Jewish self-expression and of Jewish service, far from conflicting with the objectives of social and economic improvement, is actually helpful toward their realization.

The program of the Synagogue in its broadest aspect converges on the ennoblement of individual character and the improvement of the social order. The culmination of our daily prayer is the hope "to improve the world under the Kingdom of God."

No Religion has defined daily conduct as meticulously as Judaism. Justice is defined in terms of reparation of damages when a man's cattle grazes in the field of another. Liberty is defined in terms forbidding any man to sell himself into permanent slavery. Tolerance is defined in terms of cautioning against the oppression of the stranger. Charity is defined in terms of the command that the corners of the field and the gleanings of the harvest belong to the poor, the widow and the orphan.

If the Law of Moses is a textbook in practical idealism, the utterances of the Hebrew Prophets project the ultimate goals. They were the first to envisage and proclaim universal Peace, Brotherhood, Justice, the ideals of which have been invoked and repeated since their time by all the protagonists of a better dispensation for humanity.

Jewish youth, with the greater part of life still in prospect, still weaving the fabric of their careers, are called upon in the tradition of Judaism, to evidence those personal qualities and social ideals which mark the Jew in his best traditions. Jews cannot afford to bask in the light of a few sporadic luminaries. A national reputation cannot long subsist in vicarious glory upon the reputations of single saints. The reputation of the Jew will rest upon the characters and reputations of great numbers of Jews.

While the exhortation upon the individual Jew to reflect credit upon his people is both proper and necessary, its fulfillment in the midst of an environment of daily struggle for existence is fraught with hazards. It is with special zest therefore that the Zionist points to the Jewish community in Palestine where the quality of living and the concept of social idealism is of the highest grade to be found anywhere.

That these manifestations are not merely individual characteristics but programs of organized groups is all the more to the credit of the Jew. Zionism, therefore, serves the ultimate ends of social idealism.

For the American Jewish youth the suggested program of self-expression and of service in a time such as this accomplishes more than appears on the surface. He receives in far greater measure than he gives.

Jewish consciousness can be aroused either by positive or by negative stimulations. To feel one's Jewishness only when an insult is hurled, or an alarm is sounded, to be subjected constantly to negative stimulations, to be always on the defensive, answering attacks, is bad for the nerves. It has made many of us highly nervous and hypersensitive. How much more wholesome it is to nourish one's Jewishness by positive values, not by alarm but by assurance, not by fear but by faith, not by indignation but by inspiration. Youth requires it most of all,—to be able to stand up and face the world with dignity and self-assurance.

The benefits of wholesome stimulation are not confined to the Jewish part of the personality of the youth. Spiritual vitality is not a departmental phenomenon. Once generated, it suffuses the entire personality with the wholesome glow of confidence, hope and faith. The rehabilitated Jew becomes the more vigorous and useful citizen. It is not to be wondered at that the leaders in constructive Jewish efforts are the men who at the same time render valiant service to all the other aspects of community life.

In the Hebrew tongue the word "banayich" meaning "children," is similar in sound and spelling to "bonayich" meaning "builders." The Rabbis make the most of the coincidence, calling upon the children of Israel to become its upbuilders.

For the Jewish youth of our troubled world the same high challenge is offered, to build up the life of their people both here and in Palestine. Their reward lies in the doing of the work which builds up in their inner selves, wholesomeness, confidence and dignity.

Modern Jewish Questions

Address delivered before a Conference on "The Jew and the World Crisis," held under the auspices of the Jewish Theological Seminary of America, New York, May 14, 1939.

Modern Jewish Questions

In this perplexing, harassing period in the life of the Jewish people, there is a fundamental question which even a child, if he is intelligent enough to observe the kind of world in which we live, must feel impelled to ask, "Wherefore is this people different from all other peoples?"

While the child may feel disturbed in a general way, a maturer consideration would analyze the general question into its component parts. There are four arresting questions for the modern Jew to ask and answer.

The first question is, why is the Jew singled out for special attack? Is there something really wrong with him that in so many lands he, more than any other group, draws the hatred of men?

The second question is, can the Jew throw off his burden and free himself from whatever it is which causes his troubles, so that at least his children, if not he, may be freed from them?

The third question is, should he throw off this burden?

The fourth question is, if this burden is not to be thrown off, either because it cannot be done or it should not be done, what is there that can be done to solve his problem or at least to alleviate it?

A full answer to the questions, assuming that it is possible, could hardly be attempted within these limited confines. Indeed, libraries of volumes might be cited as references. If only the mere outlines of an answer can be suggested, it may be worth the effort.

Why is the Jew singled out for special attack? Is there something really wrong with him that in so many lands he more than any other group draws the hatred of men?

In a world which is sick and troubled, the Jew is singled out for attack because it is easier to find a scapegoat than to find a remedy.

The last thing which human nature cares to do is to blame itself. Therefore, the first available pretext is seized upon. Dictators and demagogues who are experts in mob psychology, have in anti-Semitism, a ready-made alibi. It is ready-made because it has a history and a tradition. The Christian story of the crucifixion has attached the label "villain" to the Jew. The label is readily transferable from the realm of religion to the realm of politics and economics. References to the Jew as international capitalist plotting the financial control of the world, or as international Communist plotting the ruin of the present order, belong to the same villain pattern which nineteen hundred years of unChristian Christian teaching has built up. As long as the Jew persists as a distinct entity among the nations, clinging to religious traditions, cultural patterns and folk ways which are unlike those of his neighbors, and maintaining a sense of kinship with "K'lal Israel," "catholic" Israel, so long will he continue to be easily distinguishable, so long will it continue to be easy to single him out and to use him as the scapegoat, so long will he continue to be a convenient target of malevolence.

That does not mean to say that the Jew is actually a paragon of virtue, without blemish or without sin. He is only human and all too fallible. There are bad Jews who make the Jewish lot harder than it need be. There are Jews who are dishonorable in business, reprobate in personal morals and obnoxious in manners. For such Jews the rest of the Jewish community pays a heavy price because they furnish an additional pretext to the mouthings of the anti-Semites. We have learned from sad experience the world's peculiar system of bookkeeping, that if one among us sins, its obloquy is visited upon all of us. Jewish sinners should consider that they are not only disgracing themselves as human beings, but they are injuring the Jewish people as a people.

Even if all Jews, however, were paragons of virtue, they would still be vilified, condemned, and hounded, because it would suit the purposes of the misleaders of society who need a villain for the melodrama which they are concocting. In the Jew they have someone whom they consider to be a ready-made candidate for the role. There is more psychological truth than fiction in the story concerning an official in high authority in Fascist Japan, who is reported to have cabled to his ally, Germany's Minister of Propaganda, "We are starting an anti-Semitic movement in Japan. Please send us some Jews."

The second question is, can the Jew throw off his burden and thereby gain reprieve for himself, or at least for his children? The question is not whether he should but whether he can throw this burden off, whether it is a physical possibility.

Contrary to the impression which has become current since Hitler's declared policy of visiting the Jewishness of ancestors upon the children unto the third generation, it is still possible in many lands for a Jew to renounce his birthright and thus to ensure that his children or his grandchildren, if not he himself, should be accepted in non-Jewish society and spared the tragic price which Jewish identity entails in the kind of world in which we live.

There are Christian families in Europe and in America today, whose lineage from Jewish ancestry is relatively recent. Their ancestors, having left the Jewish fold, having married out of their Faith, and having reared their children as Catholics or Protestants, succeeded in extinguishing the Jewish identity of the family tree. There is no inexorable law which prevents it. It has been done in thousands of instances and will continue to be done, Hitler's proclamations to the contrary notwithstanding.

Being a Jew, is in the long range, a matter of choice. By his own act of will, an American Jew can determine today to leave the fold and take the first step which will ensure for his grandchildren, if not for himself and his children, a liberation from the burden of being a Jew, if an unwelcome burden it be.

The third question is, should the Jew throw off his burden? That there are some who would like to do it hardly needs to be argued. There are young people, embittered by their disappointments in the quest for employment because they are Jews, who revile their parents for having visited upon them their Jewish birth. Their ambition is to disentangle themselves from the handicap which hampers their economic and social progress. The material advantages of such a step are apparent on the surface.

What prevents most of them from taking that step? Is it the force of habit, the reluctance to change the direction of their lives, their associations and their social "milieu"? Are they deterred by the fear of incurring the illwill and rebuke of friends or of hurting the sensibilities of parents and relatives?

When the question is asked, should they throw off this burden, it is placed upon moral and ethical grounds, not upon the ground of convenience and expediency. If there are Jews who would like to throw off the yoke and who hesitate to do so because they do not wish to risk being looked down upon as renegades, such Jews do not come within the purview of the question. "Should," implies moral and ethical justification.

The answer to that question is a categorical "no." There is that much of the Divine quality in human nature, that almost instinctively it condemns cowardice and honors fortitude, disapproves of betrayal and applauds resistance to the forces of evil. We call it the "conscience" of mankind. Men often do things against their consciences, but inwardly they are ashamed. It did not require a manual of social ethics to tell the men on the *Titanic* that women and children must go to the lifeboats first. It is not necessary to cite legal authorities to convince us that a kidnaper or an assaulter of women is a foul creature. It does not require any lengthy exposition to arouse our admiration for the martyr and the saint, be his name Akiba, Joan of Arc, Edith Cavell, or Albert Einstein. Such is the difference between "should" and "would." "Would" is a statement of desire; "should" is a statement of moral and ethical justification.

Should the Jew throw off his burden? It would be a betrayal of his moral and ethical self-respect. Has not the Jew a right to exist? Has not the Jewish people the right to go on? Even if it had no special purpose to serve in the world, even if it had no Torah to espouse, no cultural contribution to make, it would still have a right to exist. Life is its own justification, even the life of an individual, how much more the life of a people. Civilized opinion sanctions the right of undistinguished peoples such as the Albanians or the Ethiopians to exist. Though theirs is a relatively humble place in the cultural hierarchy of the nations, the aggressions upon their land and life were vehemently condemned by the conscience of humanity.

Is the Jew, the sponsor of the Torah which is the acknowledged textbook of personal and social ethics and morality, a people whose noteworthy record of intellectual and spiritual achievement is recognized, less entitled to survive? It is not only his right but his duty toward humanity as well as toward himself, to carry on. For the Jewish people to capitulate to the forces of evil, to commit national suicide, would be an act of betrayal not only against its own past and future, but against civilization. It would be to accept the evil world upon its evil terms instead of standing by Jewish values of ethical worth which hold the key to the salvation of the human race.

Therefore, if any individual Jew would abandon his people in order to save his own skin or that of his offspring, let him know that he is doing something which he has no moral right to do, that morally and ethically he is the betrayer of his people's birthright, and stands convicted at the bar of conscience.

The final question is the most important because the answer

to it implies a program of action. If the burden of Jewish identity is not to be thrown off either because it cannot be done or because it should not be done, what can be done to solve the Jewish problem or at least to alleviate it?

The answer to this question is two-fold. The first is directed outwardly toward the world, the second is directed inwardly toward the Jew himself.

If the root of the Jewish tragedy is the sickness of the world in which he lives, then obviously the fundamental solution must be in the direction of curing the ills of humanity. By making a contribution toward the cure of humanity's ills, the Jew would be helping himself as well as his fellowmen.

What is the cure? Is it the economic reconstruction of the social order to the end that poverty and unemployment shall be abolished and all men be freed from the terrorism of insecurity, and thus one of the prime causes of war be removed? Then let the Jew do his share toward effectuating that cure. Does the cure consist in safeguarding democracy and democratic institutions against the menace of totalitarianism? Then let the Jew be found in the front ranks of the battles for democracy. Is the solution of humanity's ills to be found in the strengthening of the moral fiber and ethical sinews of men and women? Then let the Jew espouse every movement, religious, educational, philanthropic, which is calculated to train men and women from childhood up, for the highest type of citizenship.

Every Jew has a duty to society directly, and to himself as a Jew, indirectly, to take part in those programs which in his opinion offer the cure or a cure for the sick world. When the world becomes a wholesome place in which to live, when there will be enough food and shelter to go around, when nations will not need to fight over markets, and men over jobs, when it will no longer be necessary to whip up hatreds of group against group and nation against nation, then the lot of the Jew will be correspondingly easier. At the present moment, it may seem to be a remote prospect, but one day the goal will be realized. To the realization of that goal, the Jew has both ordinary and extraordinary reason to dedicate himself. This is the outward phase of the program, the Jew in relation to the world.

The second phase has to do with the Jew in relation to himself and to his own people.

If one may borrow a term from the field of international relations, one might say that the fundamental issue of Jewish life is isolationism versus collective security.

Who is the isolationist in the Jewish camp?

There is, or was, the social isolationist. He kept aloof from his brethren because he considered himself as belonging to the "bessere Juden," too good to mingle with the common folk. For the Jewish masses he felt disdain, or at best, pity. In the presence of those folk whose grandfathers happened to be born in the "wrong" part of Europe, he was most uncomfortable.

In the sphere of communal responsibilities, the isolationist is, or was, the self-centered individualist whose whole existence revolved about the axis of his personal needs and concerns. He fared best in the large cities where he could hide successfully behind the anonymity of the multitude, safe from the dangers of being singled out for rebuke. Discovered and approached, his alibis were inexhaustible. When approached for local charities, he would say that the situation overseas is more pressing. Approached for overseas relief, he would say that charity begins at home. For religion in general or for Judaism in particular, he had no use, considering himself too enlightened for religious commitments and too cosmopolitan for Synagogue affiliation. His favorite rationalization was his doctrine of Americanism, that America is a melting pot and that Jewish loyalty is a narrowing, stultifying influence inconsistent with the spirit of true Americanism. Zionism, his pet aversion, he condemned with charges of dual allegiance. He was as opposed to it as unalterably as a centrifugal force is opposed to a centripetal force. He both hated and feared it.

Such are the earmarks of the isolationist in the Jewish camp.

Every community has had them. If they are less numerous and less vocal today than they were yesterday, it is because the force of events has exposed the speciousness of their position and has discredited their rationalizations.

The social snob has been shocked by the discovery that in the eyes of the anti-Semite there are no "bessere Juden," and that all Jews are smeared with the same brush of vilification.

The shirker of communal responsibilities has found it increasingly embarrassing to play the part of a parasite receiving privileges without bearing responsibilities, letting others fight the battles for Jewish honor and Jewish rights, in which he has a stake, without lending his aid.

The pseudo-enlightened abstainer from the Synagogue has lived to see Religion become not only intellectually respectable as the erstwhile conflict between Religion and Science was resolved, but elevated by the leaders of public opinion to the "must" list of civilization, as the torchbearer in an age threatened with darkness. Moreover, as a Jew he has come to the realization that his children, reared in a spiritual "no man's land," were empty of inner resources with which to meet the world's insinuations. They have been bereft of their birthright, a lost generation. He could not have helped noticing that the "melting-pot" theory of Americanism was only a superficial phrase without cultural validity, and that the leaders of American thought were invoking Professor John Dewey's phrase, "cultural pluralism," to describe an American civilization not in terms of a melting-pot producing a characterless amalgam, but a symphony orchestra in which every instrument makes its best contribution by producing its most characteristic tones.

Likewise anti-Zionism has lost its rationalization. The "bogey" of dual allegiance and unAmericanism has been punctured by the personal example of leading Zionists of the stamp of Louis D. Brandeis, Julian W. Mack and Felix Frankfurter. Modern Palestine, whose foundation stones, laid by Zionists two generations ago, were spurned by the "practical" builders, has become pre-eminent as a home and haven for refugees.

On all counts, isolationism has been discredited. It has failed to bring the expected immunity to the individual Jew. It has impoverished and debased him as a human being. For the Jewish community it has been a force of corrosiveness and disruption.

There was insight as well as foresight in the comment of the Passover Haggadah that the villainy of the wicked son, the "rasha" lay in his isolationism, "in that he removed himself from the community." The isolationist is the "rasha" in Jewish life.

Collective security is the only policy which holds promise for the Jew in the solution of inner problems of Jewish life. "All Israel are responsible one for the other." In collective responsibility lies our strength and our hope. Benjamin Franklin's caution uttered to his American contemporaries long ago applies ever more poignantly to us as Jews today. We must hang together or we shall hang separately.

Upon American Jews there devolves a special responsibility. In the desperate plight of the Jewish people today, American Jewry, strong, free and relatively comfortable, represents the one strong staff of support. The student of history must go back to the Jews of Mohammedan Spain to find a parallel to the favorable position of American Israel in comparison with other Jewries today.

As one after another of the great Jewish communities in Europe are laid low, the finger of destiny points to us. It is as if the voice of Mordecai were challenging us, "Who knows but that for just such a time as this hast thou attained thy royal estate?"

Our power to bear this responsibility will depend on how far American Jews will stop being individualists and isolationists and will become infused with a sense of collective responsibility. An organized, integrated American Jewry of four and a half millions can become a tremendous force. A disorganized, disintegrated American Jewry is impotent.

It will also depend upon the program to which we dedicate our collective effort. The policy of collective security needs to be implemented by a program. It will have to be something more than a program of philanthropy. Help to the poor, the sick, the orphaned, the aged,—of course! Relief to Jews abroad as well as here,—of course! That is elementary. Our record as philanthropists, however, is not enough for a community which is to be considered a successor to the great Jewries of the past. We remember Babylonian Jewry for the Talmud it produced, Spanish Jewry for its Jehudah Halevi and Moses Maimonides, German Jewry for its Moses Mendelssohn, Russian and Polish Jewry for its Elijah Gaon, and the Baal Shem Tov. Shall American Jewry be remembered only for its million dollar hospitals and its efficient Federations of Charities?

We are called upon here to develop a program of Jewish education that should be more than the smattering which a Sunday School curriculum imparts. To our shame, a great majority of our children receive no Jewish education and belong to the class, "who do not even know enough to ask a Jewish question." Ours should be a system of education based on the weekday instruction that should prepare the child to read and understand Hebrew, to follow the right side of the Prayerbook, and to be conversant with the history and literature of our people. It should be a system of education culminating in popular and well-supported institutions of higher Jewish learning. Such a program of Jewish education should receive at the hands of American Jewry at least the same recognition, consideration and support as Federations of Charities are now receiving.

We are called upon to make of the Synagogue and Jewish Congregational life something more than a static weekend assembly confined to religious worship. The Synagogue and the Congregation should become a dynamic institution teeming with

Jewish activity, religious, educational, philanthropic,—the train-ing ground for Jewish leadership, a recruiting station for work-ers in important communal enterprises, and a vital link in the collective effort of American Jewish life.

We are called upon to develop strong instrumentalities for the defense of Jewish rights both here and abroad. Stormy days may be ahead, which may threaten the security of Jewish life even here. One voice speaking for a united Israel is needed both for our problems here and for Jewish problems abroad. Is it too much to hope that under the stress of the emergency, a way to unity may be found?

We are called upon to continue and increase the collective responsibility of the Jewish people for the upbuilding of Pal-estine. As a refugee haven alone Eretz Israel has a claim upon Jewish philanthropy, all other considerations apart. There are, however, other considerations which cannot be ignored by a peo-ple that lives "not by bread alone." Modern Palestine, settled and developed by Jews, has made the most significant contribu-tion to the good name of the Jew. It has demonstrated what the Jew as Jew is, how he lives, works, thinks, visions, plays, and meets danger,—when left to his own resources. It has refuted the libel that the Jew is allergic to agriculture, is incapable of co-operative living, and is congenitally a "luftmensch." It has given the Jewish people in our time its best credentials. The support and the development of Jewish life in Palestine is there-fore a collective responsibility for all Israel, redounding to the credit of the Jew everywhere.

A program based upon comprehensive Jewish philanthropy, contentful Jewish education, dynamic Synagogue organization, unified defense of Jewish rights, and energetic devotion to the upbuilding of Eretz Israel would redound to the collective security of Jews and Judaism both here and abroad.

Wherefore is this people different from all other peoples?

The four modern Jewish questions which have been posed under this rubric, and the suggested answers, indicate the nature of the Jewish problem. The theme of collective security versus isolationism points toward the policy and the program called for by the condition of the times in which we live.

If we fail of the goal, let it not be said of our generation, that we did not try the road.

A Rabbi's Score

Address delivered before Congregation
B'nai Jeshurun, January 19, 1939, in ac-
knowledgment of the celebration of its
Rabbi's ministry of twenty years in the
Congregation and in the community.

A Rabbi's Score

I<small>F ANOTHER RABBI</small> came to me at the close of a ministry of twenty years and sought my reaction to him and to his work, and if I knew him well enough to confront him with a frank challenge instead of petting him with platitudes, I should ask him a few questions which I believe to be the fundamental criteria by which to measure a Rabbi's career. Why should I not confront myself with the same questions?

The first question a Rabbi ought to ask himself is what does God mean to him, seeing that his life work is to teach the word of God, and to serve the cause of God. For the answer to that question, the Scriptural portions of these weeks, the early chapters of the Book of Exodus, offer an excellent approach.

When Moses, having undertaken the difficult mission to his people, sought enlightenment on the problem of how to identify for them the God in whose name he was sent, he was given the mandate to say that he came in the name of "Eheyeh asher Eheyeh," "I shall be that which I shall be." This phrase is etymologically the core of the name "Jehovah." The Godhead has never been in Judaism a fixed concept as much as it has been an ever continuing unfoldment, "I shall be that which I shall be."

Another aspect of the same question is treated in these Scriptural texts. Speaking in the name of God, Moses says to the people, "To Abraham, Isaac and Jacob, I appeared as 'El Shaddai.' By my name Jehovah I was not known to them."

The Rabbis have interpreted the name "Shaddai" as a connoting power and might, whereas the name "Jehovah" denotes compassion. To a people in bondage, crying out of their misery, the compassionate aspect of God was the most appealing one.

The God idea is not a static idea in Judaism. Every generation catches new glimpses of the Divine. He is in turn Warrior, Shepherd, King, Judge, Father, depending on what aspect satisfies the people's greatest need at the time. The Rabbis say in connection with these chapters of Exodus, "According to the needs of the hour ,am I named." (Leviticus Rabbah, Chap. XI, sec. 5.) There is no congealed theological formula in Judaism. He who would confine the God idea within the frame of a static definition is in a sense guilty of the sin of idolatry.

Moreover, according to Judaism, the emphasis in defining the meaning of God is not on metaphysics or theology but on ethics. "Acknowledge Him in all thy ways." "This is my God whom I shall glorify." These texts the Rabbis invoke as a basis for pointing out the importance of deed rather than creed. (Sabbath 133b.) "Emulate his ways." "Glorify him with deeds." Not what God is but what God wills is the paramount issue. Properly enough, theological expositions have occupied a relatively minor place in Jewish preaching.

The next question which a Rabbi should ask himself is, how does he translate God in the terms of human experience?

Again our scriptural portion furnishes the clew, "Send forth My people that they may serve Me." It was the first time that the sovereignty of a potentate was challenged in the name of a higher force. The identification of that force with human freedom is the foundation of the Ten Commandments. "I am the Lord thy God who brought thee out of the land of Egypt, out of the house of bondage." The prelude to the Commandments sets the pattern for the character of our religion as a religion of social justice and of universal human values. The ringing words of Micah may still be quoted as the greatest definition of religion in action, "What doth the Lord require of thee O Man, but to do justice, love mercy and walk humbly with thy God." The prophets of Israel and of Judah would not hesitate to excoriate their rulers when their rulers violated the just rights of even their humblest citizens, witness the Prophet Nathan's rebuke to King David, and the Prophet Elijah's castigation of King Ahab.

The Rabbi who shies away from proclaiming to the house of Jacob its transgression, and prefers to be a flunkey rather than a teacher, hardly belongs to the Rabbinical tradition, however pleasant a person he may be to have around at a dinner party. The price of truth is often unpopularity. The converse, however, is not necessarily true. Unpopularity is not necessarily a mark of moral excellence.

In exhorting people to ethical and moral conduct, not only in their personal relations but in group and class relations, pleading for justice between equals, and for solicitude on the part of the strong toward the weak, is part of the Rabbi's function.

Israel's purpose in the world is by its self-dedication to the moral and ethical commandments, to attest to the reality and potency of these ideals. To do that is to do God's Will on earth, is to make life holy, is to sanctify His Name. That is the meaning of "Kiddush Hashem," the sanctification of God's Name.

The third question, therefore, which a Rabbi should ask himself is, how he can help the Jewish people maintain its identity and its character. The existence of the Jewish people is not an end in itself. The physical survival of the Jew may be the prime concern of the philanthropists. Israel's spiritual survival is the prime concern of the Rabbi.

If we are going to survive merely on a socio-biological basis, it may be enough reason to justify condemning those who would annihilate us, but it is hardly enough reason for us to justify to ourselves the price we must pay for our survival. Indeed, if there had been no spiritual "raison d'etre" we should have ceased to exist long ago. Under the pressure of adverse circumstances, our survival has been a psycho-spiritual phenomenon much more than a socio-biological phenomenon. By every law of biology, we should have joined the ancient Egyptians, Babylonians and Persians in the limbo of antiquity. Our plight was much more difficult than theirs and certainly seemed at the time much more hopeless.

We survive because of the vitalizing push of a conscious purpose and destiny. What is that conscious purpose and destiny? It is that the Jewish people is the carrier of a set of ideals and a mode of living embodied in the Torah and in the "mitzvoth." "They are our life and the reason for the length of our days." The ceremonies and institutions of Jewish life are devices by which that spiritual consciousness is maintained which assures self-preservation on the highest level. Thus, by means of the Torah and the "mitzvoth," education and observance, the Jewish people can and should maintain its character and identity.

In the demonstration and fulfillment of the identity of the Jewish people, as a people, Zionism is an indispensable ideal. It is more than concentration of Jewish energies upon the building of Palestine. It is the building of a norm of Jewish living which might serve as a stimulus and standard for Jewish communities throughout the world. The Rabbis tell us that until Israel returns to Eretz Israel the "Shechinah" is in exile. (Megillah 29a.) Translated into tangible terms, it means that the highest values of Jewish life can function only in Eretz Israel. The best example of social idealism to which the Jew can point today is furnished by the workers and farmers of the Jewish National Home. To help in its upbuilding is a contribution to the spiritual as well as the physical well-being of Israel.

These are the criteria by which a Rabbi should be judged and should judge himself. What does God mean to him? How does he translate the God-idea into a program of living? How does he serve the cause of Israel's self-expression and survival?

You will have noticed that nothing has been said about Hitler, about the Jewish tragedy abroad, or about the fighting of anti-

Semitism here. These are obvious responsibilities. Every Jew is concerned with them. To the extent that the Rabbi is looked upon as a Jewish leader, he too must concern himself with these problems. What has been dwelt upon here are the special obligations which devolve upon the Rabbi as Rabbi.

When I review the various causes and purposes within the Synagogue and outside the Synagogue which have claimed me during these years, the retrospect impresses upon me the realization that these have not been haphazard interests seized upon in a "catch-as-catch-can" fashion. Gravitation toward them must have been both in conscious and sub-conscious fulfillment of a set purpose. Permit me to quote from my Valedictory address upon graduation from the Jewish Theological Seminary, more than twenty years ago.

"We realize that the responsibility of a Rabbi in America is tremendous. It involves the upbuilding of a Jewish life in this country. At present that life is in a chaotic state. The Jewish population here is far from homogeneous. A Babel of types and conditions prevails. Jewish public opinion is scarcely perceptible. Jewish life is constantly on the defensive against an overwhelming host of adverse factors, social, economic and intellectual. In the ranks of the 'defenders of the faith,' are some who have stubbornly intrenched themselves, and will not bend nor yield, mindless of the fact that that which will not yield must break. Others are pursuing a policy of indiscriminate assimilation with external cultures, heedless of the axiom that their first duty is to assimilate their own. Neither of these methods seems to promise a solution. The first seems to render Judaism repellent to the younger generation, because it severs religion from life. It refuses to reckon with the demands of life which are manifold. The second seems to end by severing life from religion.

"The hope for the restoration of Eretz Israel to the people of Israel, now the promise of a world power, has quickened the Jewish pulse the world over. With a center for Judaism in the Jewish land, the constructive work of the Rabbi throughout the

Diaspora will gain stimulus and animation. Then the upbuilding of a Jewish life in this country will proceed all the more readily; it will take on warmth and color under the rays that shall radiate from Zion.

"Here then is the problem which faces us as Rabbis,—to make Judaism a part of the life of the Jews, not alone in the Synagogue, but in all of their social relations, in every phase of their activity, whether it be physical, intellectual or recreational.

"We should be disappointed and heartbroken if our dreams and aspirations were not to be realized in some measure in actual life. But we have faith in the ultimate and we also have a vision of what that ultimate is to be. The mere possession of an ideal is in itself of great value. It gives direction and purpose to effort so that one is saved from being tossed about on the waves of contingency."

The Synagogue historically has cradled all the activities which now exist in independent institutions, the Beth Din, teaching Jews how to live at peace with one another, the program of philanthropy, the cultivation of amicable relations with our non-Jewish neighbors, the call to the vigorous exercise of the American way of life, and the espousal of Zionism in all its implications both for Palestine and for ourselves. Whatever opportunities may have come to my lot to serve these causes, outside the immediate premises of the Congregation, have also served the purposes of the Synagogue in its broadest sense.

During these twenty years, the Synagogue may have lost some of its former sway over the life of the Jewish community, as activities which formerly were nurtured under its wing have developed into separate institutions with their own identities, sometimes in competition to their "alma mater." There are Jews whose affiliation with the life of their people begins and ends with philanthropy, or Zionism, or Christian-Jewish goodwill. In this age of specialization, Jews are becoming specialists with relation to Jewish matters. If it makes for the intensification of Jewish activity, it also makes for confusion and disorganization.

The average Jewish layman is pulled hither and yon by a number of different groups and movements, each of which professes to have the solution to the Jewish problem.

On the other hand, the Synagogue has gained something in this score of years. It has become less sectarian. The theological controversies between Reform and Orthodoxy which raged in former decades, no longer figure prominently in the arena of public discussion. What accounts for the change of temper? In the first place, the Reform movement in the Synagogue has lost a good deal of its edge as a result of the lesson that negations and omissions are hardly a recipe for religious enthusiasm. Moreover, Reform could never become a mass movement as long as it existed in a vacuum of rationalization rather than in the soil of sentiment and tradition. A number of leading Reform Rabbis have recognized and sought to correct these inadequacies. Even more compelling has been the fact that the fundamental problems which have arisen in recent years affecting the vitals of the Jewish people have made questions of ritual and theology seem hardly worth fighting over in the face of the larger concerns calling for a united Israel.

The Synagogue in these two decades has become not only less sectarian but it has come closer to the everyday life of the people. This is the real significance of the Synagogue Center movement of the past two decades. It may not have achieved the success which had been predicted for it twenty years ago. The gymnasium may not have led the youth straight from the basketball to the prayerbook. Yet, behind even the mistakes of the Synagogue Center movement, there was a commendable motivation, namely, to bring the Synagogue closer to the people. Ministering not only as a house of worship, but as a social, cultural, and recreational center for children and adults, the Synagogue, especially in the smaller communities, has touched the lives of Jewish families at many points. If particular techniques have been ill-considered, or if mistakes of misplaced emphasis have been committed, the mistakes are being corrected, as experience teaches. Our Synagogues had become too formalized and too over-awing. This is not the Jewish way. The Jew always felt at home in his Synagogue. The Synagogue today is tending in the direction of less formality. Its program is being extended beyond the Sabbath-Festival-High Holy Day schedule. The voices of the children resound within its walls more frequently. The Synagogue has come to mean more in the daily lives of people than it had meant in the American scene of a generation ago.

Compared with old European Jewries which had their roots in a thousand years of local history, the Synagogue in America and the Jewish community here are relatively young institutions. American Judaism is not a finished product. It is still in the making. We have just begun to compose and assimilate the variegated elements in the local scene. The names which many Congregations took upon their establishment here, or by which they were popularly known, such as "Spanish and Portuguese," "Bohemian," "Russian," "Galician," "Roumanian," "Bialestoker," bear witness to the diversity of the American Jewish constituency. They bear witness also to the initial feeling of strangeness on the part of the immigrants in their new environment. Gradually the geographical reminiscences referring to the Old World are wearing off. The erstwhile immigrants having struck root here feel eagerly and gratefully committed to the American scene. They are becoming integrated into one American Jewish community.

There are problems, adjustments and tasks indigenous to the American environment. American Judaism cannot be expected to lean altogether on Palestine for the determination of its character, however much inspiration and nourishment must inevitably come out of Zion. A community of nearly five million Jews must inevitably in the course of time generate forms of Jewish living that will bear its own unique stamp. We have here the resources of numbers, economic strength, and religious freedom. Possessing these advantages, we have every reason to give a good account of ourselves, to fashion here a link that should be worthy of the Jewish tradition.

We have made some progress, scant though it be, toward the achievement of unity with reference to our common concerns. The Joint Distribution Committee, the United Palestine and the United Jewish Appeal nationally, and the Jewish Community Welfare Chests locally, have fulfilled a measure of unity in fund-raising. The General Jewish Council, integrating the American Jewish Congress, the American Jewish Committee, the B'nai B'rith, and the Jewish Labor Committee, has endeavored to establish unity in the defense of Jewish rights and Jewish honor. It is still a weak vessel, little more than nominal in effect. A great part of the road toward the desired goal still lies before us. Pride of authority and pride of opinion among the top stratum of American Jewry will have to be yielded, before we can expect to be well on our way toward American Jewish unity.

The achievement of greater Jewish content is an even more difficult task, because it entails a process of education for young and old. We need to recognize frankly the woeful lack of Jewish knowledge which is characteristic of the American Jews by and large. One can understand the phenomenon without indulging it. Many of our generation grew up in homes where Jewish education was negligible or altogether absent either because of deliberate omission by the parents or the economic exigencies which preoccupied their time and their minds. In any event the situation is deplorable.

What is even more deplorable than ignorance, is complacency therein which disregards opportunities for remedying the fault in oneself and, what is more serious, remedying it in the growing generation. The indifference of the "am-haaretz" is bad enough. His arrogance is vicious. An attitude of respect for Jewish learning would go far toward atonement. Esteem for the Jewish scholar, instead of an attitude of disdain which is something shown by the man of "kemach," material substance, toward the man of Torah, would be a great encouragement for

Jewish scholarship in America. It would reflect itself not only in the proper maintenance of Talmud Torahs and Congregational schools but in a more adequate support of institutions of higher Jewish learning such as the Jewish Theological Seminary of America, the Yeshivah College, the Hebrew Union College, and the Jewish Institute of Religion, where the torch of the Torah is kept alive. Jews must learn that it is not enough to be "good Jews at heart."

In view of the world-shaking events of our time, an extraordinary responsibility devolves upon us. There is a law of compensation which applies to the organism of a people no less than to the organism of an individual. When one member of the body becomes impaired or destroyed, the strength of the other members increases. The catastrophe which has befallen European Jewry summons us to strengthen our sinews. It is more than a temporary emergency which challenges us. Whatever developments in the international situation may be in store, it is certain, so far as the Jewish situation is concerned, that American Jewry will become more and more, the mainstay of Jewish life in the Diaspora.

What Jewish life achieves here is therefore a gain as well for Jewish life everywhere. Upon us, the Jews of America, rests a burden of responsibility for the Jewish people abroad, such as has not devolved in centuries upon any one community. We are fortunate to have the physical power to bear the burden. What we need is spiritual power, vision, initiative, statesmanship, and capacity for self-sacrifice, commensurate with the greatness and urgency of the task.

At this twentieth anniversary milestone, I should be less than human if I did not feel warmed by the personal aspect of the celebration, the outpouring of friendship which greets me. I see before me men, women, young people and children to whom I have been privileged to minister in sorrow and in joy. Their lives have punctuated my life. Their individual experiences under the wing of this beloved Congregation,—Bar Mitzvah,

Confirmation, Marriage, sorrowful partings when the ultimate summons called, Religious School, Sisterhood, Men's Club and youth group affiliations, Synagogue attendance, are woven into the pattern of my Rabbinate in B'nai Jeshurun. You who are here, and others like you who are not here, have poured content into the mold of my aspirations, have filled my score of years with purpose.

To this hour of reminiscence belongs also the remembrance of my parents who taught me to respect the Book, my father of blessed memory, one of the greatest scholars and keenest minds I have ever known, and my mother, God bless her, a woman who did not have the benefits of any formal education but who appreciated Torah as the best "sehorah."

To be confronted by the living witnesses of one's lifework, makes one both glad and humble, glad to have had the privilege of touching the lives of so many during a ministry of twenty years, and humble at the realization of how many oversights have been committed, how many opportunities have been neglected, and how much better that ministry might have been fulfilled.

When some years ago I delved into the archives of the Congregation and noted that Rabbi Morris Raphall had served this Congregation for nineteen years, and that Rabbi Henry S. Jacobs had served it for seventeen years, I wondered whether I should have the "zechuth," the privilege to equal that length of service. Yet here I find myself suddenly confronted by the incontrovertible figure, 1919—1939.

It is inevitable that one should be conscious of the Congregational and communal changes which the score of years has brought. Every milestone in life is a point of vantage from which to observe and survey the road which has been traversed.

1919 was in the midst of America's war year. Jews rallied here, as they did in every land, around their country's flag in numbers far exceeding their proportion to the population. Their blood soaked the soil of every battlefield. A universal hope filled the hearts of men that out of the crucible of affliction would come forth something better for the future of mankind.

The Balfour Declaration, issued at the end of 1917, was taken by many to be an earnest of a hoped-for, happier dispensation for the Jew and for all humanity. American Jewry, secure and untroubled in its own position, had organized a great relief action to save the lives and heal the wounds of the afflicted of our people in the war ravaged lands abroad. It came to be known as the Joint Distribution Committee, representing the joining of forces, the union of American Israel on a program of overseas philanthropy. That was 1919.

1939 finds disillusionment in the place of hope. The most terrible of wars is in the offing. The whittling down of the Balfour Declaration is in keeping with the "let-down" in all the great promises of 1919. If the Jewish settlement of Palestine has grown substantially in spite of all obstacles, it is an amazing tribute to the indomitable will of a stiff-necked people.

The Joint Distribution Committee is still "in business," alleviating distress on a greater scale than ever before. On many fronts a relentless war is being waged against the Jewish people. Even American Jewry, the Joseph among the brethren, favored by a benign Providence, even this prince in the house of Jacob, does not feel too secure and is not untroubled.

In these twenty years an indigenous generation of American Israel has grown up. The strictures upon immigration have thrown us upon our own resources in a greater degree than ever before. We are no longer tied as closely as we used to be to the religious and cultural apron strings of European Jewries. It remains to be seen whether we can stand on our own feet. That our Jewish youth of today is more Jewishly conscious than was the Jewish youth of twenty years ago is apparent, though it must be admitted with contrition that they have not voluntarily risen into this consciousness as much as they have been kicked into it by the boot of anti-Semitism.

Whether the new sense of Jewish awareness will take the form of creative, positive Jewish thinking and Jewish living, or will be limited to apologetics and "damn Hitler" meetings, remains to be seen. We have before us a serious responsibility in the field of Jewish education in its broadest sense, for the Children of Israel of all classes, ages and conditions.

Such is the outer frame in which our Congregational picture of the score of years is set.

In May, 1918, our present Synagogue edifice was dedicated. The new influx of members and seatholders was a revitalizing influence, justifying the judgment of the leaders of the Congregation who had advocated the change of location. In the civilian war-time program of non-sectarian and Jewish relief, our congregants rendered substantial aid. In the maintenance of institutions of Jewish learning in the community our support was a source of strength. In the fund raising efforts on behalf of the New Palestine, our man-power and woman-power took a leading part. In the local Federation campaigns, and in every great philanthropic endeavor both for local and overseas needs our Congregation was eminently helpful.

While doing our share for the community, we set our own house in order. The beauty of our Synagogue edifice was enhanced by the exquisite decoration of the interior, adding the holiness of beauty to the beauty of holiness. Into our educational program a weekday Hebrew school was introduced for our children, and evening classes for our men and women. As the religious, cultural and social life of our community expanded beyond the available physical accommodations, a magnificent Community Center was erected.

The new facilities stimulated new activities—the organization of a Men's Club, a Parents' Association, adult classes, youth groups, the establishment of a Junior Congregation, provisions for an overflow High Holy Day Congregation, and the development of higher standards for our Religious School program. The Synagogue itself extended its scope by the addition of a Sunday Lecture Service which soon attracted city-wide interest.

Thus, the coefficient of our service as a powerhouse for Judaism in this community has increased and multiplied during this score of years.

It is a source of considerable satisfaction that one's standards still hold, that one's banner is still aloft after the clashes with the realities of daily tasks and the grips with the limitations of human nature which sometimes leave in their wake disillusionment and heartbreak.

No Rabbi can pay a greater compliment to his Congregation than to say at the end of twenty years of preaching and teaching that in the main direction of his leading, it walked with him, that even when it did not follow the Rabbi it tried to understand him, and even when it did not understand him, it tried to respect him.

For every opportunity which has come to me during this score of years to touch the life of this splendid Congregation in Israel and the lives of its individual families, to make of B'nai Jeshurun a fruitful branch in the vineyard of American Judaism, and to lend a helpful word or deed redounding to the interests of "K'lal Israel," and to the benefit of the American community as a whole, I feel humbly grateful.

I dislike the word "cleric" and "clergyman" because it carries a connotation of the ministry of religion as something apart from week-a-day life, something reserved for Saturdays and Sundays. "Catholic Judaism," a term popularized by the late Professor Solomon Schechter, conveys the all inclusive nature of the Rabbi's function. I am proud to bear the title "Rabbi" because it is all inclusive, a comprehensive concern with everything that is important and worthwhile.

There is a special zest in being a Rabbi today, in being a spokesman of religion at such a time as this. It has been charged against organized religion in the past that it has often stood on the side of reaction. Few would level that charge against organized religion today. It is in the front line of defense against the forces of darkness. The foremost needs of our time and the profoundest principles of our civilization are served by religion today. It is the champion of the rights of the individual, the defender of freedom of conscience and the perennial reminder that material progress without spiritual motivation is a bane and not a boon for humanity. Morally motivated, our science and invention are blessings. Otherwise, they can become the curse of our civilization.

In the battle between the contending forces, the Jew belongs inevitably on the side of democracy in all its political and spiritual implications. It is his choice as well as his necessity. Since 1933, the Jew has borne the brunt of the attack against Democracy. He should accept the commitment with pride and passion. His struggle is thus lifted to a plane far beyond the struggle for self-preservation.

To have been able to serve as Rabbi in the American setting, and to serve America thereby, has been a doubly happy portion. This blessed land, cynosure of the eyes of the harassed world, is still young, fresh and relatively unspoiled. The decadence which has corroded Europe has as yet not infected us. Sporadically depressed by pessimism, we have a youthful resiliency which comes to our aid in a crisis. Diverted now and then, here and there, by seductive voices appealing to our basest instincts of fear and provincialism, we recover our sanity and our soundness, when the authentic voice of American tradition exhorts us. In this congenial atmosphere, Jewish life has a chance to flourish, and by flourishing, to add valuable qualities to the whole of American life and civilization.

When Rabbis Get Together

Delivered as past President of the New York Board of Jewish Ministers at its Fiftieth Anniversary Celebration held at the Young Men's Hebrew Association, New York, November 1, 1931.

When Rabbis Get Together

It is not an easy task to be an historian without archives, for one is then compelled to rely either upon his imagination or upon his memory. The Board of Jewish Ministers, though it embraces Orthodox, Conservative and Reform Rabbis seems, so far as its historical sense is concerned, to attach undue importance to oral tradition, because its written records are conspicuously sparse. Maybe some day they will turn up in full, as happened once to a Code of the Law in the days of Josiah, King of Judah. That may help our Centennial Jubilee but it cannot retroactively help our semi-centennial celebration tonight. Hence I have been obliged to rely a little upon memory, not my memory but the memory of some of my younger colleagues such as H. Pereira Mendes, a little upon research into files of contemporary Jewish periodicals, and a little upon imagination in filling in gaps and in collating facts.

There is a school of historians who believe that it is history which makes men rather than men who make history. I doubt if even the most patriotic member of our Board would venture the claim that the Board of Jewish Ministers has made history. The truth is rather that Jewish history in New York has made the New York Board of Jewish Ministers. This rabbinical association reflects the history of the past fifty years of Jewish life in our great metropolis, the new Jerusalem of the Diaspora, successor to Cordova, Mayence and Wilno.

1881, the year of our founding, is a milestone year in American Jewish history. Although social processes move in flux and cannot be fixed by dry termini, the year 1881 is usually accepted as inaugurating a new period in the American Jewish scene, a period of vast immigration different from the preceding periods both in its unprecedented numbers and in its predominantly East European origin. During this period the economic, philanthropic and religious life of American Jewry took on a new complexion, and became the multifarious community which it is today. American Israel before 1881 was a relatively simple family compared to what it has become since that time.

And New York, more than any other city in the land, has experienced these epochal transformations. Being the main port of entry, it retained the bulk of the newcomers. Its Jewish population in 1880 was 60,000. Its present population represents an increase of 3,000 per cent, not counting this morning's birth announcements in the New York *Times*. Its problems have increased almost in proportion.

While Jewish problems have changed very much, the Jewish problem has not changed materially. The New York Board of Jewish Ministers soon after its organization, opened a course of lectures in the Young Men's Hebrew Association. The first lecture was delivered by Rev. Dr. Gottheil, upon the subject, "Why I am a Jew." I doubt if much fundamentally new material bearing upon this question has been discovered during the past five decades.

1881 was the heyday of agnosticism. Darwin, Huxley and Spencer were the major prophets of the day. Their disciples, all too eager and some half-baked, illustrating the Rabbinic principle of "erroneous learning makes mischief," went far beyond their masters in the dethronement of God. Ingersoll's "Mistakes of Moses," published two years earlier, was a "best seller." On the opposite side, panicky Orthodox theologians, unaccustomed to challenge from scientific or even pseudo-scientific quarters, were making themselves ludicrous by choosing ludicrous issues for the combat. Rev. De Witt Talmadge, a stalwart defender of the Faith, preached an impassioned sermon attacking the heretics who claimed that the gullet of the whale, by positive measurement, is too small to swallow a prophet.

The Jewish camp was not free from theological agitation. The controversy was not so much between the forces of religion and the forces of agnosticism, as between the liberal and orthodox elements within the religious category. Within the Synagogue, Reform insurgency was being met by Orthodox resistance. Forensic thunderbolts were hurled from the Olympian pulpits of Isaac M. Wise and Sabato Morais, Kaufman Kohler and Samuel M. Isaacs. In the columns of periodicals, the polemic storms were continuous. Truly it was the "contention for the sake of Heaven," a controversy on the highest possible ground, actuated by sincerity on both sides.

The founding of the New York Board of Jewish Ministers in 1881 was therefore a remarkable phenomenon and a happy augury. It was a remarkable phenomenon because it was the first attempt in the Jewish camp to establish a common denominator of religious unity across the sharp differences. It was a happy augury because it foreshadowed the present condition of mutual respect which obtains on a national scale among the several branches of the American Synagogue, Orthodox, Conservative and Reform.

Jews often indulge in self-depreciation. One of the favorite points of their self-disparagement is the matter of Jewish unity. Yet to confound the defeatists there are the Synagogue Council of America, the Jewish War Relief drives, and the Jewish Agency for Palestine, signs not of disunion but of union. The New York Board of Jewish Ministers, embracing as it did from the very beginning, Orthodox, Conservative and Reform avowals, has in its humble way served these fifty years as token and aid for the transcendent major Jewish unity in the midst of inevitable minor diversities.

The founders of the Board should be recalled at this anniversary gathering. One of them, thank God, graces our assembly tonight. They were Kaufman Kohler of Beth El, Gustav Gottheil of Emanuel, Henry S. Jacobs of B'nai Jeshurun, Adolph Huebsch of Ahawath Chesed, H. Pereira Mendes of Shearith Israel, and F. de Sola Mendes of Shaaray Tefilla. They were called in those days, "the big six." The title should have been patented as it was subsequently appropriated by a firm of clothing manufacturers, now defunct. The first President of the Board who served until the time of his death in 1893, was Henry S. Jacobs of B'nai Jeshurun, who was recognized as the senior among his colleagues. The first secretary was a very young man, Rev. H. Pereira Mendes. May he be recorded in the Book of Life for many years to come.

Among the first acts of this newly organized body was the formation of a "normal class" for the instruction of teachers in religious schools. Classes were conducted on Monday and Thursday afternoons, the traditional weekdays for religious instruction as far back as the origin of the Synagogue. The subjects taught were the history of Judaism, Jewish literature, post-Biblical history and the art of teaching. The Board was also deeply interested in the administration of the Hebrew Free Schools of the City which had been organized originally to combat the Christian missionary activity. The "mitzvah" of Jewish education came naturally to the Board of Jewish Ministers as its first responsibility. Feeling a concern also for the problem of abnormal children, the Board of Jewish Ministers sounded a plea at the Lord Montefiore centenary celebration in 1884 for a Jewish children's protectory which later came into being.

Pastoral visits to the sick and dying were arranged for the larger Jewish institutions in the city, of which the most eminent were the Mount Sinai Hospital and the Montefiore Home for Incurables. In 1891, the Board issued an appeal to the New York Congregations for the establishment of a Chaplaincy Fund to be administered under its supervision. Dr. Raden was the first Chaplain to serve in that capacity.

Everything which touched the religious well-being of the Jewish community came within the purview of the Board's discussions. Sometimes the matter ended with the discussion, for the Board was not in a position to carry through any large projects. Its main function was to clarify ideas by the interchange of opinions. At other times, the discussions culminated in action.

The seed of many an important Jewish and communal enterprise was sown at these meetings. Questions related to Sabbath observance, and the problem of establishing uniform procedure in the case of marriages and divorce, were among the more difficult matters which engaged the attention of the Board during the early years of its history. To a degree, these questions are chronic and are as far from solution today as ever they were.

There were also special problems which challenged the Board's attention then and have continued throughout these fifty years of its existence. The Christian missionary challenge was an acute problem in the early years of the Board's history. Another was a flagrant case of anti-Jewish discrimination such as appeared recently at the Kings County Hospital. Sometimes a problem of world-wide consequence to Jewry would arise. A conspicuous example was the recent proposal of Calendar Reform by the League of Nations' Committee. Whatever other disadvantages the proposal may have had, it endangered the observance of the Jewish Sabbath. The united stand of the Jewish people in opposition to the proposed Calendar Reform was one of the important factors in its ultimate failure. The New York Board of Jewish Ministers was the first Jewish body in America before whom the League of Nations' representative appeared. The committee appointed by the Board, headed by Dr. Hyamson gave the impetus to what developed into a crystallized public opinion of American Israel. This opinion, joined to that of other groups, helped to bring about the negative attitude of American public opinion generally.

The Board of Jewish Ministers has several publications to its credit, which offer testimony of its aim and purpose as a unifying factor among the English-speaking Rabbis of our community. Its earliest publication entitled "The Door of Hope" was a manual of religious devotionals for the hours of sorrow and bereavement. Its latest publication bears the title of "The Practical Problems of the Jewish Ministry," a symposium to which no less than thirty Rabbis and three "Rebbitzins" have contributed. Between these two titles and what they represent, lies a vast domain of Jewish questions which the Board of Jewish Ministers has touched. If the resolutions which it has formulated and addressed upon hundreds of occasions could be compiled, they would form a running commentary, a "Tosafot" upon the history of the Jews of New York and of America.

Out of this body there grew in 1884 a larger association known as the Jewish Ministers Association of America, which, embracing rabbis of other cities, marked the earliest attempt at the organization of a rabbinical body of nation-wide proportions. The establishment of major unity above minor differences, has consciously and unconsciously been the motivation of our entire corporate existence.

Perhaps the greatest value which this association has had for us, its members today and for those who preceded us a generation and two generations ago, has been on the personal side. It means much to a Rabbi to meet his colleagues as brothers and friends. Rabbis are a much harassed folk. Because the rabbinate is the most public of all callings, it is emotionally the most taxing. In the Board of Jewish Ministers, Rabbis came together not only as Rabbis but as men. Often the bitter antagonists in public controversies were the most affable of friends in their personal relationships.

You might be curious to know how these Rabbis spent their time in their off moments, in their private conclaves, how they found relief from the pressing duties of their public calling. So far as I can gather, they found relief from the problems of the Rabbinate and still do, by discussing the problems of the Rabbinate. Within the Board meetings, they took their excursions, and they still do, into the realm of Jewish scholarship from which their busy daily work often precluded them. The Board meetings have served for many a scholarly Rabbi as opportunities for ventilating scholastic hobbies and inviting the tonic criticism of fellow laborers in the vineyard of the Torah. It is difficult to measure how much this association has meant to its members as a refuge from the emotional strain of their work, how much it has meant in the camaraderie it has afforded, in which there are no distinctions of oratorical primacy, scholastic hierarchy, or social prestige, but in which fellowship is the only badge.

Goethe has said "What history can give us best is the enthusiasm which it raises in our hearts." The history of the New York Board of Jewish Ministers gives us Rabbis cause to look hopefully to the future. But for Rabbis and laymen alike it is a witness of the larger history of Jewish life in this city and in this country. There is much in that story to hearten us all. American Israel has grown from the least to the greatest of the branches upon the tree of Jewish life—great in numbers, great in the sense of responsibility toward other branches of that stock, however remotely removed, great also in spiritual potentialities. Our fathers hardly expected that in this land, which fifty years ago was regarded by religious leaders abroad with quizzical disdain, the Torah should find one of its few remaining stands today.

We have read in the Synagogues yesterday that God appeared to Abraham "by terebinths of Mamre." The Rabbis take the story to be a significant symbol of the Jewish people. "Judaism is like a living tree. One branch may be cut off but by its vital power another shoot comes forth and flourishes." (Midrash Haggadol to Genesis 18.1.) It seems that American Israel is destined to compensate for those branches which have been cut off, in countries where formerly the tree of Abraham flourished so well.

The influx of recent Jewish life into this country beginning with 1881, the year which we are now commemorating, was an adumbration of what has come to pass. The Board of Jewish Ministers whose career spans these five significant decades, feels highly privileged in having been able to help nurse and nourish this branch of hope and promise.

Passover Pattern

Address delivered before Congregation B'nai Jeshurun, April 23, 1940. The concluding portion was suggested in part by Isaac Nissenbaum's "Derashot le-kal Shabbetot ha-Shanah veha-Moadim," Warsaw, 1923, pp. 157 ff.

Passover Pattern

THE NUMBER FOUR is in the Passover pattern. Four types of sons are described in the Haggadah. Four questions are asked by the youngest child. Four cups of wine punctuate the Seder Service.

In explanation of the number, the Rabbis say that in the chapters of the Book of Exodus referring to the Divine promise of deliverance from Egypt four different expressions are employed, "vehotzeti" "I shall bring forth," "vehitzalti" "I shall rescue," "vegoalti" "I shall redeem," "velokahti," "I shall take." The context is as important as the text. "I shall bring you forth out of the burdens of Egypt." "I shall rescue you from their hard impositions." "I shall redeem you with an outstretched arm." "I shall take you unto Me as My people." (Exodus Rabbah, Chap. VI.)

If Rabbinic amendments are in order, it may be suggested that every one of the four expressions refers to a special phase of Israel's oppression in Egypt, and every one of the four cups is a cup of thanksgiving in commemoration of the particular phase of oppression from which our ancestors were delivered.

First, there was the problem of physical oppression in Egypt. It was a heartless bondage which racked bodies and imperiled lives. Age and weakness were not regarded. Children were not spared. Human life was held cheap. Violence and murder were widespread. Therefore, the first promise was that they would be "brought forth" out of their terrible physical oppression. When we lift the cup at the "Hodu" prayer in the Seder Service we thank God for delivering our ancestors out of that physical bondage.

There was the problem of economic oppression. The Israelites in Egypt were reduced to penury and starvation. Barred from all normal occupations, they were confined to "avodath pereh," the hardest kind of menial labor. The elemental necessities of livelihood were denied them. Therefore, the second part of the Divine promise was that they would be "delivered" out of their economic impositions. When we lift the cup at the Grace after the Passover meal, thanking God for food and sustenance, it is that phase of deliverance to which we refer.

There was the problem of social degradation, which they had to endure. They were reduced to the lowest rung in a society where the caste system prevailed. They were outcasts, without standing or position, deprived even of elementary human rights. Therefore, the third aspect of the Divine promise was that they would be "redeemed" with an outstretched arm. When we lift the cup at the point of the Seder Service where we thank God "that He has redeemed us and our fathers from serfdom to freedom," we refer to this third phase of Israel's oppression.

The fourth and final phase of Israel's condition in Egypt was their own spiritual deterioration. Added to all the difficulties which were visited upon them by their oppressors, was the craveness, the lack of faith, the absence of self-respect among some of the Israelites themselves. One of the chief obstacles which Moses had to encounter, was the lack of response on the part of his own people to his message of salvation, "Behold the children of Israel will not listen to me, how shall Pharaoh heed me?" When he spoke to them in the name of the God of Abraham, Isaac and Jacob, many turned a deaf ear. Therefore, the last and perhaps the most significant phase of the story of salvation was that expressed in the words, "And I shall take them unto Me as My people that they should know Me." When we lift the Passover cup for the "Kiddush" proclaiming Israel's

consecration to God, "Who has sanctified us by His Commandments" and recall in that "Kiddush" the exodus from Egypt,
we are reminded of that phase of deliverance whereby Israel
was delivered from its own unworthiness into a sense of self-
respect and a consciousness of dedication to God.

It is a four-fold problem and a four-fold promise which the
Passover pattern symbolizes.

This interpretation is not as dialectic or as remote as it may
sound. Egypt may be thousands of years away but this pattern
provides a good view of the entire Jewish problem, as it has
existed in every Egypt in which the Jew has found himself during his long and checkered history. The problem and the salvation of the Jew may be epitomized in the four key phrases of
the Passover story, "vehotzeti," "vehitzalti," "vegoalti," "velokahti."

No period in modern times has brought so much disillusionment as the age in which we live. It has been hailed as an age
of freedom and enlightenment. Yet a large portion of humanity is steeped in oppression and darkness. So far as the Jew is
concerned, the eighteenth century idealism under which he had
received a new dispensation of freedom in most of the countries
of Europe, has turned sour.

The four-fold condition suffered by our ancestors in Egypt is
duplicated in the tragic story of the Jew in Nazified Europe
since 1933.

Physical atrocities have been perpetrated upon thousands of
Jews with a brutality reminiscent of the Egyptian Pharaoh.
Economic persecution has been practiced with a relentlessness
and thoroughness which are unprecedented. Social degradation,
branding the Jew as an inferior race, has reduced him in those
countries to the position of "pariah."

While these hardships have been imposed from without, one
inner fault has streaked a large part of the Jewry of Central
Europe, long before Hitler came upon the scene. Once more as
in Egypt, the Jewish community had elements within it which

had deteriorated spiritually, were ashamed of their birthright, and had turned a deaf ear to the message of Jewish self-emancipation. Now their protective coloration is exposed. Their "camouflage" was to no avail.

Of all the four types of serfdom, only the last is to the discredit and shame of the Jew, because it is a serfdom self-imposed. The first three phases of the Jewish tragedy are beyond his power to control. It is beyond his power to prevent pogroms of physical violence or terrorism of economic oppression or insults of social degradation. With regard to his own spiritual condition, however, it is within his power to determine whether he shall be a slave or a free man. He may lose everything else but he need not lose his self-respect.

Consistent with the Passover pattern, the program for the Jew in an age of oppression has been hinted at by the Rabbis in a series of four possible lines of action. The children of Israel stand perplexed before the Red Sea. Peril confronts them in every direction. The raging sea is before them, the pursuing Egyptians are behind them. What should they do?

According to the Rabbis, the Jewish camp, in the face of that emergency, became divided into four parties. The first party merely stood and prayed. A second group urged the counsel of despair, to plunge into the waters of the Red Sea and at last be rid of all their troubles. A third party demanded that Moses lead them back to Egypt, to "Ghetto" and to serfdom. A fourth party, belligerent, wanted to fight the advancing Egyptians regardless of their overwhelming numbers. (Mekilta Beshalah, Chap. II, sec. 2.)

What should be the way out?

Then God commands Moses saying: "Speak unto the children of Israel that they shall march forward." They must not contemplate suicide. They must not imagine that prayer alone will save them. They must not think of turning back to Egypt. They must not engage in physical struggle against an overwhelming force. Let them go forward. A people that has just experienced a miraculous deliverance should have more faith in the future. And they marched forward. The sea opened before them, and they came through unharmed.

Thus the Rabbis have read between the lines of the Passover story. We have something to learn from their analysis.

In the Jewish camp today, there are those who, smitten with fear, can do nothing but pray. Their motor nerves are paralyzed. Riveted to the spot, they are incapable of choosing any line of action. Israel is in danger. They wrap themselves in their prayershawls, raise their voices to heaven and imagine that they are thus averting disaster.

There are those who say, "Let us go back to Egypt. Let us seek to make terms with the oppressor, accept Ghetto and serfdom. We can suffer humiliation, live as subhumans, crawl and cringe, as long as we can hold on to life."

There are those who counsel the other extreme, "Let us plunge into the waters of extinction." Some mean suicide literally. Others say, "Let us drown our identity. It is an easy solution of all our difficulties. The water of baptism will in the course of time erase every vestige of our Jewishness. Our Jewish names will be washed away. Our Jewish features will be assimilated. Our traditions will disappear. We shall find peace in the waters of oblivion."

The Jewish camp also has its bellicose contingent, who are ready to take on the adversary in physical battle even if the odds are hopelessly against them.

How evaluate the four points of view as to the best way out of the peril?

Plunging into the sea of extinction is nothing less than national suicide. Group suicide is as unworthy a solution as individual suicide. Life is an imperial command. Refusal to die when life imposes hardship is the ultimate fortitude which gives human nature its dignity. For the Jew to plunge into the sea of extinction would be a betrayal of his gallant history.

Merely to stand and pray is hardly the way out. No truer

word was said than the word of the ancient Rabbi Hillel, "If I do not endeavor to help myself, how can I expect anyone else to help me. Yet if I rely upon myself alone of what account am I?" It is man's duty in life to exercise his every resource toward the solution of his problem. There is in every person an extra reservoir of power which gives him strength far greater than he imagined he possessed. Prayer is the tapping of man's surplus resources of spiritual power at the same time that it prepares him to accept the Will of God. Prayer as a prelude to action is noble and effective. Never should it become a substitute for action.

To go back to Egypt, its serfdom and its segregation, once having tasted freedom, may be physically endurable, but is spiritually stultifying and psychologically catastrophic. Returning to Egypt is not the same as the original dwelling in Egypt. The Jew of the Middle Ages suffered neither psychologically nor spiritually as a result of the medievalism which conditioned his life. His life was self-sufficient. His modern offspring, however, having been exposed to a century and a half of the dispensations of Western liberalism and Western culture, cannot by a fiat of renunciation go back to where his forebears left off, as if nothing had happened in the interval. If no choice is given him, if he must accept Egypt under duress, then at least he is spared the remorse of having made a shameful choice. Voluntary return to a servile quarantined existence is not the way out of his dilemma, for the Jew of the Western world.

The fourth party in the Jewish camp, the belligerent party, always ready for a fight, has this much at least in its favor, that it does not lack courage. Its will to live is strong. It is not willing to rest content with prayer. It will not countenance a return to Egypt. Courage alone, however, is not enough. There is the courage of wisdom and there is the courage of reckless folly. Socrates made the distinction long ago when he deprecated the courage of the hothead fool who rushes into battle without surveying the situation, the mettle of the enemy, the chances of success, the objective at stake, and the possibility of other alternatives. The Jewish people has often in its history engaged in battles where it seemed hopelessly outnumbered. Sometimes it won, as in the time of the Maccabees against the Syrian hosts. Sometimes it lost, as in the time of Judaea against Rome. In those instances, however, there was no alternative to battle, except physical destruction and spiritual annihilation.

Today, there are hundreds of thousands of Jews who are fighting in the forces which are ranged against the Nazi-Fascist power. They are fighting as citizens of their respective countries and they are fighting as Jews. Their battle is merged with humanity's battle. Alone, however, Jews would be helpless in any physical combat against the overwhelming numbers of their foes. Only in Palestine, where their proportion is one to three, would they have a fighting chance. Would any reasonable person have counseled the five hundred thousand Jews of Germany to hurl themselves against the might of the German Reich? It might have been an heroic gesture, more heroic than to have hurled themselves into the sea, but just as futile.

What then is the way out?

"Speak unto the Children of Israel that they shall go forward."

The difference between rushing to plunge into the sea, in an act of self-extinction, and going forward even though the direction lead straight into the devouring waves, is the difference between despair and faith, between swimming and sinking, between survival and extinction.

Going forward, in these days, means the undismayed continuance of the daily program. Men and women of little faith are tempted to question the worthwhileness of planning for the future, when every day the future seems more hazardous. In the Jewish camp particularly questions are being asked, "What of the Jews in Europe? Is it worthwhile to extend help to European Jewry when they are about to be engulfed by catastrophe beyond our control? Why pour resources into Palestine when it faces the danger of being conquered by the enemy? What is the use of going on with all our Jewish exertions, when the future is so dark?"

The Jew who will proceed upon his path only when the road lies clear before him, had no right to be born a Jew. Peril and hazard have been our portion in history. There is more fortitude in moving forward along one's chosen path, in the face of hazard, than in "suicide squad" heroics. It is fortitude coupled with faith, the faith that somehow a path may be found through the sea.

There are Jews in Germany and Poland today who under all the burdens and dangers, are going on, as and when they can, going on with the rearing of their children and the daily problems of Jewish life, and at the same time refusing to renounce the culture of the Western world. That they are made of more heroic stuff than the "back to Egypt" group or the suicide group, will be readily granted. They are equally as heroic as those who would choose to die in one last stand, knowing the fatal outcome in advance. Going forward is not only an act of courage but an act of faith. One day when the fortunes of war will turn, their faith will be vindicated.

How much more reason have the Jews of America to move forward! A comparison of our plight with the plight of Jewry abroad should make us both thankful and ashamed, thankful for our portion and ashamed that we have among us those who contemplate any other alternative but to go forward.

The episode of Israel's passing through the Red Sea has been repeated more than once in the episodic story of the Jew. It has become a part of the pattern of our survival.

Let Israel go forward, with a faith that expresses itself not in standstill prayer but in directive movement, with forward looking eagerness instead of backward looking regrets, with confident poise rooted in courage rather than with sword-rattling rooted in recklessness.

The waves of the sea shall again make way for a people resolved to achieve its four-fold salvation. With the help of God and with undiminished self-help, may we one day have cause to celebrate a Passover which will mark the fulfillment of the four-fold promise, deliverance from physical persecution, from economic oppression, from social degradation and above all, emancipation from spiritual serfdom.

Kol Nidre Summons

Address delivered before Congregation
B'nai Jeshurun, October 4, 1938.

Kol Nidre Summons

K OL NIDRE, THE eve of the Day of Atonement, the holiest
night of the Jewish year, is a tribute to the stubborn quality of
Jewish faith. Its tones are mournful yet strong, sad yet determined. It is a reminder of the refusal of a stiff-necked people
to bow to the seemingly inevitable necessities.

There is a fundamental difference between Greek tragedy and
Hebrew tragedy. When the house of Agamemnon is doomed,
Electra gives up the struggle, and enters the doomed domicile
resigned to her fate. Not so with Israel. Encompassed by
calamity and surrounded by adversaries, he exclaims with the
Psalmist, "I shall not die but live, to declare the work of the
Lord." Afflicted and bereaved, he exclaims with Job, "Behold
though He slay me, yet will I trust in Him."

What Polish Jewry suffers one year, German Jewry another
year, and what nearly all of European Jewry suffers today, are
the latest links in a chain of tragedy which stretches from the
barbarity of the Roman legions in the first century, to the feroc-
ity of the Christian Crusades in the eleventh century, to the
sadistic bigotry of the Inquisition in the fifteenth and sixteenth
centuries. To all of these the answer of the Jew has been "Shema
Yisrael," "Hear Israel, the Lord is our God."

Of all peoples which have trodden the stage of world history,
the Jewish people is the one people alive today which has been
from the beginning, a people committed to a moral and ethical
purpose. The Jew is the living witness of ageless truths.

If Israel is the living witness, Kol Nidre is the living voice of the living witness. Could we but tune in with all our hearts, with all our souls, and with all our strength, we might hear in the voice of Kol Nidre the majesty of Abraham's response "Hineni," "Here am I," in response to the divine call demanding his most precious possession as the token of his faith, the daring of Moses laying the command of God upon the most powerful ruler of his time, "Release my people that they may serve Me!", the bitter sweetness of David singing out of his distress, "When I am in trouble, I cry out 'O Lord,'" the universalistic vision of Micah, "And they shall beat their swords into ploughshares," the passionate warning of Isaiah, "There is no peace for the wicked," the pathetic lament of Jeremiah, "Woe that a cloud has fallen upon Judaea's golden splendor," the nostalgic yearning of the Psalmist by the waters of Babylon, "If I forget thee, O Jerusalem, may my right arm forget its skill." These are some of the tones and overtones of the vibrations of Kol Nidre.

Every year, before Kol Nidre, Rabbis receive a letter from an organization called, "The Free Thinkers of America." The communication purports to open our eyes to see how stupid is Religion, and how unenlightened is the observance of the Day of Atonement. Here are a few sentences from the chronic free thinkers' epistle:

"An annual appeal to the Jews of America on the occasion of the observance of Yom Kippur.

"The time has come when the enlightened Jews of the world should make a step to emancipate their co-believers from the bondage of their religion.

"The Jews do not have to confess their sins; it is Jehovah who should ask forgiveness for the false banner he has given them and for the false prophets he has induced them to follow.

"'Yom Kippur' is the most humiliating day in all the

superstitious annals of religion, so use this day for religious independence, and let it be an emancipation proclamation to the world.

"Abandon your Temples and renounce your antiquated creed."

If they are sincere, they are to be pitied more than scorned. The doctrinaire "free thinkers" who challenge us are neither free nor thinkers. They are not free because they are confined in the jacket of orthodox atheism of fifty years ago. They are not thinkers because they apparently never heard of such names as Jeans and Eddington. When their epistle was first composed and circulated, probably decades ago, it may have made some impression upon the pseudo-intelligentsia of that day, who under the first shock of Darwin, Huxley and Spencer, thought immaturely that they were being confronted by a choice between Religion and Science. It did not take the honest scientists long to learn that in the presence of the ultimate mystery of the universe, Science stands in reverence. Correspondingly it did not take intelligent Religionists long to make clear that the fundamental premises of Religion have nothing to do with cosmologies, whether the world was made in six days or in six eons, nor with folk lore and folk ways, but that they have to do with a few basic ideas which Science can neither prove nor disprove.

What are these basic ideas underlying Religion in its broadest sense?

1. The universe is not an accident but the result of a creative intelligence.

2. Man is distinguished from the animal domain by virtue of an endowment of spiritual qualities.

3. There is a moral drive in human history which, though slow in fulfillment, ensures the ultimate realization of Justice, Brotherhood and Peace.

These three affirmations constitute the irreducible minimum

of Religion, the kernel which will be as safe from the invasion of Science in the year 2940 as it is in the year 1940.

The Jew is irrevocably committed to these affirmations. The more they are challenged, the more firmly he espouses them. Individual Jews may be atheists. Our charter as a people, however, is a religious mandate. Read the Bible if you would understand how the Jew conceived of himself, and of his place and purpose in the world.

In the beginning, God created the world. It was a good world. Every stage of Creation was sealed by the Divine approval. "And God saw that it was good." Into this world, He placed man, gave him woman as a companion, a paradise for them to live in, and a few simple commands to obey. Man and woman committed the sin of disobedience. They ate the forbidden fruit. For that, they were punished. Paradise was forfeited. Succeeding generations fluctuated between sin and virtue, good and evil, obedience and disobedience to God's commands. Abel obeyed, Cain disobeyed. Noah obeyed, his contemporaries disobeyed. Then arose Abraham in whom God saw great promise. He decided that out of Abraham's seed he would build the stock of a righteous people, a nation which should be dedicated to God's commands. He bade Abraham abandon his idolatrous environment, and go forth to a new land and to a new destiny, to become the founder of a new people that should be a blessing to mankind. Abraham obeyed the call. He went forth. He needed, however, an heir to carry on his heritage. Isaac became his heir. Regarding his offspring, Abraham received the divine charge that he should command them to keep the way of the Lord, "to do justice and righteousness." An object lesson of what happens when justice and righteousness are not observed, was furnished by the destruction of Sodom and Gomorrah.

The early chapters of Genesis are the preamble of Jewish history. They contain the pattern of all that has happened since. The Bible stories therefore, are not merely a congeries of

quaint fables and commendable maxims, but a connected auto-
biography of the Jewish people from Genesis to Chronicles, unified by the main theme that this people founded by Abraham,
was founded not merely in order to be another people on the
face of the earth, but to be a unique people, dedicated to God's
Law, a people whose title to Canaan rested upon its fulfillment
of the Law, but was forfeited when the Law was violated, and
whose credentials for survival today are still the same, namely,
"to do justice and righteousness in the earth."

There is no other people in the history of nations which has
even considered it necessary to justify its existence upon moral
grounds. A people is here because it is here. The Jew has
read into his destiny a moral purpose. Has he fulfilled that
purpose? To a great extent he has, at a tragic cost to himself.
He has fathered Christianity only to be recurrently crucified by
Christians. He has foster-fathered Mohammedanism only to be
sporadically reviled by Moslems.

Today, living in a world of force, the Jew is excoriated by the
high priests of force because his Bible has imposed a conscience of righteousness and justice upon the world. The
"prophets" of might want neither the New Testament nor the
Old Testament. Both Testaments are condemned as a menace
to the "Kraftanschauung" of the Aryan "Uebermensch."

So the Jew is attacked in the name of a philosophy. To proclaim high sounding reasons for hounding the Jew may seem
more civilized than bluntly and without explanations to deprive
him of jobs, businesses and careers, and brutally pogromize him.
This so-called "higher anti-Semitism" was rampant in Germany
in the nineteenth century. Now it is coupled with the lower
anti-Semitism of brute force.

There are also two ways in which the Jew can react to anti-
Semitism. There is the reaction on the higher level and the
reaction on the lower level. Reacting on the lower level, he can
cry out against the physical persecution he suffers, and his cry
is as right as the instinctive cry of an animal against its attacker.

On the higher level, however, the Jew can rededicate himself to his heritage with all the greater zeal, knowing that he stands for eternal values which will prevail long after the "Uebermensch" era will have been forgotten.

When we understand that, then we lift our burden from a low plane to a high plane. It is one thing to be hated because we are economically envied. It is quite another thing to be hated because we are intellectually and spiritually feared. It makes a great difference in the state of our souls whether we are excoriated for our faults, or we are hounded for our virtues.

There are men, sensitively-souled, high-minded men, who when their cause is just, would rather be the persecuted than the persecutors. We recall on Kol Nidre such a man in Germany, a German professor, Emil Granauer of Hanauer University, who with his wife and children embraced Judaism as a protest against Nazi persecutions. We recall the great French writer, Romaine Rolland, who said in an open letter to the Jews of Poland, "I regret I am not a Jew, because I am ashamed of the record of my Christian brothers." Let us be sure that if the world's wrath we must bear, we bear it for reasons of which we can be proud. Let us become conscious ourselves and make our children conscious of the best motives of our history, and of the highest purposes of our destiny.

Our cause is integrated in the cause which is at the core of the devastating conflict now raging abroad. Never in the history of warfare has the moral issue been more sharply defined than it is today. In the last war a moral basis was discovered three years after war had been in progress. Only in 1917 did President Wilson coin the slogan, "the war to make the world safe for democracy." In the present conflict the moral issue was defined six years before the war began. In 1933, upon assuming power, Hitler and Nazism served notice on the world that they repudiate democracy, excoriate liberalism, scoff at the principles of human equality and brotherhood, revile the religious traditions of Judaism and of Christianity, exalt nationalistic chauvinism, glorify race hatreds, defy international decencies and extol war as the highest and noblest way of life. At the same time, they proclaimed a special tenderness toward animals. The movement for the prevention of cruelty to animals is very strong in Germany. The Hebrew prophet, Hosea, had a word for it,— "the murderers of men kiss cattle."

For seven cruel years the Nazi philosophy has been dinned into the ears of the world. Therefore it needs no ministry of propaganda to teach the American people and civilized men everywhere what this war is about. It is a war to defend and maintain the gains of civilization which are threatened with a "blackout."

Anyone who maintains that this is a war between two equally undesirable imperialisms is either a fool or a villain. One need not exonerate the British Empire for its sins of omission and commission against its subject peoples in granting the premise that England today vis-a-vis Germany, is on the side of human decency and progress. Let the doubters ask themselves where they would prefer to live today, in England or in Germany. No picture is all white or all black. Life, however, demands a definitive choice between two sets of circumstances on the basis of their general complexions. We are not asked to participate in an academic debate. Civilization, as we know it, imperfect, but better on the whole than what we have known before, is at stake.

In this challenge to civilization it was no accident that the Jew became the first victim. No greater compliment has been paid the Jew than to have singled him out as the special target of Nazi sadism. Alas, it was a tragic compliment which devastated hundreds of thousands of our people. But it put upon the Jew once more the noble yoke of the suffering "Servant of the Lord."

Some Jews are heard venturing the prediction that Hitler's downfall is inevitable because it is an inexorable law of history that whoever persecutes the Jew comes to grief. To put it that way, as if the Jew were invested with some magic immunity, is to over-simplify and therefore to understate the truth. To believe that would be unworthy and unwarranted chauvinism of which the Jew, least of all, should be guilty.

If history, in the long range, seems to be on our side, it is only because and to the extent that the Jew has been a living witness of eternal truths, the truths of Sinai which other peoples have adopted in their own characteristic versions.

Israel's place in the panorama of history is quite incidental. The all-embracing theme is that there is a moral bookkeeping system in the ledger of history, that there is a moral nemesis in the affairs of men. "If ye walk in my statutes ye will survive . . . If ye transgress them ye will perish." The Jew himself is no exception. He is bound by the same moral imperatives. "Are ye not unto Me even as the children of the Ethiopians?" is the cautioning word of Amos. "Because of our sins we have been driven forth from our land," is the mentorial refrain of our Prayer Service. His defeats, as his victories, are lessons to himself and to the world. He is the witness that there is a Moral Arbiter in history.

It is no accident therefore that in the challenge which the forces of evil have hurled at Religion and Civilization, the Jew should have been singled out again as the special victim. His role is incidental but it is not accidental.

Never before in the history of our trials and tribulations has the issue been drawn so clearly. We are proud in the knowledge that Hitler is allergic to Judaism, which means also to Christianity. Never before has the ethical basis of our existence been so convincing. It makes the "Akedah," the sacrifice, worthwhile. Jews in many lands stand not only on the physical war front. They are in the front-line trenches of the spiritual war front. The story of Isaac's sacrifice at Moriah becomes a lesson in current events.

A Hitler spokesman has said, "The sword will come into its own again and the pen will be relegated to the place where it belongs." An ancient Jewish Rabbi has said, "A book and a sword have come down to the world." (Leviticus Rabbah, Chap. XXXV, sec. 5.) The Jew has chosen the book, the word, the ideal. Let those who will, espouse the sword. The future will decide as between the proponents of the book and the proponents of the sword. It is the modern phase of the irreconcilable conflict between Jacob and Esau. And the Jew knows how to wait. Hitler talks about a thousand years. He is merely talking. The Jew, when he speaks of a thousand years, has the warrant of four thousand years of history to which to point. He knows how to wait,—a thousand years if need be.

Kol Nidre summons us to remember that there are verities which transcend the changes of time, that there are ageless truths and tasks, that of all the peoples which have trodden the stage of world history, the Jew alone has been from the beginning, a people committed to a moral and ethical purpose, that we of this age must continue to hold the banner high, and refuse to bow to the seeming necessities of our age even as our forebears refused in their day.

Zionist Orientation

Substance of addresses delivered before Congregation B'nai Jeshurun, Rosh Hashanah, September 7, 1937, before Hadassah Convention at St. Louis, November 2, 1938, and before Congregation Sherith Israel of San Francisco, December 8, 1938.

Zionist Orientation

W<small>HEN ONE IS</small> beset by difficulties and perplexities in his chosen path it is useful to invoke and to review the original aim, its direction and its purpose. By doing so, one is enabled to proceed upon the path with renewed assurance and with clearer vision.

The present difficult stage through which the Zionist movement is passing is therefore a good time for an exercise in orientation.

There are two fundamental questions which we have to put to ourselves in discussing this subject. Indeed, these questions are fundamental to the discussion of the Jewish problem as a whole.

First, "Is it desired that the Jew should continue as a separate entity in the world?"

Some may answer that question in the negative. They may take the view that it would be best for the Jew to disappear from off the face of the earth, seeing that he is a man born for trouble. They may feel that the best thing we can do for our children and children's children is to help in whatever way we can to bring about the process of extinction. How can it be accomplished? By intermarriage, baptism, assimilation. Though it cannot be done in the Nazi lands, it can still be done in England, the United States, and other countries.

An examination of the Jewish Book of Numbers during the past thousand years will reveal that both prosperity and adversity have taken their toll of voluntary or quasi-voluntary decimation. The Inquisition drove thousands of Jewish families into the arms of the Catholic Church. Some of them maintained their Judaism in secret. Most of them disappeared out of Jewish life after the first generation. The sun of emancipation in Germany and Austria, in the 18th century, lured thousands of Jewish families into the embrace of Christianity. Most of them were lost to the household of Jacob. Not even Hitler's grandmother hunt could reach them because they anteceded the third generation.

The story is repeated in other lands.

Whether under the lure of prosperity, or under the drive of adversity, defections from the ranks of Israel have taken place, and can happen again.

It is to be assumed, however, for the greater portion of present day Jewry, that remaining as Jews is their choice, not their inexorable fate. They would not desert the Jewish people, even if they could, and they accept as axiomatic the proposition that Jews should accept their birthright and should strive to perpetuate it through their children and children's children.

Therefore, the answer to the first question, "Is it desired that the Jew should continue as a separate entity in the world?" is, so far as we are concerned, unmistakably in the affirmative.

The second and more relevant question is, "If it is desirable that the Jew should survive as a separate cultural, spiritual entity, what guarantee is there that he will so survive?"

Casting a long glance back over the history of the Jewish people since the destruction of the Jewish state 1870 years ago, we find that for the first sixteen or seventeen centuries, that is for the first nine-tenths of that period since the destruction of Judaea, the integrity of Jewish life was preserved and safeguarded by a fence, the "fence of the Law."

The Pharisees were not only great Rabbis, but also great statesmen. The name Pharisee, as it begins to be better understood in the light of Jewish history, begins to lose the unsavory connotation which Christian theologians had attached to it. The Rabbis who lived at the time of the destruction of the Jewish Temple and State, and shortly thereafter, the Rabbis who were the fathers of Talmudic Judaism, had the understanding and the foresight to realize that no nation can be expected to survive as a separate entity without a land, without a government and without a religious center, unless substitutes would be built up which might serve, even if temporarily, as moral equivalents for these lost assets.

Thus Jabne came to the rescue when Jerusalem was destroyed. The Talmud replaced the Temple, and the hope of the restoration of Judaea sustained the morale of the people. The separate code of law and observance governing the minutiae of Jewish life and animated by a will to maintain the group as a separate, distinctive group, was more than a penchant for legalism. The "fence of the Law" had reference to the problem of Jewish survival.

The Rabbis had the wisdom not only to formulate those laws and ceremonies, but also to plant in the heart of the people the hope of the rebuilding of Zion. It was no mere accident that centuries after the destruction of the Jewish State and Temple, Jews continued to pore over the tractates of the Talmud, which dealt with the agricultural laws of Eretz Israel, with the Temple sacrifices and with a gamut of situations which were related not to their contemporary life but to the life as it had been lived in Palestine before the Destruction. Through the Talmud and the legal codes based upon it, Jewish civil life continued to function. Through the Prayer Book, the longing and hope for the restoration of Zion was kept alive. The Pharisees were practical statesmen.

While it is true that the "fence of the Law" has kept Jews from mingling with Gentiles, it should be recognized that it was not a one-sided fence. The Christian world, on its part, scorning the Jew as the "anti-Christ," isolated and persecuted him. Thus, both by outward compulsion and by inner choice, the Jew remained a separate, distinctive people. This separatism has been the guarantee of Jewish self-preservation up to modern times, wherever Jews have lived. The Jew who ventured beyond that fence was on the way out of Jewish life.

Into that fence, however, there came a serious breach when the Emancipation movement swept over Europe in the 18th century under the impact of the revolutionary ideas of brotherhood and equality for all men, which culminated in the French Revolution and in the American Revolution. Jews in France, Germany and other countries began to be regarded as human beings with human rights. Jews in turn met the friendly approach more than half way. The beautiful friendship between Moses Mendelsohn and Lessing was the token of the fraternizing of Shem and Japheth. Mendelsohn's grandchildren, however, reared by their parents in the lap of the Christian church, were the token of what happened to many Jewish families when the fence of Jewish separatism was breached.

One may ask, "How then does it happen that Jewish life and activity flourished even in countries where Emancipation has been in effect for a long time?" That it should have flourished in Eastern Europe during the nineteenth century, was to have been expected, for the Middle Ages were never quite liquidated there and the wall around the Jew was never removed. What of England, however, or the United States, where the Jew has enjoyed equality and freedom for generations? Does not the continuing force of Jewish life and activity there invalidate the theory that Emancipation creates a problem for Jewish survival?

There are qualifying factors. Let it be remembered that even in liberal countries the emancipation of the Jew has never been carried out fully, consistently and continuously. There were hangovers of Christian prejudice, such as the Dreyfus affair in France, sporadic provocations nourished by reactionary groups, which have punctuated the course of Emancipation. It has been a fluctuating, interrupted emancipation which was never quite all that it was meant to be. Hence, the breach in the fence of

Jewish separatism in those countries was always subject to limitations.

Besides, Jews in different lands do not live in water-tight compartments isolated from one another. When there was a pogrom in Kishinev, the repercussions of it were felt in Paris, London, Amsterdam, and New York. Even the half-assimilated in these centers of emancipated Jewry became stirred out of their lethargy. If Germany persecuted its Jews, the rest of the Jewish world naturally reacted and even the half-withered limbs of Israel, stirred by anger and humiliation, became revitalized.

There is an additional factor which has interrupted the normal effects of Emancipation, namely, the Jewish immigration from unemancipated lands to emancipated lands bringing into these areas the old Jewish way of life which separatism had nurtured. Waves of immigrants from Russia and Poland have halted the process of assimilation in the American Jewish scene.

Restraining factors have impeded the forces of assimilation, which otherwise in the natural course of the process of emancipation, might have breached the fence of Jewish loyalty and Jewish self-consciousness.

This is the picture in stark and perhaps painful realism. The condition of Jewish life in Germany before Hitlerism validates our thesis. German Jewry was on the whole an assimilationist Jewry, going downward Jewishly until Hitlerism appeared. In France, Italy and the Scandinavian countries where the Jewish populations were relatively small, relatively emancipated and relatively without East European infiltrations, assimilation and intermarriage had been on the increase steadily in the past several generations until interrupted by the stimulus resulting from anti-Semitism.

The complexion of Jews and Judaism in the United States would be vastly different today if it had not been for the infiltration of East European Jewry which became the dominant element in the Jewish population here, and if it had not been for the stir created by the pogroms of Czarist Russia and by other anti-Semitic outbursts abroad. If not for these factors, American Judaism today would be a weak sister indeed, and the forces of assimilation would by this time have wrought their havoc.

The final evidence of the validity of the thesis is what is happening to Russian Jewry under the Soviet regime. A community of three millions, completely emancipated, and at the same time out of contact with the rest of the Jewish world, is gradually disappearing into the vortex of assimilation.

The argument need not be labored further. It leads to the conclusion that Emancipation, which is an unmixed blessing to the Jew as an individual, is not an unmixed blessing to Jewish group survival.

Must the alternatives be, emancipation *or* Judaism? Can emancipation *and* Judaism go together?

That, frankly, is the persistent question which haunts the Jewish problem. One can argue around it, or cut intellectual corners here and there, but in the last analysis this is our dilemma. In one breath we pray for the time, and we believe in its coming, when the forces of iniquity will be crushed, and the Jew, together with all men, will breathe the air of freedom and equality. At the same time, we are also praying and hoping for the preservation of our people and its Torah. Are the two hopes mutually contradictory? Must the choice be, Emancipation *or* Judaism? Cannot Emancipation *and* Judaism exist side by side?

There are two conceivable solutions, one of which seems more remote than the other. By no means are they mutually exclusive. Needless to say, the ideal situation would be the fulfillment of both solutions.

The solution which seems the more remote is one which would depend upon a revolutionary concept of nationhood.

Let us imagine an ideal situation here in the United States. We are a congeries of racial strains, cultural traditions and religious denominations. The free interplay of these forces can become our richest cultural and spiritual asset. Freedom to preserve their uniqueness should be not only tolerated but encouraged for the sake of the colorfulness and contentfulness of American life.

Under such a dispensation, backed by an enlightened public opinion, which would not only approve but honor each group for its contribution to the American symphony, every citizen would take pride in the spiritual, cultural heritage which is peculiar to himself and would strive to preserve it. Of course, there would develop inevitably over and above these local and personal cultures, an American civilization redolent of our geographical, climatic and sociological environment. It would be, however, a free growth of the soil, adding to, not supplanting, the other cultures.

In such a milieu, the Jew would have every reason for religious loyalty, racial pride and cultural self-sustenance.

What then would constitute the all-embracing character of our democracy? Just this kind of attitude. What would constitute the criterion of American loyalty and patriotism? Enthusiastic acceptance and practice of this way of life, and readiness to bear whatever burdens and sacrifices may be required by the welfare and safety of the state.

It is admittedly a picture which is far different from the present condition. Some Americans will claim that this is in effect what we have today. Actually, public opinion has a long way to go in order to reach the ideal condition which has been imaged. At best it tolerates differences, considering them as harmless, or moribund, or both. The only distinctions which public opinion accepts as permanently inviolate are religious creeds and forms of worship. There is a gap between the attitude which tolerates racial and cultural differences and an attitude which would invite, evoke and bless them. Until the latter point will be reached, Jews and other minorities will feel under restraint and there will be a psychological pressure in favor of adaptation instead of self-expression.

Needless to say, the intensification of nationalism which followed the last World War, and today is felt to a greater or smaller degree in every land, has put uniformity within national boundaries at a premium. Consequently, the restraint upon diversified self-expression is felt the more keenly, even though it be voluntary and not imposed restraint.

The nineteenth century Emancipation movement, even at its best, was a movement of toleration, which lifted political restraints but left psychological restraints. One day it will have a sequel which will mark a new concept of nationalism. That day is not at hand.

There is a less remote and more feasible solution of the dilemma which has been posed with reference to the problem of Jewish survival.

If a substantial population of Jews might be congregated into one land where they themselves would be the masters, they could be both free and Jewish. There would be no outside influence to interfere with their Jewishness, no outside culture to limit the full development of their own culture, no pressures either imposed or self-imposed. In such a land, there could not conceivably be the danger of their ceasing to be Jews. They could no more cease to be Jews there than the English could cease to be English in England, or the Bulgarians could cease to be Bulgarian in Bulgaria. In a Jewish State there might be changes in customs, laws, institutions, just as there are changes in the life of other nations; but the changes would be Jewish changes in response to developing Jewish needs and under the imprint of Jewish national personality. Indeed, the very process of change would be a sign of healthy growing Jewish life even as change everywhere is the sign of healthy, growing life. Whatever a Jewish nation in a Jewish State would do, would be in itself the norm of Jewish living. It would be an example to other Jewish communities of what is Jewish art, Jewish literature, Jewish law, Jewish science, Jewish government.

Obviously, it would be unreasonable to expect that all of the seventeen million Jews of the world should be congregated in that land. Not all of them would be needed to produce a Jewish civilization. After all, the Bible was the product of a Jewish population of no more than three millions. There are national entities in the world today whose numbers are a fraction of seventeen millions. What would be required is a homogeneous community, sufficient in numbers to be a living national entity, not merely a token group or a laboratory community.

It would be expected, however, that out of such a national Jewish life there should come stimulus, inspiration and new content for Jewish communities throughout the world. These communities then would not need to depend for their Jewish consciousness upon persecution in their own midst, or upon the repercussions of persecution of Jews in other lands. Their Jewishness would be nourished by the life-giving stream flowing out of the Jewish Homeland. They could at last be at the same time Jews and free men, without the danger of the one conflicting with the other.

In this entire picture, Palestine has not been mentioned by name, in order that the argument might not be prejudiced by a specific reference. It was the formula which required consideration, not its particular application. Actually, however, what other land could there be for a Jewish Homeland, or a Jewish State? What other spot could command such sentimental attachment, such historic memories, such outpouring of love and labor?

The compass needle of the Jewish heart points Palestineward. It would have been as feasible to have suggested to the Poles at the end of the World War that they should resume their national life in Brazil as to suggest to Jews that they should build their Homeland in British Guiana, Ethiopia, Biro-Bidjan or southern California.

The mere hope of returning to Zion one day in the future, a hope enshrined in our daily prayers, has been enough to bind the scattered fragments of Israel together into a sense of common destiny these 1870 years.

This, indeed, is Zionism,—the establishment in Palestine of a Jewish National Home, publicly assured and legally secured. Volumes have been written upon its manifold aspects, the relation of the Jewish National Home in Palestine to Jewish dignity everywhere, the relation of a Jewish State to the protection of Jewish rights wherever Jews dwell, the influence which the Zionist movement has exerted in the past fifty years in reclaiming Jewish artists, men of letters, scientists and musicians, and the practical achievements in Palestine during the half century in which the Zionist movement has been an organized nation-building movement furnishing in the colonies in Eretz Israel the highest example of social idealism. Much has been written and spoken of Palestine as the refuge which has absorbed more victims of German, Polish and Roumanian persecution than any other land, of the amazing way in which the Jewry of Palestine has met the years of Arab terror, Nazi intrigue and Italian provocation, and of the establishment during this period of trial and tribulation, of dozens of new Jewish settlements, of the opening the Jewish Port of Tel Aviv and of industrial and cultural advancement.

It is the fundamental principle with which we are concerned in this analysis. To understand that is to understand Palestine's power of gravitation in drawing the best and the most idealistic of the Jewish youth into a land no longer flowing with milk and honey, but barren and spoliated through the neglect of centuries, and moving them to labor as no other youth in the world has labored in order to transform this desert into a garden. Then one can understand why Eliezer ben Yehudah, forty years ago, faced insult and attack from the old "Halukah" Jews in Jerusalem rather than yield in his determination not to speak a word except in the Hebrew language until Hebrew should become the every-day language of young and old in Palestine. Then one understands why in hundreds of thousands of Jewish homes throughout the world the coin dropped into the Jewish National Fund box for redeeming the soil of Eretz Israel carries with it the tears and hopes of the Jewish people. Then one understands why the most vital, cultural and spiritual creations of the Jew today, not only in literature, art and drama but in noble living are to be found in Eretz Israel. Then one understands why the Yishuv faces Arab marauders and murderers without being daunted. Then one understands the contrast between Vienna and Hanita, between suicide and exaltation in the face of peril, between the slogan of European Jewry, which is, "Escape!" and the slogan of Palestinian Jewry, which is, "Advance!" Then one understands why we Zionists must continue our labors, whatever the difficulties and setbacks. All this is possible because we are engaged in the task of building a Jewish nation and Jewish nationhood which are to be for Jews everywhere the surest guarantee of Jewish self-preservation coupled with freedom.

Is the Zionist solution less remote and more feasible than the hope of impressing all the nations with a new concept of nationalism such as would encourage unrestrained Jewish self-expression? The history of our time bears unmistakable witness in the affirmative. The Balfour Declaration was a long step in the direction of the Zionist solution. Whittled down by subsequent compromises, it still remained a charter for a Jewish National Home. A further step was taken when the idea of a Jewish State was projected by the British Government in 1936 as a solution to the Arab-Jewish problem and almost came into realization. If England wins the present war, the proposal of a Jewish State in Palestine will come up for discussion again.

Let us look toward the day when an enlightened humanity will broaden its definitions of nationhood. In such a time, the Jewish National Home, or the Jewish State in Palestine, will serve not only as exemplar but as feeder of Jewish spiritual and cultural nourishment to Jewish communities wherever they may dwell. Its very existence and development will be, as it is already today, a source of interest and pride, and what is more, a common responsibility for Jews the world over to bear.

While the dawn of that hoped for day seems remote, a Jewish

National Home is already a reality and a Jewish State is more than a vague possibility for the realizable future. There is ample reason to warrant the espousal of Zionism with all our hearts, with all our souls and with all our might. Much as a Jew may do for Palestine and Zionism, Palestine and Zionism do infinitely more for him.

Palestine is the heart of Jewish hope and promise. Zionism is the spiritual dynamic of the Jewish people. It helps to give spiritual content to Jewish life everywhere. Zionism offers the guarantee that when democracy will triumph in the world, Judaism will not melt away under the sun of freedom. It is the supreme expression of the mystic will to live which is the stubborn fact of Jewish history.

Realism Plus Vision

Substance of addresses delivered at the Reception tendered by the Jewish Community of Belfast, Ireland, August 3, 1939, and before the National Convention of the Mizrachi Organization of America, Baltimore, May 20, 1940.

Realism Plus Vision

THE ZIONIST HAS proved to be the realist as well as the idealist in modern Jewish history. Zionism was fathered by the highest idealism of our people and mothered by its grim necessity. The one parent guaranteed its form, the other determined its substance.

Theodore Herzl, the founder of modern Zionism, had the vision to see, and what is equally important, the courage to speak. In prophecy, the quality of "Nabi," the courage to speak, is coupled with that of "Hozeh," the vision to see. Great leadership in every age requires these qualities of courage and vision. Herzl had them. With these he combined another faculty, also characteristic of the Jewish prophetic tradition, the power of realistic analysis of the contemporary scene. Theodore Herzl was the supreme realistic idealist of his generation.

As realist he said more than forty years ago, "We have honestly endeavored everywhere to merge ourselves in the social life of surrounding communities and to preserve only the faith of our fathers. We are not permitted to do so."

As idealist he said more than forty years ago, "No human being is wealthy or powerful enough to transplant a nation from one habitation to another. An idea alone can accomplish that; and this idea of a State may have the requisite power to do so. The Jews have dreamt this kingly dream all through the long nights of their history. 'Next year in Jerusalem' is our old phrase. It is now a question of showing that the dream can be converted into a living reality."

Herzl was realist enough not to accept the so-called emancipation of the Jew at its face value; therefore he sought a solution that would solve. He was realist enough to fashion instruments, financial and organizational instruments, for the implementation of this solution. Yet, he was dreamer enough to vision the "Endziel," a Jewish State. In his day, this vision must have seemed remote, if not fantastic. Yet, in our day, even the dream portion of Herzl's formula does not seem very remote, and surely not fantastic. The phrase, "Jewish State," has already come up once on the international agenda, in the report of the British Royal Commission. It will come up again.

The present juncture in the history of the Jewish people calls again, though this time in a different way, for the synthesis of realism and idealism.

If forty years ago the illusion of emancipation raised false hopes, let us beware lest today disillusionment induce specious despair. From the fool's paradise to the hysterian's inferno is the tragic sequence of illusion and disillusionment. Perhaps it is not accidental that the deepest despair in the past decade of Jewish life was to be found, not among the long-suffering Jews in Poland and Rumania, but among the "assimilationist" Jews in the liberal countries, where anti-Semitism was widespread.

Two generations ago, when the tide of nineteenth century liberalism was high, the Zionist, realist that he was, accepted it gratefully but without credulity. Today, when the tidal wave of reaction is working havoc, the Zionist, realist that he is, regards it sorrowfully, but without panic.

Does the present Jewish scene throughout the world warrant unrelieved and unmitigated despair? Was there ever before in our "Galuth" history, a Jewish community as great in numbers, as abounding in the material resources and spiritual possibilities as American Israel, capable of becoming the "yad hahazakah," the mighty arm, to help other communities? Was there ever before a time when the plight of the Jewish people was as clearly identified with the plight of civilization itself and when therefore, our cause had such powerful allies? Can freedom, once tasted, be permanently exiled from the lands which are now under the heels of oppressors? Will the tyrants who are sitting on the top of the world today sit there twenty-five years hence? Was there ever a time since Rome destroyed our Homeland, when our Homeland was as alive as it is today?

These are legitimate questions which should be pondered in any honest and intelligent evaluation of the Jewish present and future.

Assuredly, there is no reason for being at ease, but neither is there reason for panic and hysteria. If complacency corrodes, panic paralyzes.

It is a time which calls for realism coupled with vision. There is no need for assuming that the Emancipation of the Jew is inherently chimerical and fantastic, any more than there is reason for assuming that democracy is inherently chimerical and fantastic. Emancipation is a slow process. It never took hold because its concomitant conditions of democracy, justice, freedom, the rights of man, never quite took hold. The emancipation of the Jew could not flourish in a vacuum. Its effectiveness was dependent upon the effectiveness of all that was involved in nineteenth century liberalism, namely, democracy, humanity, the rights of man, peace and freedom. When these aspirations will be fulfilled, as we believe they must be fulfilled, then emancipation will also become effective at last.

When the full emancipation, however, will come, the Jewish problem will yet be short of solution. The premises of the problem will then be changed from outward to inward. The inner problem of adjusting himself to a world of freedom, democracy, and enlightment, may, in some respects, prove to be more difficult for the Jew than his present problem of adjusting himself to a world of evil and darkness. What will save him from disintegration? Will the mantle of Jewishness, as in the parable of the contest between sun and wind, be doffed in the day of the warm sun?

Zionism holds a solution for both problems. With stark realism it proposes against the present period of darkness in which the Jew is the chief victim, a Jewish Homeland where he can live, not on sufferance, but as of right. With deep idealism, looking toward the brighter day of freedom and democracy, it proposes a dispensation which will guarantee that Judaism will not melt away under the sun of freedom. The dispensation envisaged is a Jewish State, where the Jew and Jewish values can function with indigenous creativeness, infusing at the same time positive life-giving content into Jewish life everywhere.

Munich, which will be remembered ruefully as the cradle of Nazism and more recently as the scene of the shame of European democracies, should also be remembered as the place where Theodore Herzl had planned to call the first Zionist Congress in 1897, but was discouraged by the shortsighted leaders of the local Jewish community. The "Vorstand" of the "Kultus Gemeinde" would not permit the fair city of Munich to be "contaminated" with Zionism, so the first Zionist Congress was held at Basle. There is a Jewish saying to the effect that "God sends the cure before the affliction." As if by intuition Herzl sought as the place where to propose the cure, the very city which a generation later was to become the cradle of the twentieth century affliction to our people. It is one of the ironies of history that the offspring of that "Kultus Gemeinde" and of other communities like it throughout Germany, tens of thousands of whom have found a haven in Eretz Israel since 1933, should have had occasion to bless the memory of him whom their forebears spurned.

Zionism, synthesis of realism and idealism, is the highest Jewish statesmanship. Its mandate speaks to our people in accents of strength and dignity as if to say in the Voice that charged Ezekiel, "Son of man, stand upon thy feet and I shall speak unto thee."

If the synthesis of realism and vision is the characteristic of the Zionist movement, it should be expected that this same quality would distinguish the most characteristic child of the Zionist movement, the Jewish National Fund.

In the Keren Kayemeth, heaven and earth are commingled, the ideal and the practical, "haye olam" and "haye sha-ah," the immediate and the ultimate.

The Jewish National Fund was given form by two great realists who were at the same time great visionaries, one, Professor Schapira, a mathematical realist who had the vision, however, to see that a coin could be powerful enough to build a cornerstone; the other, Dr. Herzl, a political realist who had the vision, however, to envision a scattered people becoming a sovereign nation. This characteristic child of the Zionist movement was developed to its present substantial estate by another great realist-idealist of our people, Menahem Ussishkin. That one of the most realistic Zionists of our generation should have been drawn to the Presidency of the Keren Kayemeth LeIsrael, was a natural gravitation.

If we of this generation of Zionists have failed in doing all that we should have done to make our stake in Eretz Israel these twenty years more real and more substantial in accordance with the opportunities which existed, our failure can be measured in dunams of land.

Land is the fundamental commodity in the life of individuals and nations. It is the primary source of livelihood. It is the foundation upon which homes are built. It is the span of national boundaries.

The measure of a people's adequate recognition of the primacy of land in its economic and political program is the measure of its statesmanship. To the extent that a people fails to make the most of its opportunities for land acquisition, not to buy and sell but to have and hold, it evidences its shortcomings in the art and science of nation-building.

Not the least of the "Galuth" symptoms of the Jewish consciousness has been its tardiness in taking full advantage of the opportunities for "Geulath Ha-aretz," Land Redemption, which were available since modern Zionism converted a sentiment for Zion into a practical program of nation-building.

If Jewish need and Jewish self-respect have been the twin pillars upon which the motivation of the Zionist movement has rested, the soil of Palestine has supported the one as well as the other. If the refugee problem created by the Nazi policies in Europe has focused attention in recent years upon the need of footholds for the homeless in the Jewish National Home, there has also taken place at the same time a noteworthy growth of the soil in terms of wholesome modes of living, reorientation in the human values which spring from agricultural pursuits, and valuable patterns of a co-operative society. Thus, Jewish need and Jewish dignity have been served simultaneously.

Every strategically located dunam of land which is not in our possession today is an indictment of our shortcomings as realists. Every crisis which has confronted the Jewish National Home during these two decades has carried its own special penalty for our sins of omission.

Realists, however, have no time for remorse. They have time only for repentance and amendment.

That in the worst period of the Arab terror, new frontiers should have been established by our pioneers in Beisan, in Western Galilee and in the Hills of Ephraim, adding to the epic martyrology of our people such names as Hanita, En Hashofet, Tirath Zvi, indicates once more that the failures were never those of the "Yishub", but those of the "Galuth."

The present stage of trial and stress when doubts are cast upon the future of Palestine by men of little faith, is a testing period for our realism as well as for our vision. Zionism, some say, is at the crossroads. Others say an impasse has been reached. Fair-weather friends of Palestine remark with a show of regret, "it is too bad." Others, who are positively negative to Zionism exclaim with unconcealed glee, "We told you so. You have come to a dead end. You had better turn back."

To the former the idealist's answer is that the road to Palestine, from the first, has never been the short and easy one but the hard and long one and that the clash with obstacles generates its own special spark of zeal and faith which illuminates not only the ultimate aim but also the intermediate experience.

To the latter the realist's answer is that the Palestine aspect of Jewish life today is at no worse a pass than the greater part of Jewish life outside of Palestine. Actually it is in a much better state. At least the Jew in Palestine is in a better position to exercise the elementary right of a human being to fight for his ancestral home and soil. If it is to be assumed that Jewish life in most of the Diaspora lands too has come to an impasse, then we can only contemplate an escapist, Messianic mysticism, divorced from life, such as attended the Sabbetai Zevi hypnotic spell and subsequent collapse of several centuries ago.

The significant contribution of the Zionist movement in modern times has been that it has taught the Jewish people first that a vision, if it is ever to become a reality, must be implemented by a program of action, and second, that action without vision is motion without direction. The mere longing for Zion is not quite Zionism. It becomes Zionism when it actuates a program for the upbuilding of Zion. There is a world of difference between the Hebrew word, "yehi," the resolution, "let there be," and "va-yehi," the fact, "and there was." The crucial letter is the conversive "vav," converting wish into fulfillment. Only God could accomplish such a transformation by a mere word, could create a world by the "Logos." He said, "Let there be light, and there was light." Human beings must labor and toil in order to accomplish the conversion of the future tense into the past tense. Zionism addresses itself to that crucial and arduous task in relation to Zion's rebuilding.

Speaking of tenses, it is appropriate to recall that the Hebrew language is virtually without a present tense. The tense corresponding to the present tense has no defined status. It is called "benuni"—"betwixt and between"—transient between the past and the future. This too is a phase both of realism and of vision, not to be overawed by the present. The present moment in our destiny, undefined and uncertain as it may seem, should be viewed in the long-range perspective as a transition between what was and what is to be.

Let us not lose our perspective.

If forty years ago when political Zionism was in its infancy, they who fathered it could have foreseen that at the end of forty years, after a checkered course of hopes and disappointments, there would be in Palestine by 1940 a strong and vital community of nearly one-half million Jews, alive and creative economically and culturally, and capable of self-defense, but that the political future of the Jewish National Home in 1940 would be not as certain as desired, would they not have been pleased on the whole with such a prospect? "Can a land be made to travail in one day? Can a nation be born at once?" We Zionists are sometimes charged with exaggerating the importance of our achievements, of looking upon the work of our hands with magnifying glasses, and proclaiming it with megaphones. At times, in moods of severe self-scrutiny, we also take ourselves to task for setting great store by relatively small accomplishments.

Let it be understood, however, that our homeland-building program is not to be compared with that of any other people. Making bricks without straw was not more difficult than building a homeland without powers of government, nay, in the face of a corrupt Turkish government for the first half of these forty years, in the face of an indisposed British government for the second half of the period, and without the unanimous support of the Jewish people itself, throughout the entire period.

Despite these all but insuperable obstacles, we have built up the nucleus of a homeland which is a physical and spiritual oasis in the entire Near East. Let our critics scan the colonization records of history to see if they can find in the history of any other people, however favorable its circumstances and unobstructed its path, an enterprise in colonization which can compare either in its material soundness or in its idealistic quality with the record of the Jewish homeland.

From time to time other territories are suggested as Jewish "homelands." Biro-Bidjan and Ethiopia have been offered as diversions from Palestine by regimes which had ulterior motives in view. The offers were received coldly by Jewish public opinion. There can be no "Ersatz" for Eretz Israel.

In recent years territories have been suggested not as "homelands" but as havens of refuge. British Guiana, Kenya, Madagascar, Alaska, Southern California and Santo Domingo are among the territories which have been named.

There is no incompatibility between Zionism and a favorable attitude toward the settlement of other areas upon the earth's surface. The Jewish need for havens is so vast and urgent that every opportunity is to be welcomed, as long as it is understood that there is a distinction between a refuge and a national home. Zionists are realistic enough to recognize that necessity. Obviously Palestine can accommodate only a portion of all who must emigrate from European "infernos." Indeed, it is the successful experiences of the Jews in the colonization of Palestine which serve as the best credentials in giving assurance that Jews can be relied upon to cope with the problem of colonizing waste and barren territories converting them into productive areas.

If the non-Zionists were equally realistic and honest, they would recognize that every territorial proposal needs to be judged by several important criteria. Is it a "bona fide" offer? Is the proposed area habitable? Is the per capita cost of settlement reasonable? Will it accommodate hundreds, or tens of thousands? Obviously a refuge for a few hundred families hardly deserves the attention which would be merited by an opportunity for mass settlement.

Judged by such criteria the realistic and honest non-Zionist would be compelled to admit the primacy of Palestine even from the "territorialist" point of view.

What has aroused the misgivings of Zionists is the suspicion that some of the advocates of other territories are not altogether motivated by objective realistic considerations but by a conscious or subconscious prejudice against Palestine. There can be understanding and co-operation between Zionists and non-Zionists on every territorial enterprise if the premises are honestly and realistically evaluated.

An interesting observation is made in a Jewish newspaper in Jugoslavia, "Jevrejske Novine" of October 20th, 1938, contrasting the work of draining the Pontine Marshes near Rome, and drainage of land in Palestine for Jewish settlement. The writer points out that the Pontine Marshes have existed for over two thousand years, during which time they were always a vast breeding center of foul matter, and that although the union of Italy took place in 1870 it was not until nearly thirty years later that the first steps were taken to drain those marshes. The task has now been considerably advanced. The land has become suitable for settlement, and already 20,000 persons have been settled there by the Italian Government. This number represents only about half of the people who are to be settled on the land. In contrast to this work of reclamation the writer refers to the 50,000 Jews who have been settled in Palestine on land of the Jewish National Fund. He calculates that the area of the Pontine Marshes drained until the end of 1935, the latest date for which figures are available, was 41,600 hectares, which is equivalent to 416,000 dunams, and that the amount of land of the Jewish National Fund that has been drained, irrigated and cultivated amounts to 387,625 dunams. The cost incurred by the Italian Government in this reclamation work amounted to 197,000,000 Lire, which is about £3,700,000. But although the expenditure in the case of the Jewish National Fund was a little higher than that incurred by the Italian Government, the number of people settled on the land is over twice as many. The

Italian people, living in freedom in its own country, needed many decades before it could boast of having drained those famous marshes as a national achievement, whereas the Jewish people, dispersed throughout the world, without the right of imposing taxes or enforcing labor, was able to achieve better results in approximately the same time. "What a difference between the performance of a powerful government and that which was achieved by a group of pioneers of the Jewish people!", the writer properly concludes.

Would not the founders of our movement have felt that in a long and difficult process of rebuilding a nation after nineteen centuries of dispersion, the Zionist record over a brief span of two-score years is a great achievement and warrants looking forward with confidence to the ultimate fulfillment of our hopes? That should be our sober judgment today. The important thing is to know that we are on the right road—the road back to Zion.

In the long perspective, the present period of political uncertainty, government restrictions, and war hazards, may prove to have been a transition during which the gains of twenty years have been consolidated and a way paved for a new advance.

For the Jewish people these fateful, catastrophic days hold much instruction. One lesson above all seems to cry out for emphasis. It is a lesson in what it means for a people to have a land and a home.

When the little Finnish nation of three and a half millions was invaded and attacked by a vastly greater power, the world's indignation was aroused, its sympathy flowed out and its generous help went forth to the victim. When, however, three and a half million Jews in Poland were consigned to massacre and spoliation on one side and to material and spiritual dispossession on the other, the world's conscience was not outraged, its sensibilities were not shocked and its practical sympathies were not aroused. The Jews of conquered Poland were deprived even of the privilege of heroic death. In our contemporary Book of

Lamentations, this is the saddest page, namely, that a people uprooted and divorced from its historic soil can only look for a beggar's crumb at the table of humanity's understanding, consideration and respect.

Had three and a half million Jews lived on their national soil in Eretz Israel there might be a different story to tell today,—witness the story that has been told by the Yishub of less than five hundred thousand souls during the troubles they have had to face since 1936.

Some will say that all this is in the subjunctive mood, a hypothetical contingency. This mood can and needs to be converted from the subjunctive to the optative. The means for doing it is the old Herzlian formula, "if you will it, it is not a myth." If the present tragedy of the homelessness and landlessness of the Jewish people can stir the sections of Jewry who are still strong and free, to hasten the ultimate solution, the pain and the labor will not have been in vain.

In a world shaken by war, it would be fatuous to imagine that we alone can determine the fate of Palestine, regardless of the larger world forces. Yet, it is nothing more than realism to believe that the determining influence of that which we can do is not to be underestimated; and it is nothing more than sober statesmanship to make use of every day for doing that which in our power lies to strengthen and extend the dimensions of Israel in Eretz Israel.

The timeliness of the Zionist thesis is hardly affected by recent war developments. The war is a sad interlude. Israel's passion for Eretz Israel is a permanent attachment which may be impeded but never frustrated.

Who can predict how this war will develop, what changes it will bring forth, what new lines and boundaries will be written upon the map of the world, or how the problems of small nations and minority groups will be disposed of?

As the war proceeds the minds of men are turned toward the peace which will follow the war, inquiring what the complexion of affairs is going to be when the war shall have come to an end. War aims and peace aims is the subject which has been agitating people everywhere.

The Jewish people has no aims which are different from those which it has pleaded for all these years; first, that Jews as individuals wherever they may live, be treated as human beings on terms of equality with other human beings; and second, that the Jewish people, as a people, be accorded the right to which any people is entitled, to have a place which it can call home, and to which its members can come as of right. These have been and will continue to be our peace aims.

That these aims have no chance of being realized unless the Allies are victorious goes without saying. That they will be realized when the Allies are victorious, there is no assurance, but there is hope for it if the peace will be one founded on justice to all.

Is it fantastic to believe that the consideration of our just aspirations in Palestine may be on the agenda of the Peace Conference after this war, as it was on the agenda of the Peace Conference following the last war? Is it Utopian to hope that the next Peace Conference may produce a sequel to the Balfour Declaration?

Let us be sure that when the time is opportune, our credentials will be impressive. In a realistic world, the most realistic validations of our claims to Eretz Israel will be not only the strong urgings by Jewish communities outside of Palestine, but our numbers and influence in Palestine, the amount of land there in our possession and the strategic locations of that land.

It would therefore be an unforgivable sin against the destiny of our people if because of "kotzer ruah," a shortage not of means but of spirit, vision and will, we fail to make ours every dunam of land which can be bought, every industrial position which can be gained, and every immigration influx which can be accomplished.

"To some," say the Rabbis, "it is given to win their world

at one stroke, properly timed." (Abodah Zarah 17a.) Shall we be ready if and when our hour should strike?

If the old legend is more than a legend, that "Israel's Messiah will come when the cup of Israel's tears standing on God's throne will be full to overflowing," then surely our time of redemption cannot be far off.

We need to turn our vision and faith toward tomorrow to help us over the tragic realities of today.

Faith is the supreme need for our time, as real and as sustaining as bread. We more than any other people are expected to be well supplied with resources of faith. Has it not sustained us through a thousand crises? From the time of Abraham it has been the badge of our tribe. "Get thee forth out of thy home and birthplace . . . unto the land which I shall show thee." The new land was not even specified. How different was the reaction af another contemporary, Lot's wife. She was bidden to flee from Sodom and Gomorrah, but in order to be sure of the necessity for flight she turned her eyes back for a moment,— and was petrified. It is an old, old story. Faith moves men, while doubt petrifies them.

The thirty-second chapter of Jeremiah, the realistic idealist of his time, is the text for our time. While the armies of Babylon were battering at the gates of Jerusalem, the Prophet of Lamentations conveying the doleful message of the impending fall of the city, in the same breath of prophecy conveyed the comforting reassuring message of restoration. As a token of his faith in the future he proceeded to buy a field in Anathoth, in the vicinity of the besieged city. "For thus saith the Lord of Hosts, the God of Israel, 'Houses and fields and vineyards shall yet again be bought in this land.'"

In the face of a world of "hurban," destruction, we continue to address ourselves to the theme of "binyan," upbuilding.

These are "Sephirah" days for our people, and every day must count. Zionists in the present world crisis have no time for self-pity and no time for wailing and weeping.

We have time only for building.

At the heart of the Zionist attitude toward life is an indefeasible will to master untoward circumstance and hew out a path for the self-expression and the self-realization of the Jewish people not only in Palestine but everywhere.

An estimable leader of a Jewish community in the peroration to his charity appeal was heard to say, "If we Jews are doomed, if we must perish, then at least let us meet our fate with noble tragedy." He was probably thinking of the end of the classic Greek tragedies in which the central characters resign themselves with noble dignity to their fate. There is another way, which the "Maccabee" has taught. The word "Maccabee" means "hammer."

Let those who will, adopt the "anvil" philosophy, of noble submission to the blows of fate. Zionists build their lives and their hopes upon the assumption that the Jewish will to live is the hammer which will break through every obstacle. Perhaps philosophically considered, one assumption is as reasonable as the other. Psychologically considered, they are as far apart as life and death, "the hair's breadth," which according to the Rabbis, separates heaven from hell.

Jewish history vindicates the Zionist way of life.

Bialik—The Hebrew Poet Laureate

Address delivered at the Bialik Memorial
Meeting held in Carnegie Hall, New
York, July 20, 1938.

Bialik–The Hebrew Poet Laureate

CHAIM NACHMAN BIALIK was truly the poet laureate of the Jewish people.

He has made it possible for us to say that Hebrew is not a dead language but a living tongue. He has taken the language of the Prophets and the Psalmists, of the sages and the scholars, and has so molded it and fashioned it and wrought it that it has become an instrument, both delicate and versatile, capable of expressing the finest shades of thought and feeling, the most delicate nuances of light, sound and color. He has taken the old forms of speech and breathed into them new life and meaning.

It was Ahad Ha-am, the great teacher whom Bialik esteemed above all others, who, speaking of the distinction between the sacred and the secular, made the discerning observation that what is sacred endures in its form from generation to generation, though its content and the interpretation of its content may vary from age to age. The contrast between the Bible and Plato is cited as an example. How many meanings have been read into the Holy Book, how many different interpretations it has received. To one age, it meant one thing, to another age it had a new and different meaning. Yet, it always remained the Holy Book, the sacred Scriptures, however its interpretation may have changed from age to age. On the other hand, the great works of Plato which at one time commanded the homage of the whole intellectual world, when Plato's philosophy was the vogue and Plato's metaphysics were the accepted science, are today superseded and hold an interest only for special students of the subject.

The Hebrew tongue is the "Lashon Kodesh," the holy tongue. Its content, its constituent elements, may change, but the vessel, the language as such has always been revered.

Bialik has poured new wine into the old vessels of the Hebrew speech, a new life-stream into the old arteries. He has taken the sacred heritage of an ancient tongue and made it live. It has become in our time the modern counterpart of Ezekiel's vision of the "dry bones." For that miracle of rejuvenation we lift the voice of gratitude to Chaim Nachman Bialik. He is the great master of the Hebrew tongue whose lips have been touched by the burning coals from the sacred altar.

Bialik has done more. He has made it possible for us to say not only that we have a living national speech, but that we have a contemporary national poetry which compares with the great poetry of our time. He has expressed the soul of his people as only one or two others have done in a thousand years of Jewish history.

We Jews have been all too long content to shine in reflected glory, to feel second-hand pride. When Heine sang the sweet lyrics of Germany, we boasted; when Antokolsky carved the marble masterpieces of Russian theme, we gloried; when Israels painted lovely Dutch pictures, we prided ourselves. Is it always to be the glory of the Jew that he should bring his talent and offering to the altars of all the nations except his own and pour the libations of his genius into every shrine except his own? Isaiah's rebuke is not obsolete, "In the children of strangers do they take abundant delight."

Bialik did not go to alien shrines. He made the offering of his genius at the altar of the Jewish people in whose lap he was reared, from whose breasts he was nourished. Therefore we hail Bialik as Israel's national poet.

Perhaps the greatest service that Bialik has rendered his people has been that he has stirred the Jew to a sense of self-respect as did no other poet of his time. With prophetic fury he lashed the weakling and the coward. With burning indignation he excoriated the "mah yofisnik," the sycophant who would sell his heritage for a smile from the non-Jew. With bitter rebuke he chided the anemic passivity of those who accepted the hooligan's kick as if they were dogs, and bore the yoke of oppression as if they were cattle. Bialik has taught the Jew to stand up and battle for his life and for his rights. Bialik has taught the Jew to understand that his greatest tragedy is not his sad plight but his supine attitude toward it.

> *"My father—bitter exile, my mother—want,*
> *'Tis not my staff or the shameful scrip I dread!*
> *More cruel than these, more bitter sevenfold*
> *Is life without hope or brightness for the eyes;*
> *The life of a hungry dog, bound by its rope*
> *How art thou cursed, thou life without a hope!*
> *Illumine, star, my soul that has despaired*
> *Through pagan worship and 'neath exile's weight."*

Bialik has lifted the vision of the Jew to a star, the star of Zion which points the way of hope. In "El Hazipor," "To the Bird," he has given winged expression to his yearning for the hills of Judaea, the Valley of the Sharon, and the dews of Hermon. It is a paradox, of which only genius is capable, that he, the product of the Yeshivah, the "Mathmid," should have been able to feel the call of the soil and to give his people a fore-taste of the song of the soil, with which Jewish life in Palestine was to hum a generation later.

Regarding Jehudah Halevi, with whom Bialik has been most often compared, it is told that after a life-time of yearning and longing for Eretz Israel, he realized at last his hope to visit that beloved land, but his moment of realization was tragically brief, for as he threw himself to kiss the earth he loved, an Arab horse-man trampled him to death.

Bialik has been more fortunate. The fulfillment of his dream lasted not a moment but a decade and more. Now, after years of life and labor upon the soil of his fatherland, he is gathered unto his fathers. His body becomes one with the soil he hailed and longed for and blessed in the very first winged expression of his poetic genius. Bialik's heart has stopped beating, but the heart of Israel, which he has done so much to quicken and to strengthen, has caught up his pulse-beat, and will carry it on.

We are indebted to Chaim Nachman Bialik, who has given us a tongue to speak with, a national song to cherish and a national hope by which to live.

We who have been born in America, or, if not born here, at least reared upon the lap of this new continent, we who have not ourselves lived through the "shehitah" and the "harega," the ordeals of pogrom, tragic experiences which have moved Bialik to utter his immortal threnodies, we who cannot identify from first-hand experiences the rich picturization of the Mathmid, the student, and of the old "Beth Hamidrash," where he studied, we too, of this American generation, are profoundly indebted to Chaim Nachman Bialik.

Can we repay the debt? No more than we can repay the sun for shining, or the dew for bringing refreshment to the earth. For us it is to prove that we deserve to call him our own. We must give a sign that the flame of his soul has touched us. We must let him see that we are not as the withered grass, of which he sings in plaintive tones, when he says: "Verily the people is grass, it has become as dry as wood."

Let us give proof that American Israel, which used to be regarded as the withered branch of the Jewish tree, is not without vitality. Let us show that this branch can give forth blossoms and bear fruit. Let us give the sign that the star of Zion to which he turned our gaze has captured our hearts, that Eretz Israel is our "Eretz Hemdah," the land in which we delight because it is the cradle of renascent Hebrew speech, renascent Hebrew genius and renascent self-respect.

In the same words with which Bialik hailed Ahad Haam, his teacher, do we hail his memory, our teacher and our poet.

"Accept our blessing, o teacher, our blessing sincere,
The blessing which years without end our hearts did contain;
Now in pure untarnished love we bear thee thanks
For every seed of nobleness thou didst implant
Which in our barren hearts did blossom into fruit.
And if it should in our generation come to pass
That the sacred spark will glow in Israel's soul,
It will be because among all the sons of Exile
In thy noble soul it first did flash."

In Bialik's great masterpiece, "The Dead of the Wilderness," he makes those ancient speak a mighty word. "We are to be the last generation under bondage and the first to be free."

Would that it might become our fate to be that generation which shall be the last to bear the yoke and the first to see the light of redemption, when the land of our past shall become the land of our present and of our future. Then it will be time for the poet of that day to write a sequel to Bialik's doleful "Evening Song." It will be the "Song of the Morning," the song of the new awakening.

Jew and Moslem

Address delivered before the Moslem
Brotherhood Association, New York, January 6, 1935.

Jew and Moslem

As a son of the West, I invariably feel a sense of humility and contrition in the presence of sons of the East. One should be humble knowing that the great words which have sustained the spirit and still sustain the spirit of mankind, have emanated out of the East, whether they have been the utterances of Confucius, Zoroaster, Buddha, Moses, Jesus, or Mohammed. One should be contrite at the effrontery of our Western World when it presumes to impose its standards and its civilization upon peoples who have more to teach than they have to learn.

The Jew, however, has at least this compensation, that there is enough of the Orient in him to make him view with a wholesome skepticism our mechanical Western civilization. We may be experts in sanitation but not in sanity, in achievement of comforts and conveniences, but not in the achievement of happiness, in speed of transportation and communication, but not in the quickening of the soul, in winning a livelihood, but not in achieving a life.

There is an historic kinship between Judaism and Mohammedanism, which warrants a closer understanding and fellowship between the respective adherents of these two religions and cultures today.

Mohammed, in the early part of his career, came under Jewish influence. Many of the Old Testament stories and characters appear in the Koran. The ritual and legal codes of Islam contain some elements which are traceable to older Jewish sources.

Judaism in turn has much reason to acknowledge a debt to Mohammedanism.

Believe me, it is not mere courtesy or gallantry, which prompts me to say to you that the Jewish people looks back upon its association with Mohammedan culture and institutions as one of the most satisfactory periods of its history since the loss of its sovereignty in Palestine.

The period in Mohammedan Spain from the tenth to the thirteenth century, with few exceptions, is known as the "golden" period of Jewish literature. Jews rose to high positions in political, economic and cultural life and rendered signal services to the communities in which they dwelt. Hasdai ibn Shaprut and Samuel ha-Nagid were viziers to the Caliphs. Under the stimulus of Arab poets, scientists, physicians, philosophers and philologists, Jewish poets, scientists, philosophers and philologists produced their best work. Cordova, Granada, Lucena, Malaga, Saragossa, Seville and Toledo were seats of Jewish culture. Menahem son of Saruk, Dunash son of Labrat, Solomon ibn Gabirol, Bahye ibn Bakudah, Abraham and Moses ibn Ezra, Jehudah Halevi, and the versatile Maimonides, are only a few of many luminaries who illuminated the firmament of Jewish life in Mohammedan Spain.

We are about to observe the 800th anniversary of Maimonides, our greatest philosopher, scientist and physician. His chief work, "The Guide to the Perplexed", was written in Arabic.

The association between Jew and Arab brought mutual enrichment. Jews became the carriers of Arabic civilization and culture to Europe in the Middle Ages, spreading that civilization and culture wherever they went.

It is well to recall these historic chapters because they point a lesson for the possibilities of the future. In Palestine of tomorrow, Jew and Arab may again live in harmony and in friendship, cultivating each his own best resources to their mutual advantage.

If Palestine in recent years, as a result of Jewish enterprise and industry, has enjoyed more favorable conditions than any of the neighboring countries, Arabs have had their share of the benefits. Economically they have benefited by higher wages and better employment opportunities. From Transjordania, Syria and Iraq, thousands of Arabs have gravitated to Palestine because of its economic advantages. In the field of health and sanitation, the well-being of all the inhabitants of the land was aimed for and in a measure has been achieved. In the Hadassah clinics and hospitals there are no sectarian restrictions. In the cultural realm there is a growing awareness of the need for cultural intercourse between Jew and Arab. The Hebrew University classes and facilities are open to Moslems as well as Jews. A Chair in Arabic literature has been established there as a token of esteem for Moslem civilization.

The Jew in Palestine desires to live in peace and amity with his neighbors, and to raise the standard of living, physically, economically and culturally, for all the inhabitants of the land.

It would be less than frank, however, for one who is a Zionist, not to make mention of his fundamental belief that Zionist aspirations are compatible both with Arab welfare and with international justice.

If international justice is a concept to be honored in the observance rather than in the breach thereof, it should give consideration to the relation between need and possession.

The Arabs have national homes in Egypt, Iraq, Yemen, Syria, Transjordan and Saudia, areas twenty times the size of little Palestine. The Jewish people, most homeless and dispossessed of all peoples, asks that one little corner, hallowed by its ancient traditions, should be acknowledged as the Jewish National Home which Jews should be entitled to enter, settle, and cultivate and administer as of right. That is what home should mean to a people as to an individual. In the exercise of its rights in Palestine, the Jewish people will never abuse the rights of the other elements of the population be they Arab or Christian. Is the Jewish people to be denied that little portion of justice?

Palestine can never mean to any other people what it means to the Jew. During all the centuries when Jews in large numbers did not inhabit it, Palestine was neglected. During the few present decades following the Balfour Declaration when Jews flocked to it, it has become rehabilitated as no other soil has been rehabilitated in so short a span of time.

From any normal point of view, the price paid by the Jewish people for its relatively small foothold in Palestine, seven per cent of the total area, has been beyond all reason. The price paid has been not only in money, many times the intrinsic value of the land. Far heavier has been the price paid in labor, suffering, blood, life itself. Only Palestine is worth that price to the Jew and only to the Jew is Palestine worth such a price.

It is to be hoped that with frank mutual understanding the difficulties and frictions which may exist between Jews and Arabs in Palestine are not insuperable, that they will be solved in the course of time as both realize how much more they have in common than they hold in difference. If there are some Jewish extremists who incite to friction, they should be silenced. If there are some Moslem hot-heads and politicians who incite to friction, they should be silenced. Let there be no false issues injected into the normal processes of neighborly intercourse. Gradually the recognition must grow on all sides that a successful Palestine means a better, happier life for everybody.

We are called upon, by the challenge of the times in which we live, to bear testimony together. We should stand together to testify that what the world needs today far more than machines, which are the outstanding achievement of Western civilization, is prophecy, which is the outstanding achievement of Eastern civilization. The great prophets of humanity have all hailed from the East. Their message of brotherhood, peace, love and righteousness are still the guiding banner. In this day when nationalism has gone mad, and when ethics and morals are being interpreted not as absolute values but as conditioned by national considerations, let us stand together to testify that ethics and morals are not bounded by geographical or racial lines.

We have in common another message to proclaim, that the chief concern of human endeavor should be to make this world a better world and that the vision of men should be focused on the improvement of the here rather than on the beatitudes of the hereafter, that man is not born with "original sin," that physical pleasures in and for themselves are not sinful provided they are disciplined and regulated so as to serve the social common weal, that the highest life is that in which flesh and spirit are integrated into a wholesome harmony, that man's chief purpose and duty is to make life on earth fit to bear the name and blessing of God.

Roger Williams—New England —New Palestine

A Tercentenary Tribute delivered at Providence, Rhode Island, July 5, 1936.

Roger Williams–New England–New Palestine

 I T IS WITH deep reverence that we stand upon this holy ground, dedicated as a memorial to one of America's immortals. The dimensions of this occasion are not limited by local boundaries. They are as wide as the human brotherhood. It is human brotherhood which we glorify today.

The Jewish citizens of America are gratefully cognizant of the designation of this day by the illustrious Governor of your State, as Jewish Day in your Tercentenary celebration; and the Zionist Organization of America feels it as a high privilege that the day has been fixed so as to coincide with its annual convention.

Every minority group in American life has reason gratefully to commemorate the name of Roger Williams and the year 1636. In that year he founded here a settlement upon the basis of complete religious toleration, with a view to its becoming "a shelter for persons distressed for conscience."

In the chorus of thanksgiving, the voice of the American Jew vibrates with a special fervor and pride. With thanksgiving he recalls that Roger Williams was the first on this continent to grant liberty to Jews, together with other minorities, though it was not until 1684 that the right of Jews to settle in Rhode Island was specifically affirmed by the General Assembly of the State.

With pride, the Jew recalls the part played by his forebears in the development of this commonwealth. It was in Rhode Island, in the city of Newport, that there grew up a Jewish community in the Colonial period, which was the largest and most influential in the country, having established there the oldest Synagogue on the North American continent. Its contribution to the economic development of the young Colonial Commonwealth was substantial. It was, therefore, a romantic coincidence that nearly one hundred years later, when the General Assembly of the State of Rhode Island was to be convened for the first time after the evacuation of the city in the face of the British invasion, it was in the historic Synagogue of that historic Congregation that the General Assembly of the State convened.

Roger Williams more than any other individual of his time, fathered and fostered those principles which were the antecedents and precedents for the guarantees of religious freedom and racial equality, which distinguish the Constitution of the United States. If one considers where Roger Williams found his antecedents and precedents, one is led to the Book of Books, which gave this courageous preacher his spiritual nourishment and his motive power. The law of his life and the law of the living corporate society which he established here, were derived from the law which came out of Zion. "And ye shall love the stranger for ye were strangers in the land of Egypt." "Have we not all one father, hath not one God created us all?" In the soil of Palestine had been conceived the original seed of the ideal of love for the stranger and of human brotherhood, which he espoused.

In 1636 Roger Williams was himself a victim of intolerance. Banished from one part of New England because of his views, he found refuge in this colony. Less than a century and a half later, his views had become woven into the consciousness of all the colonies and were written into the charter of the new American nation.

These United States were the first nation to be founded upon the rights of man. No other nation in modern history was so ideal-conscious at its birth. In the formation of no other nation in modern times did a declaration of liberal principles and ideals precede the establishment of nationhood.

The only precedent in history is that of the Jewish people. The Torah, their declaration of independence and their set of ideals and principles, preceded their establishment as a nation in Palestine. Before a single foot of the soil of Canaan was occupied, Israel was pledged to the moral and ethical Law. It is an analogy which binds the Jew to America with ties of spiritual kinship and understanding.

If in the world of 1936 there are peoples and governments which are shamefully remiss to the recognition of human rights, there should be some solace in the knowledge that our America at least still honors the cause which Roger Williams espoused. On this Memorial Day therefore, let our hopes be mingled with our memories.

The Bible has been one link between Palestine and America. There is another. Just as many generations ago upon the soil of this continent there was built up a New England, so in our time there is being built up a New Palestine, a new edifice upon the ancient soil. Just as men came to this New England three hundred years ago to find and to found not only a new livelihood but a new life that should be freer, better, and happier than the old life, so in our day Jews from the Old World are coming to the New Palestine, to find and to found not only a new livelihood, but a new life that should be freer, better and happier than the life in the old countries.

The modern pioneers in Palestine, like their ancient forebears, also came to the land with a set of ideals and a reckless selflessness in its behalf. A nobler chapter of colonization is not to be found. The men and the women who drained the swamps, planted the trees and builded the roads of the New Palestine are the intellectual and spiritual aristocracy of our race.

The quest by an ancient people for fountains of self-renewal, is worth every price, every hardship. Nothing will daunt him. With the patience of Job he will yet teach his Arab neighbor to grasp his hand in fellowship. He will yet bring the day to pass when the two Semitic peoples will dwell side by side in peace, "each under his vine and under his fig tree, with none to make him afraid."

Twenty years ago, when the nations of the world endorsed Great Britain's covenant with the Jewish people to establish in Palestine a Jewish National Home, it was upon a resolution offered by a Senator from New England, Henry Cabot Lodge, that the Congress of the United States gave its unanimous vote of approval. This approval has been renewed by every one of our Presidents since that time, Wilson, Harding, Coolidge, Hoover, and Roosevelt.

Thus Palestine and what has come out of Palestine are linked with this day and with this place.

The Jewish people has a book of remembrance in which are inscribed the names of great figures, Jew and Gentile, living and dead, whose life and work have touched with blessing the destiny of our people and the welfare of all mankind. This book, the Golden Book of the Jewish National Fund, rests in Jerusalem, the Holy City in the Holy Land, the cradle of the religion which Roger Williams preached and practiced, and of the religion which the Jew has lived and taught. For every name therein entered a handsome gift is made by some individual or organization in honor of the one thus inscribed. With these gifts land is purchased in Palestine, to remain forever as the property of the Jewish people, serving as a foothold for those who come to New Palestine to build a new life. For every name thus inscribed a scroll of honor is issued.

Judge Letts and members of the Rhode Island Tercentenary Committee, on this day which has been proclaimed by your Commonwealth as Jewish Day, in the presence of delegates to the annual convention of the Zionist Organization of America which is dedicated to the ideal of a Jewish Homeland in Palestine, and in the presence of this entire distinguished gathering, I have the honor, in behalf of the Jewish National Fund which represents all Zionist groups and parties, to present to you and through you to the State of Rhode Island, this scroll, bearing the immortal name of Roger Williams as one inscribed in Israel's Golden Book of Remembrance. Please accept it as the tribute of an ancient race which has suffered and still suffers from bigotry and oppression.

May the Providence that guided the founder of this community in his courageous adventure upon a new path, guide our nation today in the path he blazed, and bring the light of better understanding to all the dark corners of the earth.

Palestine at the World's Fair

Address as Chairman of the Board of Directors of the Jewish Palestine Pavilion at the New York World's Fair, delivered before the Convention of the Zionist Organization of America, Detroit, July 3, 1938.

The Pavilion was projected in 1938 and completed in 1939.

Palestine at the World's Fair

A HAD HA-AM, in one of his most penetrating essays, says that Adam, the first man, was unconsciously a great philosopher when he uttered the word, "I." Indeed, philosophers since his time have created mountains of argument in order to explain this little word, and they have not yet arrived at a clear understanding of what is "self."

The modern philosopher of Zionism goes on to say that in his opinion, self, the essence of personality in an individual and in a people, is the combination of memory and will, the union of past and future.

Everyone of us, on the basis of a personal self-analysis, can identify the observation that the ego unites the past and the future, so that memories merge into will and experiences become interwoven with hopes. This is the essential meaning of personality.

The achievements which the Jewish people has to its credit in Eretz Israel today represent, more than any other set of facts and achievements can possibly represent, the truest expression of the Jewish national ego, of Jewish national selfhood. Nowhere else in the world is there, or can there be, such a union between our past and our future, between Jewish memories and Jewish will.

Even if one were to propose the hypothesis that there might conceivably be a future for the Jewish people in some other land, yet the ineluctable historic fact remains that Palestine, and Palestine alone, has been the most characteristic scene of the Jewish past, the Old Testament past, the Maccabean past, and, in part, the Talmudic past. That historic fact would rule out any other land from consideration as the land of Jewish selfhood, of the Jewish ego composed as it must be both of past and of future.

If the Jewish self has not yet come to full flower in modern Palestine, if it is still somewhat raw and unseasoned, it is because there has not yet been enough time. Half a century in the life of a nation is hardly enough time for the reorientation after an interruption of more than eighteen centuries. Yet, even in this brief union between Israel and Eretz Israel amazing things have happened,—the revival of the ancient Hebrew tongue, the renaissance of a culture and a literature, the reclamation of the earth and of human beings living upon it, the creation of noble patterns of human relations represented by the co-operative agricultural groups, the "kibbutzim" and "kvutzoth." More than enough has happened to justify the hopes and the sacrifices, the toil and the tears which have been poured into it; more than enough to vindicate the Zionist contention that only upon that soil can Israel's soul "flourish as the rose and strike root as the Lebanon."

Another test of collective selfhood is the sense of responsibility felt by one segment of the group toward all the other segments. The Jewish community in Palestine has given a noble demonstration during the years of Arab terror. Had they been concerned only for their own security they could have had peace with the Arabs long ago by consenting to immigration restrictions upon newcomers and a permanent minority status for the Jew in Palestine. That they refused to do. They risked their lives in order to keep the doors of Palestine open so that myriads of other Jews might come. While in other lands, the existing Jewish communities grow uneasy when large additional numbers of Jews enter, Palestine Jewry rejoices at the entry of every additional immigrant. It sets at naught the artificial distinctions between "legal" and "illegal" immigration, recognizing that a

Jew coming to his national home can never be "illegal," but that "illegal" is the hand that would bar to a man the door of his home. Such an attitude is a fundamental test of national selfhood.

The ultimate test of selfhood has been met there, namely, the readiness to offer life in defense not merely of physical self but of all that spiritual self implies, the values of the past and the hopes of the future. The soil of Eretz Israel is still moist with the blood of those who have given that ultimate testimony,—witness the martyrs of Hanita, Ain Hashofet, Tirath Zwi.

Enough has happened in this short experience of half a century of reunion in Eretz Israel to touch even Jewish life outside of Palestine, in Galuth lands, with the glow of self-discovery. A new meaning has been poured into the Jewish self-cognition of our time. Like the reviving limbs of a sick man whose heart has begun to function normally again, the members of the world-wide body of Israel have taken on new life. What else is the meaning of such youth groups as Young Judaea, Junior Hadassah, Avukah, Masada, and others, drawing American-born Jewish youth? What is the meaning of the Hebrew-speaking youth who sometimes embarrasses his less Hebraically-tutored elders, if not the stirrings of the Jewish "anochi," self-awareness? Youth is a crucial test of national selfhood. When we have the youth, our self-preservation is assured. We have a future to link with the past. We must continue to reclaim our youth. "Ani yeshenah velibi er," "I am asleep but my heart is awake." Many of them have been dormant but the pulse still beats. It can be quickened, it must be quickened by the lifegiving vitality streaming from the fountainhead of the Jewish selfhood, Eretz Israel.

The Palestine Pavilion which we are to erect at the World's Fair will be an opportunity to demonstrate before the eyes of the world, focused upon that international exposition, what the Jewish national ego is and what it has created in this brief period of its renaissance.

From the design of the building, which will be the work of

Palestinian artists, to the last piece of fabric in the exhibit itself, which is to be produced by craftsmen and artisans of the Yishub, the Palestine Pavilion will be characteristically Jewish. There used to be a time in the history of our people when we contented ourselves with the slogan, "the beauty of Japheth in the tents of Shem," to bring the beauty of the Occident into our Semitic premises. Today, the Jewish national ego is more confident about its artistic expression. The Palestine Pavilion will bring the beauty of Shem into the tents of Japheth, into the World's Fair.

The Palestine Pavilion will tell the story of Jewish labor, Jewish industry, Jewish agriculture, Jewish town-planning, Jewish arts and crafts, Jewish public health, Jewish co-operative enterprises, Jewish culture and education. It will dramatize in pictorial and plastic form the miracle of the transformation of the soil and the soul of a people. The Palestine Pavilion will be a physical token of how the Jew, as Jew, lives and creates. It will show his present as a link between his past and future. It will tell the story of religion and nationalism interwoven. It will hint at a future which the Rabbis have foreshadowed when they said that Messiah will come when Mount Tabor, the scene of national self-defense under Barak, will be united with Mount Sinai, the scene of religious Revelation.

At the World's Fair nations and governments from all parts of the world will endeavor by their buildings and exhibits to convey to the American people something of their respective personalities, something of their national selfhoods, something of their characteristic achievements and contributions. Thank God for our great democracy where such an international project can still be held. Thank God that these United States are free from the "ruah ra-ah," the evil wind which has poisoned other lands.

That among these buildings bodying forth the personalities of nations and governments there is also to be a building bodying forth the personality of Israel and Eretz Israel, is reason for all

Zionists to say "sheheheyanu." "Thank God that we are privileged to witness it."

Let the assimilationists rage and fume. Let them muster all their shafts of dialectic and polemic to deny reality. Let them protest to the high heavens that they are "Americans of the Mosaic persuasion," that Jews are nothing more than a religious sect, though many of these so-called religious sectarians give their religion the absent treatment and lead their children to alien altars. "Baal korham yaanu amen," perforce they must say "amen." They will be among the multitudes of American Christians and Jews who will come to the Jewish Palestine Pavilion out of curiosity, but who will remain to admire. I predict that they will have a hard time hiding their thrill, that their pseudo-logic will capitulate to their emotions.

The Jewish Palestine Pavilion at the World's Fair will demonstrate in undeniable brick and mortar, in tangible fabric and visible colors, that there is a Jewish national selfhood and that it is growing and flourishing in the Jewish National Home.

For twenty years now, ever since the Balfour Declaration, we Zionists have been telling the American people, Jews and non-Jews, what is being done by our institutions in Palestine. Some have taken our declaration on faith and have responded to our appeals. Others have remained skeptical and aloof. Here will be our first great opportunity to offer an exhibit in evidence, to bring a replica of Palestine to America. It will validate in the eyes of millions who will visit the Fair all that the United Palestine Appeal, the Jewish National Fund, the Keren Hayesod, Hadassah and all other fund raising institutions have been proclaiming.

The Palestine Exhibit will indirectly hurl back the charges which are being leveled against our people by those who, with malice aforethought, vilify us by generalizing the traits of some individuals and by labeling as characteristic, manifestations which are abnormal, the result of abnormal conditions to which Jewish life has been subjected.

We affirm that we are ready to be judged by that which is the Jewish norm, the true Jewish self. We demand to be judged by that which we have created in our National Home.

Those who exhort the Jew to live up to his "mission" as a "holy people," exemplar of justice and righteousness wherever he dwells, and who, affirming that dispersion is his destiny, condemn Zionism as Jewish separatism, are indulging themselves in a naïve or willful "non-sequitur." Where is the Jew most likely to reveal his best traits if not in the environment where he can be most truly himself? Do they expect that Jewish communities in the Diaspora, living in the midst of a non-Jewish world will be able to live as islands of justice and righteousness in a sea of greed and injustice? It is a noble mandate, a high sense of responsibility, but is not the possibility of its fulfillment infinitely enhanced by the existence of a Jewish community in Eretz Israel where every span of earth and sky calls to him in the name of his great past, to be his best self? "Out of Zion shall come forth the Torah," the light to illumine the path of Israel everywhere.

Fifty years of revitalized Jewish life in Palestine have produced greater evidences of his capacity to fulfill his "mission" than five hundred years outside of Palestine.

In a World's Fair whose theme will be, "the World of Tomorrow," our building, surrounded by great and magnificent structures, will be striking by its simplicity. Its modest proportions will convey a message of the past and a lesson for the future.

The message of the past is that out of modest little Palestine, wedged in between great empires, have come forth civilization's greatest boons, the God concept, the Moral Law and the Messianic hope. Our foes may burn our books, they cannot burn our ideas, for our ideas and ideals have been handed down "in letters of flaming fire" which will for all time illumine the path of mankind.

The lesson for the future is that the world of tomorrow,

abounding in mechanical inventions and scientific findings, will need desperately that spiritual nourishment which has come out of Palestine. It is not difficult to see that without God, without a Moral Law and without a Messianic hope the world of to-morrow is doomed. The warning which, according to our Rabbis, was given at the Revelation of Sinai, still holds, "either you accept the Torah or your doom is here." (Talmud, Sabbath 88a.)

Out of the Menorah which will surmount our Pavilion will shine forth the etefnal message, "not by force, nor by might but by My spirit." Force may gain temporary victories; only Justice can determine enduring dispensations. In the world of to-morrow science and invention will transform the face of cities and change the modes of living, but the definitions of life's purpose, once formulated upon the soil of Palestine, will never become obsolete.

To bring about the realization of the Palestine Pavilion is a great and beautiful task. Those who were present at the corner-stone laying, a few months ago, will never forget that scene. The cornerstone was a stone brought from Hanita, a silent wit-ness of Jewish heroism and martyrdom. It was touching to see how Jews reacted. Some came to it reverently and bent down to kiss it. Others were content to merely touch it. Others simply gazed upon it and wept. It represented to them all the labor and sacrifice, the toil and the tears and the blood which the Jewish people has poured into its own land.

That scene brought to mind the beautiful comment of the Rabbis on the story of Jacob's dream. They say that when Jacob was lying upon the stone, a fugitive from home, he dreamed of a ladder reaching to heaven with angels running up and down taunting him and mocking him with the words, "Art thou the Jacob whose image is engraved in the heavenly throne? Art thou the Jacob of whom the Divine voice spoke, 'Israel in whom I am glorified?' Art thou that Jacob who art now lying pros-trate upon the ground?" (Genesis Rabbah, Chap. LXVIII.)

It is the taunt which reflects the recurrent self-introspection of the Jew. Self-criticism, the transitional moment of doubt, is also a part of selfhood reacting to a crisis.

Jacob today is prostrate. In many lands he is writhing in the dust like a worm, lowly, humiliated. Even in Palestine he is not untroubled. It is not strange that doubts and misgivings should sometimes torment him. But it is only a passing phase. It has never been more than a passing phase. Perhaps it is a necessary transition in the growth and development of personality, transition from the past to the future. For out of that moment of trouble and doubt springs a resilient will and faith for facing the future. It was expressed in the Divine reassurance that Jacob felt as he was lying there upon the stony earth. "The land on which thou liest shall I give to thee and to thy children." That same reassurance fills his soul today in the midst of the ordeal through which he is passing in the Galuth lands, and also in Palestine. "The Jewish Homeland shall be ours and our children's."

Come and let us together build this building fraught with so many overtones of Jewish selfhood.

William Green—Leon Blum—Palestine

Address delivered at the Leon Blum Colony Dinner in honor of William Green, New York, June 26, 1940.

William Green–Leon Blum–Palestine

T HE OVERTONES OF tonight's gathering are as broad as the theme of democracy itself, and the basis of tonight's symposium is as fundamental as the foundations of civilization which are being threatened in our day.

This is an harmonious blending of a three-fold theme. First, this is a demonstration of our high regard for America's foremost labor leader, William Green. I do not consider myself as qualified as some of the others who have spoken and will speak, to discuss the subject as one of the labor ranks associated with our guest of honor in his daily responsibilities. I can only claim a very technical and literal common denominator, consisting of the fact that I believe in labor unions, and Mr. Green, I trust, believes in marital unions. And I suppose that in my career I have organized as many of the latter as he has of the former. I trust that my unions have been as productive as his.

Speaking as a citizen, I recognize that the strength and dignity of a democracy are in direct proportion to the strength and dignity enjoyed by its labor ranks. If that be the touchstone, then William Green, who has done so much for his generation in achieving a stronger position for labor in America than it has ever enjoyed before, is truly one of the statesmen of American democracy.

He is a statesman also because he has not confined his energies to his primary responsibilities, but has lifted his voice courageously and consistently in condemnation of injustice and aggression whether they were perpetrated by an individual or by a nation, whether they wore the label of Nazi, Fascist, or Communist dictatorship. He has earned the right to be called a friend of humanity.

He is a statesman also because, and not least because, he recognized in the ideal of Palestine as a Jewish National Home something which was akin to all the spiritual values that he had espoused. He recognized and recognizes in Palestine, not merely a haven for the homeless but a corner of the earth where a cooperative society, with a democratic way of life, an emphasis upon the rights of labor and an impetus to spiritual creativeness, is being cultivated not under the whip of compulsion but by the free will of a free people.

The second theme tonight, congenial to the first, is Leon Blum.

That Leon Blum should have declared himself years ago in favor of the establishment of the Jewish National Home in Palestine and identified himself as one of the founders of the Jewish Agency for Palestine, was to be expected of one of the great exponents of democracy in our time. That a colony in Palestine should be founded in his honor and designated by his name, is a fitting tribute both to him and to Eretz Israel. That the Leon Blum Colony should be established on Jewish National Fund land, the inalienable property of the Jewish people where only they who labor on it may live on it, makes the kinship between the name and the enterprise complete.

Leon Blum has stood in his land and for his people as the champion of the same ideals with which the career of our guest of honor is identified. Today, he is spurned by the regime in power in the land which he served with unexcelled patriotism and unsurpassed devotion. If Leon Blum is spurned, then all that is best in the life of the French people is or will soon be repudiated, the France of Henri Bergson, Romain Rolland and Leon Blum. Physically, this France may be crushed, for a time it may be subjugated under the heel of the conqueror, but the torch that that victim has been compelled to drop, we here in

America are resolved to take up and carry aloft. That is our mission in this, the dark age of modern history.

Not least of all, our theme tonight is Palestine. Palestine is now one of the remaining battlefronts of Democracy. That little land has thus far escaped the fate which has befallen other little lands. If the war should come to Palestine, we know that there will be 500,000 Jewish men, women and children who will be found ready to defend every inch of its soil. It will be the first time since the days of Bar Kochbah, 1800 years ago, that a substantial Jewish population will be ready to fight in and for its ancient and historic soil.

It should be a source of satisfaction to all friends of Labor to know that in the building of its national home in Palestine the Jewish people has embodied a measure of social idealism, cooperative economy and dignity of labor, unique in the annals of colonization.

The Leon Blum Colony in Palestine, established by the contributions of American labor, will be the witness of the understanding and support which a great democratic segment of American life has consistently given to the aspirations of the Jewish people for a Jewish national home. Goodwill, understanding and support coming from any quarter is welcome. Coming, however, from the ranks of labor they are especially welcome, and, we believe, not undeserved.

Because land is the fundamental commodity of life, the manner in which a people's land is acquired, owned, occupied and used, is the best criterion for evaluating a people's moral caliber and its title to the respect and goodwill of other nations.

The right of the Jew to Palestine is three thousand years old. Let it be assumed, however, that history began only twenty years ago. An international covenant was made with the Jewish people twenty years ago, which later received the sanction of King Feisal, the then Arab spokesman. Not only his formal sanction but his warm approval was expressed in a letter to Dr. Chaim Weizmann. This covenant, pledging a national home for the Jewish people to be established in Palestine under the mandate of Great Britain, was recognized as an act of justice to a people which alone among the peoples had no homeland, and for whom Palestine alone could be a homeland.

It might have been expected that thereupon the mandatory government would proceed to make substantial grants of state lands in Palestine for settlement by Jews. This was indeed promised but it was not fulfilled. Instead, the Jews had to pay exorbitantly for every square foot. It might have been expected that Jewish gain would mean Arab loss, as sometimes happens when a new population enters an old country. Instead, Jews have actually increased the habitable, cultivable area of Palestine by curing land that was diseased, making fruitful places that were waste, and teaching the Arabs by example how to make the earth yield more abundantly.

It might have been expected that the land acquired by Jews would, as land among other nations, become the object of struggle between the strong and the weak, and, as usually happens, would gradually fall into the hands of the rapacious and the rich. Instead, what has happened? To the extent that organized representative Jewish bodies such as the Keren Kayemeth which is the Jewish national land fund, the Keren Hayesod which is the colonization fund, and the Jewish Agency for Palestine, the supreme administrative body, have administered Jewish affairs in Palestine, and to the extent that these bodies are vested with powers, resources and authority,—to that extent the land is owned, not privately but publicly, as a national possession, and its settlement and use are conducted upon lines of co-operation not exploitation, collective welfare not individual aggrandizement, justice not rapacity.

Thus the frontiers of the Jewish people in Palestine, which have been achieved under the aegis of the Zionist movement, are the frontiers of justice, in keeping with the Prophetic exhortation that "Zion shall be redeemed with justice." Four plains have been redeemed from waste and sterility, the plain of

Jezreel extending from Haifa southward, the plain of Zebulun skirting the Mediterranean, the plain of Hepher in the Sharon, and the plain of Beisan near the upper Jordan. And now a fifth frontier in upper Galilee consisting of the Huleh swamps and their environs, is being reclaimed. These five plains are the five gains we have to show for our labor. They are gains not alone for the Jewish people, not alone for scores of thousands of homeless and oppressed of our race, but for the whole of Palestine, adding areas which heretofore have been almost desolate. They are gains for the Near East adding health spots which heretofore have been breeding grounds of disease. They are gains for civilization adding model communities of social justice in a part of the world where feudalism still obtains.

It is with good reason that the Zionist enterprise in Palestine is regarded as the idealistic leaven in the life of the Jewish people, the saving remnant in the spiritual as well as in the physical sense, the one instance to which we as a people can point, of a national practical enterprise conducted by Jews as Jews and bearing the authentic stamp of the Jewish will and the Jewish personality.

Jewish Palestine, built upon democratic principles, belongs to the orbit of Democracy and is now one of the battlefronts of Democracy. Every bit of strength we add to the people who are engaged in its defense, every barren acre we help convert into an acre of food and subsistence, every foothold we provide for the settlement of a new refugee, is an added bit of strength for the forces of Democracy. At a time when the American slogan is, "all aid to England short of war," our effort for the benefit of Palestine assumes a broad significance.

There are countless friends of liberty and lovers of Democracy today under the heel of Hitler who, alas, cannot speak for themselves. Our voice is their voice, too. The expression of our faith in the ultimate victory of the democratic principles is the expression of their suppressed prayers.

Palestine, Leon Blum and William Green belong together in

tonight's theme. From its inception, the Leon Blum Colony project has had the enthusiastic support of the President of the American Federation of Labor. Tonight's tribute to William Green will be translated into a sum which will complete the financial obligation entailed in the establishment of the Leon Blum Colony in Palestine.

William Green, by his presence here tonight, has not only made possible the completion of the Leon Blum Colony project, but has channelled our thoughts and utterances toward the consideration of fundamentals which are the basis of the lives of free men everywhere. This is the meaning of our threefold theme tonight.

Our faith in the future derives new reinforcement here. We are resolved to implement that faith by our readiness to do whatever may be within our power, so that truth, honor, freedom, justice, equality and democracy shall not perish from the earth.

STUDIES IN BACKGROUNDS

The Function of the Church in the State

Substance of address as Chairman of the Social Justice Committee of the Rabbinical Assembly of America, delivered before the University of Minnesota Convocation, Minneapolis, May 2, 1935.

The studies in backgrounds commencing with this essay are for the most part related to the general purport of the volume, conveying historical backgrounds for several of the problems which come under the scope of "Toward a Solution."

The Function of the Church in the State

The conflict between Church and State, which in our day has had its most pointed expression in the totalitarian states, is deeply rooted in the evolution of the Western world. Competition between secular and religious institutions for authority and prestige has punctuated the history of nations and continents. It is a thousand year old struggle.

"Going to Canossa" is a phrase which had for its setting the dramatic clash between two strong personalities, one a Pope, the other an Emperor, who dominated eleventh century Europe. Pope Gregory VII made and deposed emperors. Henry IV was the strong-willed ruler of Prussia. Threatened with dethronement by the German princes acting on orders from Rome in consequence of his defiance of the Pope, he hastened to make peace with the head of the Church. In the middle of winter he crossed the Alps and waited three long days outside the Pope's castle at Canossa. Finally allowed to enter, he begged pardon for his sins and was forgiven. The King's penitence, however, was short-lived. At the head of a large army he later entered Rome, seized the city and forced Pope Gregory into exile. Conflicts between Popes and Kings continued.

In fifteenth century England, there was another dramatic episode in the struggle between Church and State. Henry VIII, failing to receive papal sanction for his divorce from his first wife, flouted the authority of Rome and declared himself the head of the Church as well as of the State. Thus came into existence the Church of England as a Nationalist Church where higher ecclesiastics are appointed by the Crown and have seats in Parliament.

The conflict broke out again with Napoleon as the central figure. In a march on Rome, he had the Pope seized and carried away to Fontainebleau. With the fall of Napoleon, the Papacy was restored to its power.

A further decline in the temporal power of the Pope took place in 1870 at the unification of Italy when his status as ruler was confined to the Vatican area, the Lateran palaces, and a Swiss guard. The situation in Italy remained in a condition of confusion until 1929 when Mussolini recognized by a treaty the Papal sovereignty, limited to the Vatican City, and accompanied the treaty by a concordat which recognized Roman Catholicism as the only State religion and the only form of religious education.

The relationship between Church and State can be one of four types:

1. The Church controls the State. The extreme example of this type of relationship was the position of the Catholic Church in the Middle Ages, before the Protestant Reformation and the rise of Nationalism challenged and weakened its control.

2. The State controls the Church. The extreme example is Russia, where a hostile government is in complete control. In Nazi Germany the aim is the same though in effect it has not been altogether successful.

3. A compromise arrangement, such as operates in England where the National Church though subject to the State, enjoys a special official status.

4. Official separation between Church and State, prohibiting an "established" Church but permitting Churches of all denominations to function freely.

The United States offers the best example of the free Church within a free State. Here the legal position of the Church is that of a voluntary association with its own jurisdiction, subject, however, to the laws of the State. The Constitution provides that "Congress shall make no law respecting an establishment of a Religion or prohibiting the free exercise thereof."

While there is no official relationship between Church and State in the United States, there is, however, a friendly co-operation. Religious bodies receive special privileges from the Government. They are exempt from taxes. The sessions of our Congress are opened by prayer. Important Christian holidays are recognized as legal holidays. Chaplains are appointed in the army.

In everyday life it is hardly feasible to draw a hard and fast line of separation between secular and spiritual institutions. Life is of one piece, not separable into strictly demarcated departments. Contacts and overlappings between the functions of the Church and those of the State in American life, are inevitable. Without any official relationship, the Church has profoundly affected the course and character of American life.

The Church has been the foster mother of education. Many of the institutions of higher learning have been founded under the auspices of religious institutions, or have been directed by religious personalities. On the Samuel Johnson gate of Harvard Yard, there are inscribed the following lines, which indicate the purposes for which Harvard University was established by its founders:

"Dreading to leave an illiterate Ministry to the Churches
When our present Ministry shall lie in the dust."

Samuel Johnson, who was the first President of Columbia College, declared it as his hope that the studies of nature there pursued, lead the students to "a knowledge of the God of Nature, and of their duty to Him, to themselves, and to everything that contributes to their true happiness, both here and hereafter."

Also in the field of elementary education the Church has been a dominant influence. As late as 1850, the children of the best families derived their secular training mainly under the auspices of the Church, in institutions which combined secular and religious instruction. It was so in Jewish Congregations as well as in Christian communities. The Public School system did not become widespread and efficient until well on in the second half of the nineteenth century.

If the Church has been the foster mother of education, it has been the natural mother of philanthropy. Within its walls, social welfare programs were conceived and the administration of charity had its birth. To refer again to the Jewish community as an illustration, some of our most important institutions in New York, such as the Hebrew Orphan Asylum founded in 1822, the Mt. Sinai Hospital established in 1852 and the Federation of Jewish Philanthropic Societies organized in 1917, originated under the direct inspiration and guidance of the Synagogue.

The Church has always played an important role in the molding of public opinion upon moral issues. The movement for the abolition of slavery owed much to the inspiration and guidance of religious leaders and institutions. Beecher and Brooks in the Christian pulpit were outstanding abolitionists. Rabbi David Einhorn preached anti-slavery sermons in the face of pro-slavery sentiment in Baltimore, and was finally compelled to leave the city. Countless civic and political leaders in America have derived their moral philosophy and their spiritual outlook from the Church. High public officials, including many of the Presidents, were the sons of clergymen or were in other ways reared in a religious atmosphere.

The part which the Church has played in American life is therefore not to be underestimated. It is doubtful if the Church will ever again be as closely woven into the texture of the American State. Some of its former prerogatives have been usurped by secular agencies. With the exception of the Catholic community, secular education has been taken almost entirely out of its sphere. The elementary school system has been secularized.

Institutions of higher learning are in the main under secular control. The work of social welfare has also, in great measure, become dissociated from the Church, and has been assumed either by the states and municipalities or by voluntary secular associations. The social welfare work which is still being conducted by the Church, is a very small fraction of the total.

It is evident, therefore, that in the field of education as well as philanthropy, there has been a progressive secularization and specialization away from the Church. These areas of endeavor have grown in size and efficiency. On the other hand, the Church, while it may have lost some of its hold on the life of the community, may also have gained in being left free to develop with all the greater vigor those fields where its place and function remain unchallenged.

What is the function of the Church in American life at the present time?

It is an invaluable auxiliary in making for a better and more wholesome State.

Its first responsibility lies in the sphere of religious education. Secular education is not enough. The purpose of education is to develop the complete personality of the child, moral and spiritual as well as intellectual. Thus the child can be properly fitted to take his place as a useful citizen. Characterless Apollos and cynical Minervas, splendid physical specimens, who have had the advantages of education and culture, but who lack character, whose attitude toward parents is arrogant, toward the duties of citizenship—indifferent, toward moral obligations—flippant, and toward the ethical code—recalcitrant, are not an asset to the State. The most important element in the training of the child is character training. While it is a responsibility which should, in the first instance, devolve upon the home, it is natural, however, for parents to turn to the Church for assistance and co-operation. Each of the great religious denominations is addressing itself to this problem through its own methods. Thus the Church serves the cause of moral and spiritual training without which the future of any state is not safe.

The Church also plays an important part in generating and maintaining the civic morale which is essential to the stability of the State. What is the guarantee of law and order in a community? Surely it is not alone the fear of the penalty attaching to violation of laws which makes for a law-abiding community. There are spheres of conduct which are not within the province of legislation. Laws prohibit the extremes of greed, and lust, and vulgarity. The milder manifestations of these evils are not subject to the jurisdiction of the law, yet they affect the tone of the community. The Commandment, "Thou shalt not covet," is not a legal injunction. The most effective guarantee of law and order in a community is the sense of civic duty and moral responsibility prevalent among its citizens. In this sphere the Church is an indispensable factor making for the stability of the modern State. Not only does it teach and preach obedience in the law, but it devotes itself especially to the inculcation of the plus elements, above the irreducible minimum. Law guarantees the minimum; Religion exhorts the maximum. It is the plus elements inculcated by Religion which make the difference between a high level and a low level of statehood.

The Church, finally, is the propagator of Faith, faith in God and in Humanity, faith of men in one another and in the development of their God-given possibilities, which is a binding cohesive force in the life of the community and a sanction for co-operative fellowship. Churches and Synagogues are growing away from interdenominational contention. They are instead addressing themselves with growing emphasis to interdenominational understanding and co-operation. The Interdenominational Goodwill Movement, including Catholics, Protestants and Jews, has made substantial progress in recent years. It has been a wholesome antidote, though not effective enough, against unAmerican efforts to foment suspicion and illwill. Thus the Church is a unifying force in American life.

One of the most important areas in our national life where the influence of the Church has been exercised on the side of progress is the sphere of economic relations. Its exhortations to economic justice have not stopped at the point of the pronouncement of general principles, but have ventured upon the advocacy of a program.

For the past decade the public mind has been occupied with the question of economic justice more than in any previous period in our history. The prolonged depression which has made poverty our greatest common denominator, has made economic problems and policies matters of acute public concern, witness the popularity of Mr. Upton Sinclair's "Epic," Mr. Townsend's "De Senectute" proposals, and Father Coughlin's "radiocinations." Any economic panacea gets a wide hearing nowadays.

When so large a section of the population is concerned, it is natural to ask, "Where does the Church stand?" Has Organized Religion, which claims more than fifty million communicants in this country, any word to pronounce, any guidance to give in these problems which agitate the public mind, and which are paramountly real and vital in the life of our nation?

In considering where the Church stands, it is pertinent to examine not only where it stands today, but where it stood before the depression brought economic questions into sharp, persistent focus and made economic liberalism a popular philosophy.

Although strictly speaking, the problems of international peace, race relations, decent housing and community health, would also come properly under the same heading, it is industrial relations which have been the kernel of the social economic problem in our industrial civilization, and are therefore the most telling criterion and the crucial test in determining where Organized Religion stands.

In a matter of such vital import general observations may not be convincing unless they are supplemented by factual evidence. A summary of the pronouncements and activities of Church and Synagogue groups would speak for itself in conveying the deepening sense of concern with the economic injustices of our time.

For the Catholic Church, the official pronouncements on Social Justice stem from the encyclicals of the Popes Leo XIII and Pius XI. The first, issued in 1891, dealing with the condition of labor, is regarded by the Catholic Church as the "Magna Charta" of the rights of labor. The second, issued in 1931 on the fortieth anniversary of the first encyclical, deals with the reconstruction of the social order. For the Protestant Church, the official pronouncements emanate mainly from the Federal Council of the Churches of Christ in America, which includes nearly all the important Protestant denominations. For the Synagogue, the official pronouncements derive from the Central Conference of American Rabbis, which is the Reform group in the Synagogue, and the Rabbinical Assembly of America, which is the Conservative group. The Orthodox group has not as yet developed an official medium and method for the articulation and propagation of its social justice principles.

Every one of these three major religious denominations has a special commission whose purpose it is to study social and economic questions, formulate the proper attitudes and policies on behalf of their Church organization, strive to gain for that formulation the adherence of the denomination as a whole, and then seek to make that formula publicly known and accepted as far as possible. The Department of Social Action of the National Catholic Welfare Conference for the Catholics, the Social Service Commission of the Federal Council of the Churches of Christ in America for the Protestants, and for the Jews the Commission of Social Justice of the Central Conference of American Rabbis and the Committee on Social Justice of the Rabbinical Assembly of America, are the official Church agencies in this field.

The first significant fact to note is that Organized Religion assumes the right and feels the duty to offer its sanctions and its guidance in the economic realm. It is noteworthy because there has been and there still is a powerful element, in the pulpit as well as in the pew, which holds that Religion and Economics are independent spheres which ought to keep a respectful distance away from each other. Under the aegis of theological "laissez faire," some eminent lay pillars of the Church have been able to do what they pleased in the economic realm without embarrassment to their religious conscience and without prejudice to their Church standing.

Therefore, it is significant that the pronouncements and activities of official Church bodies, Catholic, Protestant and Jewish, leave no room for doubt as to the attitude of the Church regarding its right and duty to concern itself with social economic questions.

The Papal encyclicals lay down the broad principle that "it is the right and duty of the Church to deal authoritatively with social and economic problems, not in technical matters for which she has neither the equipment nor the mission, but in all matters that have a bearing on moral conduct." On the same point, the Protestant principle promulgated by the Federal Council of the Churches of Christ in America, declares that "it is the duty of all Christian people to concern themselves directly with certain practical industrial problems." The Committee on Social Justice of the Rabbinical Assembly of America declares "that discussion of problems of social and economic justice and the evaluation of movements to abolish exploitation, poverty and other social evils are not only the legitimate but the necessary concerns of the Synagogue." The Commission on Social Justice of the Central Conference of American Rabbis declares that "the function of the pulpit is not to raise charity funds to patch up social ills while keeping silent concerning the wounds which fester underneath the patches, but that the more permanent function of religious groups is to evoke a social conscience concerning our economic life whereby through social economic reconstruction, the periodic pauperizing of masses of human beings through charity and relief will become unnecessary."

On the specific problems within the sphere of industrial relations, the Church pronouncements deal with industrial democracy, wages, hours, and conditions of labor, women and children in industry, unemployment, social insurance, and the general evaluation of the present economic system.

All three creeds commend trade unionism, or as it is more commonly called, collective bargaining. They hold that the workers have the same right as the employers to organize and to be represented by those of their own free choice, for only in that way the workers, who individually do not possess equal bargaining power with the individual employer, can treat as economic equals with their employers. The Catholic position goes so far as to suggest that it is the obligation of the State to protect the organizations whose purpose it is to safeguard the rights of the workers, for the reason that the State should protect the weak whereas the strong can take care of themselves.

On the question of wages, all the creeds agree that there should be a minimum wage adequate to support the worker and his family in reasonable comfort. The Catholic view states that the right to a living wage is as "a dictate more imperious than any bargain between man and man," and that in the face of this dictate the law of supply and demand must recede. It also defines a living wage, as including not only the immediate needs of the family, but also savings to provide for future contingencies, such as sickness and old age. The other two creeds regard such provision for contingencies as an obligation resting chiefly upon industry and the State. The Protestant view favors the highest wage that each industry can afford. It too holds that a free contract which requires that the worker sign away his elementary rights, is an unjustifiable perversion. A decent wage should in its opinion, be the first charge on industry, having priority over interest. The Jewish point of view coincides, in putting human rights above property rights, and declares also that there must be not only a minimum wage for the workers, but a limitation on the maximum income for the employers.

On the subject of unemployment, all the creeds agree that the right to work is a fundamental right and a spiritual necessity. In January, 1932, the three denominations issued a joint statement using the occasion of the industrial crisis to reiterate some of their previously stated views. They assert that the cure for unemployment is not relief but employment, that a large program of public works construction is needed, that the hours of work must be reduced without reduction in wages, that industry should bear the costs of the problems it creates, namely, insurance against unemployment, sickness and old age, instead of having the burden borne as heretofore by the individual workers or by the charity organizations of the community, and they stress the point that unemployment is linked up with the general evils of our economic system, such as the improper distribution of wealth and the resulting lack of balance between production and consumption.

With reference to the general evaluation of the character of the present system as a whole, there is some divergence of opinion. The Catholic view, while denouncing the "laissez faire" policy of the Manchester School of Economics, which sanctioned unbridled individualistic competition at the expense of the workers, is just as emphatic, however, in its deprecation of socialism. It believes in private ownership, and urges the workers to save and to aspire to becoming owners. Although the right of private property is upheld as a natural right, a distinction is drawn between ownership of property which should be private, and the use of property which should be guided by social considerations. State ownership is opposed except in certain forms of property which are too important to the public welfare, and carry with them the danger of domination. The concentration of wealth in the hands of a few is condemned as placing immense power and economic domination in the hands of a small group, and as leading to the domination of the State by financial interests and even to clashes between States because of the financial interests involved.

The Protestant view declares for "equal rights for all men in all stations of life, the abatement and prevention of poverty, a new emphasis upon the application of Christian principles to the acquisition and use of property, and the most equitable provision of the product of industry that can ultimately be devised." The present economic system is condemned because of its recurrent depressions and prolonged unemployment cycles, the failure of the industrial mechanism to function properly in the use of natural resources and in the productive capacity of the nation, and the shocking inequalities of income which result in overcapitalization on the one hand, and underconsumption on the other, thus creating vicious circles of depression. It inveighs against the concentration of wealth which carries with it a dangerous concentration of power. It points to the fact that the present distribution of wealth and income, which is so unbrotherly in the light of Christian ethics, is also unscientific in that it does not furnish purchasing power to the masses to balance consumption and production. What is needed is a planned economic system in which co-operation shall supplant competition as the fundamental method, and in which the principle shall be operative that the personalities of human beings deserve first consideration.

The view reflected in the statements of the American rabbinical organizations holds that the unrestrained exercise of private ownership without regard for social results, is morally untenable, that the profit system with its appeal to basically unworthy motives has been shown to be not only irreligious but anti-economic, that the instruments of production and distribution as well as the system of profits, must be placed increasingly within the powers of society as a whole, that pending the socialization of the economic system, certain basic enterprises such as banking, transportation, communication and power production, which are too important to be left in the control of private groups, must be immediately socialized. It is pointed out that the total national income even today, reduced as it is, is still sufficient, if properly distributed, to maintain every family on a decent standard of living, and that until such adjustment is made, we must have a radically revised system of taxation. Our individualistically inspired economy has degraded human character and has led to the verge of collapse. Our economic system must be reorganized, so that co-operation instead of competition shall be the guiding principle. It can and should be changed by orderly procedure. "The old order is coming to an end. What we are witnessing is nothing less than the breaking up of a whole social system. We are now at the end of one of the great epochs in history as truly as men and women were at the decline and fall of the Roman Empire or the collapse and disintegration of the Feudal System.

"Future generations will marvel at our mechanical inventions and also wonder at our lack of social creativeness and vision. Not one factor is missing today out of which to construct a world of social comfort and justice. We have natural resources, unmatched machinery, men trained to a high degree of skill and efficiency, vast reservoirs of wealth dammed up in vaults and banks and corporations, and great markets here and abroad. The one thing we lack is the vision and the will to mold this unprecedented mass of riches into an order of social justice.

"If the Jewish religion does not identify itself with the movement for the better economic order, it will be, by default, condoning the present order, and will have to resign itself to the fate of all those institutions of the old order which must some day be abolished when the old order perishes."

These pronouncements of the Churches touching the main problems of our industrial economy, have not been permitted to remain static verbiage. Conferences and seminars are held, at which both laity and clergy participate in the discussion of social and economic questions. The medium of the printed word is also used extensively. Thus, the social justice message of the Church reaches ever widening circles and educates public opinion.

The Church has felt itself called upon not only to adopt, declare and propagate the principles of economic justice, but also to apply these principles to specific industrial situations. Many members of the clergy of all the denominations have taken sides in industrial conflicts, usually on the side of labor, or have been entrusted by both sides with the power to make decisions in crucial questions at issue. In a number of important situations, official representatives of the Catholic, Protestant and Jewish denominations have spoken or acted jointly. The following are a few selected instances:

1. In connection with the steel strike of 1920, an investigation commission, sponsored by the Inter-Church Movement, a Protestant organization, issued a report supporting the grievances which occasioned the strike, namely, long hours, the "boss" system, and the restrictions upon the right of collective bargaining. Following a report by the Iron and Steel Institute which justified the twelve-hour day, a joint statement was issued in 1923 by the Catholic, Protestant and Jewish bodies, condemning the twelve-hour day as morally indefensible. Shortly thereafter, the twelve-hour day was modified.

2. In connection with the strike on the Western Maryland Railroad in 1926, the three denominations joined again in an effort to clarify the ethical issues in the controversy. Their joint report was commended by the press of the country "as a courageous and significant act on the part of organized religion in focusing public opinion in the ethical aspects and social implications of economic frictions that could and should be prevented directly by the parties concerned."

3. In 1928, the three religious bodies attempted jointly to mediate upon the conflict between the American Federation of Hosiery Workers and the Real Silk Corporation. In the same year they jointly investigated the Bituminous Coal Strike, and issued a statement condemning the violation of the right to a living wage and collective bargaining. They urged the President

and Congress to bring about a fair and just mediation of the issues at stake.

4. In 1929 they undertook an investigation of the conflicts in the textile industry in the South.   In a joint statement which aroused widespread public attention, they condemned the working conditions in the Southern textile mills and the violence against the workers.

It should be borne in mind that the greater part of these Church pronouncements and activities in the field of social justice, were undertaken before the economic collapse made the evils of our economic system tragically patent, and before the logic of events brought a political party to victory on the campaign slogan of "a New Deal for the forgotten man." The social justice principles and programs of the Churches were arrived at in the main not under the stress of an emergency, but by a sober analysis of the normal functioning of our present social order, and are therefore, on the whole, the well-considered opinion of the Church upon the social economic issues of our time.

It is evident that the indictment which is sometimes leveled at the Church that it is a protector of the privileged and a defender of the vested interests, is not generally true so far as concerns the Church as we in this country and of this generation have known it.   If a radical change in the economic pattern of our society were to overcome this nation tomorrow, the Church would not be in the vulnerable position in which it has been in some other countries, such as Russia, Spain and Mexico, of being liable to be singled out as the bulwark of reactionism.

Here in the United States, it is to the credit of Organized Religion as a whole, Catholic, Protestant and Jewish, that it has taken cognizance of the social economic problems by the appointment of official agencies to study and observe the workings of our present system, that it has pointed out the weaknesses and evils of the present order, that it has clearly enunciated the principles upon which a just social order must rest, that it has given moral evaluations of specific industrial situations, and that it has endeavored to be of service in the solution of industrial conflicts. Nor is it less noteworthy that these three major groups have co-operated so closely in the fulfillment of this mission as the common obligation of all the creeds. In no other country has such co-operation been so well effectuated.

Far from preoccupying itself with "otherworldly" matters or with "apocalyptic and millenarial visions," the Church in this country has addressed itself to the challenging realities of the present order.

Of transcendent importance for the present crisis in world history is the role of Organized Religion in resisting the totalitarian trend of our time. This aspect of the role of the Church is of epochal significance and deserves separate consideration. Few will fail to acknowledge that the protesting voice of Religion has been raised, even where there was risk of danger. The rights of the individual have found stalwart defenders among the spokesmen of all the religious denominations. To the ultimate hoped-for vindication of the fundamental principles which are the landmarks of our civilization, the forces of Organized Religion are making a valiant contribution.

For Church and Synagogue in the American scene, it can be justly said that on the whole their relationship with the State has been a happy one for both sides. Here they have not been subjected to dogmatic opposition born of an unreasoning reaction to the abuse of ecclesiastical power. At the same time there has been a wholesome recognition by religious bodies that they are functioning in a free State where there is no "established Religion." Out of these mutually agreed conditions there has evolved mutual respect, cordiality and co-operation.

Earlier Settlements of
German Jews in America

Substance of address delivered before the Institute of Jewish Affairs of the Jewish Theological Seminary of America, New York, December 12, 1933, based on the author's work, "A Century of Judaism in New York," where the source references may be found.

Earlier Settlements of German Jews in America

In the history of American Israel, the chapter dealing with the years following 1933, will dwell on the immigration of tens of thousands of Jewish refugees from Nazi Germany, their adjustment to the new environment and their influence upon the existing communities. If that chapter is to have permanent value, the writing of it will wait not only until the new influx will have abated, but also until the social adjustments and interactions will have had time to work out, and the new elements will have had the opportunity to become integrated into the context of American-Jewish life.

While the process is going on, it may be of some interest, historically as well as sociologically, to cast a retrospective glimpse upon the earlier settlements of German Jews in America.

It has become conventional for writers on the subject of American-Jewish history to divide the subject into three simple categories, the earliest period of the settlement of Spanish and Portuguese Jews, the next period of the immigration of Jews from Central Europe and the latest period of the arrival of Jews from Eastern Europe.

Strictly speaking, it is not quite correct to make categoried divisions. History does not so readily accommodate itself to logic. There were German Jews who came here during the Spanish-Portuguese period. There were East European Jews who came here during the so-called German period, and there have been Jews, both of German origin and of Spanish and Portuguese origin, who have come here during the East European immigration period,—much to the confusion of the strait-jacket historian.

For the purposes of clarity, however, divisions may be drawn more sharply than historical accuracy would permit. Labels may be affixed to periods in accordance with their main trends, regardless of the exceptions.

Although the earliest Jewish communities on the American continent were composed chiefly of Spanish and Portuguese Jews, there were a sprinkling of German Jews among them. A few came directly from the German provinces. Others came from England. Some came from Holland, which had a community of Ashkenazim in addition to the more important community of Sephardim. (The terms "Sephardi" and "Ashkenazi" are used interchangeably with "Spanish Portuguese" and "German," although they are not exactly synonymous. The words "Ashkenaz" and "Sepharad" occurring in the Hebrew Scriptures, Genesis, 10:3, and Obadiah, 1:20, are generally employed to designate Germany and Spain respectively. These terms are also used to describe not only the Jewries from these two lands respectively, but also the Synagogue rituals which trace their developments to these two sources.)

Names which are unmistakably German are found in the records of the Jews martyred by the Inquisition in Mexico at the end of the sixteenth century and during the seventeenth century. German Jews settled in the Dutch West Indies, Dutch Guiana and the British West Indies, particularly in Curaçao, Surinam and Jamaica, during the latter part of the seventeenth century and the early part of the eighteenth century. A letter from the Sephardic community in Curaçao accompanying a contribution to the Sephardic community in New York toward the building of its Synagogue in 1729, states that at that time already the German Jews in Curaçao outnumbered the Spanish and Portuguese Jews.

The record of German Jews in the United States goes back therefore to the earliest period of Jewish settlement here, the year 1654, when the first Jews arrived in New York, then New Amsterdam.

The first German Jew to come to New Amsterdam was Asser Levy who arrived from Holland in 1654. He was the first Jew to stand up for his rights as citizen. When Peter Stuyvesant, Governor of New Amsterdam, and his council, passed an ordinance "that Jews cannot be permitted to serve as soldiers, but shall instead pay a monthly contribution for the exemption," Asser Levy and his comrades refused to abide by the order, and petitioned for leave to stand guard like other burghers, or to be relieved from the tax. The petition was rejected with the comment that if the petitioners were not satisfied with the law, they might go elsewhere. Levy carried his appeal successfully to Holland, so that he was permitted to do guard duty like other citizens. Subsequently, he requested to be admitted as a burgher, showing a burgher's certificate from the city of Amsterdam. The application was denied by the subordinate officials, who were sure that such a privilege could not be granted a Jew. Asser Levy at once brought the matter before Stuyvesant and his council, who, mindful of the previous experience, ordered that Jews should be admitted as burghers.

Thus Levy achieved important victories for the civil rights of the earliest Jewish settlers in New York. He appeared as litigant on many occasions, invariably argued his own case, and usually won. Instead of being unpopular on account of his many lawsuits, the contrary seems to have been the case. The Court records attest to the confidence which his Christian fellow-citizens reposed in his honesty, and the respect in which they held him. He was also the first Jew in New York to own real estate.

In Philadelphia, the first Jewish settler on record is a German Jew, Jonas Aaron, mentioned in a record of 1703; and the second Jewish settler on record is also a German Jew, Arnold Bamberger, mentioned in a record of 1726. German Jews were to be found in all the important Jewish communities of that period, which were the communities in the cities along the seaboard, namely, Newport, New York, Philadelphia, Richmond, Charleston and Savannah. It was not until 1802, however, that the first Congregation of German Jews was organized, Congregation Rodeph Sholom, of Philadelphia.

The tone and leadership of the Jewish communities in the important cities, was, of course, set by the Spanish and Portuguese Jews by virtue of the fact that they were usually the original settlers. As the earliest Congregations were Sephardic, the Ashkenazic Jews had no choice but to join them, until their numbers were large enough and strong enough to organize their own Congregations.

There were, however, several groups of German Jews in Lancaster, Schafferstown and Easton, who having settled in the interior of Pennsylvania, as early as 1735, maintained their distinct identity. The record of the German Jews in this early period would be far more impressive were it not for the fact that they did not exist as separate groups, but were counted in with the Spanish and Portuguese communities.

The period which is usually referred to as the main period of German-Jewish immigration into this country is the one between 1815 and 1880. The year 1815 marked the defeat of Napoleon, resulting in the end of the breathing spell of toleration which the Jews of Germany enjoyed under his regime. With the collapse of that regime the disabilities and restrictions which Jews had suffered before were reinstated. The hardships upon the Jewish population included not only civil disabilities but commercial restrictions, restrictions upon the number of Jewish marriages and conscriptions to military service. The New World offered an escape from all of these. Toward the middle of the century, the revolutionary movement in Central Europe found Jews in the ranks of the revolutionaries and therefore in the ranks of the victims of the reaction which followed. Many of them fled to America where they developed into some of the most useful citizens.

The year 1880 is used as the terminal date for two reasons. Conditions of Jewish life in Germany had by that time improved considerably, with the result that the exodus abated. Secondly, the year 1880 marked the beginning of the large scale persecutions and pogroms in Russia which brought about a huge Jewish exodus from Russia to the United States, changing the whole complexion of Jewish life in this country. 1815 to 1880, is therefore, the usually accepted period associated with the main settlements of German Jewry in this country.

In 1817, the immigration from Europe to America reached the then unprecedented figure of 20,000. The numbers increased steadily. After 1845, the rate was 100,000 a year. In 1854, it reached 450,000. German Jews constituted a substantial portion of this immigration wave. The Civil War, of course, interrupted the trend. By 1870, due to improved conditions of Jewish life in Germany, the decline of the Jewish immigration tide set in.

The rapid growth of the Jewish population in the United States during this period can be surmised from the available estimates which place the Jewish population in the United States in 1818 at 3,000; 1826, at 6,000; 1840, at 15,000; 1848, at 50,000. Between 1850 and 1870, the Jewish population in the United States quadrupled.

Where did these new German immigrants settle? Most of them, as might be expected, settled in the cities along the Atlantic seaboard. That was the easiest thing to do. Many, however, ventured forth to newer fields. The country was expanding westward. Many of the new immigrants followed the westward trail. Arriving here mostly without means, their first resort was usually to peddling as a means to livelihood. Both by temperament and by economic necessity, these immigrants were more venturesome than their Spanish-Portuguese predecessors had been before them. Gradually they penetrated the middle west, the southwest, and eventually, the far west. The chronology of the founding of Congregations of German Jews reflects this westward movement. New Congregations were organized in Cincinnati in 1837, in Chicago in 1846, and in San Francisco in 1850.

The first Jewish settlement west of the Alleghenies, was in Cincinnati. Joseph Jonas, who arrived from England in 1817, was the first Jewish settler there and the Jewish pioneer of the Ohio Valley. To many of the natives who had never seen a Jew before, he was an object of curiosity. He told of an old Quakeress who said to him: "Art thou a Jew? Thou art one of God's chosen people. Wilt thou let me examine thee?" She turned him round and round and at last exclaimed; "Well, thou art no different to other people."

In the meantime, German Jewish communities were growing rapidly in the larger cities on the Atlantic seaboard. In New York, a Congregation of English, Dutch and German Jews, who wished to worship according to the Ashkenazic rite, seceded from the Sephardic Congregation and organized in 1825, under the name, "Congregation B'nai Jeshurun," as the first Ashkenazic Congregation in New York. The number of Ashkenazim living in New York would have warranted the organization of a Congregation of their own long before. Although sporadic attempts had been made previously, they did not succeed until 1825.

Among the Jews of German or partly German origin in the New York community during the first quarter of the nineteenth century, two names stand out from all the others. One is the name of Sampson Simson, who had the distinction of being the first Jewish graduate of Columbia College and the first Jewish member of the bar. Later he became the founder of the Jews' Hospital, known subsequently as Mt. Sinai Hospital. The other was Mordecai Noah, half Sephardic and half Ashkenazic. He was unquestionably the outstanding American Jew of his generation, a brilliant orator, publicist, jurist, playwright and statesman. He was the author of an interesting project, never realized, to establish on Grand Island near Niagara Falls, a colony for persecuted Jews of Europe, which might serve as a training ground for Jewish self-government preparatory to the return of the Jews to Palestine.

Neither Noah nor Simson joined the new Ashkenazic Congregation, though they gave it their blessing. The new Congregation had the goodwill of the whole Sephardic community. It was a mutually agreeable secession.

If it took one hundred and fifty years for a second Jewish Congregation to emerge in New York, it took only five years longer for the third Congregation to come into being. It was also Ashkenazic and bore the name "Ansche Chesed." Its makeup was uniformly German unlike B'nai Jeshurun which had been composed of English, Dutch and German Jews. Between 1830 and 1850, ten new Congregations were organized in New York, all Ashkenazic. By 1862, there were twenty-three Congregations in the city, and the only Sephardic Congregation was still the original one. These figures are a commentary on the growth of German Jewry.

What of the character and development of the new element in the Jewish population? In comparison with the Spanish Portuguese settlers, they were for the most part humble folk. The Spanish Portuguese Jews had come to America with a cultural background and with commercial experience, sometimes combined with substantial financial resources. While contingencies of misfortune may have destroyed their security and even wrecked their fortunes, they brought with them a personal endowment rooted in generations of proud and successful ancestry. In this new land, they formed communities which tended to become closely knit, and even ingrown, as had been their community life in the old homesteads. Indeed, their meager numbers in this country, which probably did not exceed 1500 at the beginning of the nineteenth century, consisted largely of family kindred.

One can understand, therefore, why there was a social cleavage between the Sephardic Jews and their Ashkenazic neighbors. Their relations were in no wise different from those which had obtained in the mother communities of London and Amsterdam. It is significant that at a later period, similar social relations obtained between the German Jews and the newcomers who were the East European Jews. Social preferences are often based upon no greater merit than the accident of chronological priority. Jews are not exempt from the foibles of human nature.

The venturesomeness of the German Jews in their geographical scope of settlement and in their commercial enterprise, was rewarded. The time was in their favor. It was the great expansion period of American history, the period of the covered wagon, the steam locomotive, and "the gold rush." They soon graduated from their erstwhile poverty. Neither were they slow in improving their education. Many of them who came here as illiterates, did not long remain in that condition. All of them sought to compensate in the education of their children for their own lack or limitation of educational opportunities.

Their social life was active and abundant. Whereas among the older Sephardic settlers, the Synagogue had been the social meeting place as well as the religious center, the German Jews, because of their larger numbers and because of their greater sociability, found it necessary to establish special organizations for social purposes. The Jewish fraternal order as a social and benevolent institution, originated during this period. The oldest and largest of these was the Independent Order of B'nai B'rith, founded in New York in 1843.

The philanthropic activity of the German Jews was widespread and well-organized. Jewish communities, no longer the small homogeneous groups they had been during the Spanish Portuguese period, required more extensive provisions for the poor, the aged, the orphaned and the sick. Whereas formerly the provision for all these needs was either centered in the Synagogue and Congregational life or arose directly out of it, now the philanthropic needs of the community made independent claims and developed their character and support, to a large degree, independently of the Synagogue. Some of the outstanding philanthropic institutions of today originated in the third quarter of the nineteenth century under the leadership chiefly of German Jews. In New York, the Jews' Hospital, later known as Mt. Sinai Hospital, was organized in 1852. The Young Men's Hebrew Association was formed in 1874.

The Synagogue during this period was not the all-embracing institution which it had been in the Spanish-Portuguese period. Formerly the Synagogue and the Synagogue officials had exercised a control over the life of the individual Jew, from the cradle to the grave. Births had to be registered in the Synagogue. The license to marry had to be secured from the Parnass (lay head) of the Congregation. "Kashruth" (Dietary Code) was under the administration of the Congregation. Passover "matzoth" were baked and distributed under Congregational auspices. Philanthropy was a Congregational activity. Even a burial permit could be gotten only with the approval of the head of the Congregation, and often served, as did the granting of the marriage license, as a means of forcing the payment of delinquent dues. Such close control by the Synagogue could have been possible only in a community which was small, homogeneous and closely knit, as had been the Sephardic communities in America. With the coming of the German immigration, as the community became more heterogeneous, the Synagogue's scope of power was diminished.

To say that the German Jewish period was marked by a receding trend in the domination of Jewish life by the Synagogue, does not mean that the Synagogue did not function effectively or that it did not flourish abundantly. It only means that Jewish life was becoming so vast, so extensive, so diverse and so complicated, and the needs of the Jewish community outside of religious worship were becoming so great, that they inevitably grew beyond the confines of the Synagogue and the Congregation.

Congregations increased rapidly and Synagogues grew into large and magnificent institutions. In New York alone, where up to 1825 there had been but one Congregation, there were twelve Congregations by 1850 and twenty-three Congregations by 1862. As German Jewry prospered, they erected more and more beautiful edifices. Congregation Emanuel, which had been organized as a modest group in 1843, erected its magnificent house of worship on Fifth Avenue and Forty-third Street, twenty-five years later, at a cost of more than $600,000 for the land and structure, and succeeded in raising more than the sum required from the sale of pews to members.

There was also a change in the function of the Rabbi. In the Spanish and Portuguese Congregations, the religious officials, bearing the title of "Hazan," were not preachers as much as they were teachers and officiating ministers. Some of the early Ashkenazic Congregations managed to get along for a time without Rabbis, although they did employ cantors. The first Congregation in New York, in which sermons in English were delivered on frequent occasions, was in Congregation B'nai Jeshurun, fourteen years after its organization. Its first minister was Rev. Samuel M. Isaacs, who came from Holland. The first Rabbi in New York who preached regular Sabbath and Festival discourses in English was Dr. Morris J. Raphall, who came to Congregation B'nai Jeshurun from Birmingham, England, in 1849. In a number of Congregations sermons were delivered in German.

It was characteristic of the early Jewish Congregational life in the United States, both among the Ashkenazim and the Sephardim, that there was no central religious authority to whom all the Congregations could look for guidance. The Sephardim leaned on the mother Congregations and the religious authorities in London and Amsterdam. Congregation B'nai Jeshurun, from 1825 to 1849, acknowledged the spiritual authority of the Ashkenazic Chief Rabbi of England until the scholarly Dr. Raphall became their Rabbi. Other Ashkenazic

Congregations did likewise. The first attempt to establish a chief Rabbinate in New York was not made until the period of the Russian Polish influx, in the last quarter of the century.

Jewish religious education for children was provided for by only a few Congregations. Some of the larger Congregations attempted educational programs which offered not only religious but also secular instruction. The Public School system was not yet sufficiently developed to command the confidence of the people. In the more affluent families secular instruction was provided either in private schools or in Congregational weekday schools. Admission was open, upon the payment of tuition fees, to the children of the community as a whole, regardless of Congregational affiliations. One of the best known institutions of its kind was the B'nai Jeshurun Educational Institute established in 1852 by Congregation B'nai Jeshurun, as a separate building adjoining the Synagogue. The success of these institutions, however, was short-lived. With the improvement and spread of the public school system, they declined and soon disappeared.

For the purposes of religious instruction, city-wide chains of religious schools were organized in many communities. The first attempt at religious school instruction on a communal scale was launched in Philadelphia with the organization in 1838 of the Hebrew Sunday School Association, by Miss Rebecca Gratz, after whom the character of Rebecca in Sir Walter Scott's "Ivanhoe" was modeled, daughter of Michael Gratz, a German Jew who became an eminent merchant. Similar movements followed in other cities, both for Sunday and weekday religious instruction. The first institution for higher Jewish learning in America was Maimonides College, founded by Rev. Isaac Leeser in Philadelphia in 1867.

Many occasions presented themselves for co-operation among the various Congregations. The dedication of new Synagogues, in the establishment of which Congregations often assisted one another, the problem of Sabbath observance and of "Kashruth," the maintenance of Hebrew Free Schools and the philanthropic needs of the community, as well as occasional appeals from Palestine, found the Congregations usually willing to consult and to co-operate.

It was during this period also that there was formed a body to protect Jewish rights for American Jewry as a whole, as well as to defend the rights of Jewry abroad. It was formed in New York in 1859 under the name of the "Board of Delegates of American Israelites." It was the first national organization prepared to speak and to act for American Israel as a whole, and so recognized by the American Government. From the time of its inception up to the time that it was finally merged in the Union of American Hebrew Congregations in 1878, the Board of Delegates of American Israelites rendered important services to the Jewish cause. Its leading spirits were for the most part, Jews of German descent.

The discussion of the relation of German Jewry to the Synagogue cannot be disposed of without dwelling on the Reform movement.

It is not unlikely that some kind of movement for the reform of the Synagogue ritual would have taken place of its own accord and quite independently of influences emanating from Germany. It is doubtful, however, if an indigenous movement for Reform would have taken the same course or developed the same characteristics as marked the Reform movement under the influence of German Rabbis.

That some kind of Synagogue reform would have developed here without the benefit of outside stimulation, is evidenced by the fact that the first stirrings in that direction in this country took place in a Sephardic Congregation, Congregation Beth Elohim of Charleston, and under the leadership of a Sephardic Jew, Isaac Harby, who in 1924 organized in Charleston, the Reformed Society of Israelites. He and his followers presented to the Congregational authorities demands for the improvement of the liturgy. They were rejected. Thereupon, the Society formed its own Congregation on Conservative Reform principles. Its membership consisted of Sephardic Jews. In 1840, however, the old Congregation under the guidance of Rev. Gustav Posnanski, a German Jew, finally introduced an organ into its Service and adopted a prayer ritual modified after the German Reform model. It was, therefore, the German influence which did finally affect, even if it did not originally cause the first movement for Synagogue reform in this country.

The German Reform movement, propagated in this country by German Rabbis who came to minister to American Congregations, had a profoundly disturbing effect upon the currents of Congregational life and Synagogue ritual in America. Many new Congregations were organized on Reform principles to start with. In New York, the first Congregation organized as a Reform Congregation, was Emanu-El. Many other Congregations previously Orthodox, modified their mode of worship, usually after bitter controversies and at the cost of secessions, sometimes involving litigation in the civil courts. More than once it fell to a Gentile judge to pass on matters of Jewish ritual and theology.

It was a time of great religious controversy in American life. Jewish pulpits and Jewish periodicals resounded with theological debates. On the side of Reform, the outstanding figures in that controversy were David Einhorn, who held pulpits in Baltimore, Philadelphia and New York, and Isaac M. Wise, who held pulpits in Albany and Cincinnati, edited "The American Israelite," and was chiefly instrumental as the organizing genius of the Reform movement in America, having organized the Union of American Hebrew Congregations, the Hebrew Union College and the Central Conference of American Rabbis. The chief protaganists on the side of Orthodoxy were Isaac Leeser, of German birth, who held positions in the Sephardic Congregations of Richmond and Philadelphia, edited "The Occident," and was the prime mover in the organization of the Board of Delegates of American Israelites, the American Jewish Publication Society and Maimonides College, Morris J. Raphall, noted orator and scholar who held the pulpit of Congregation B'nai Jeshurun in New York, and Samuel M. Isaacs, editor of "The Jewish Messenger," who had served Congregation B'nai Jeshurun for a time and subsequently became the Rabbi of Congregation Shaaray Tefila, an offspring of B'nai Jeshurun.

The third quarter of the century was the most heated period of the controversy. As a reaction against the extremists of the Reform movement a "Conservative" trend developed in which Marcus Jastrow, Rabbi of Congregation Rodeph Sholom in Philadelphia and Henry S. Jacobs, Rabbi of Congregation B'nai Jeshurun in New York, were among the leaders. The organization of the Jewish Theological Seminary of America owed much of its strength to this reaction against extreme and doctrinaire Reform. Most important in stemming the tide of Reform was the influx of East European Jewry which, during the last quarter of the nineteenth century, changed the whole complexion of Jewish life in America.

The story of the East European immigration to the United States, its adjustment to the American environment, its significant contributions to the Synagogue in the strengthening of Orthodoxy, to Yiddish literature, Hebrew culure and Talmudic scholarship, to the Zionist movement and to the American Labor movement, and its permanent effects upon the American Jewish scene, is another chapter. It may be said, however, that the settlement of German Jews in this country prepared the ground for the East European immigration, in the form of a well-organized community life, alive with religious, social and philanthropic activity, just as in the earlier period the Spanish and Portuguese Jews had prepared the ground for the newcomers from Germany. The German Jews found here a Jewish community, dignified and influential, which helped the refugees from the Old World to feel that Jews had a place in the New World. It was a community which by virtue of its conduct, its allegiance to the Synagogue, and its contribution to civic and political life, out of all proportion to its meager numbers, made the name of the Jew respected wherever the Sephardic Jews settled.

Thus each group which settled here has provided the fabric upon which the next group could weave its own design. The debt which American Israel today owes to German Jewry, is one which even our children's children will have to acknowledge. Jewish life in this country today, with all that has intervened, since the German immigration abated and the East European tide came in, is still in many of its aspects under the influence of institutions which the German Jews have created in this country, and of personalities whom German Jewry in America has produced.

The history of the Jews of New York contains a curious sequence of events which might well be taken as symbolic of the whole sequence of American Jewish life. Just as in 1825, Harmon Hendricks, a Sephardic Jew, then Parnass of the Spanish and Portuguese Congregation Shearith Israel, expedited by his financial assistance the establishment of the Synagogue of Congregation B'nai Jeshurun, so, years later, Sampson Simson, a Jew of German descent, under the influence of John I. Hart who had been the first Parnass of Congregation B'nai Jeshurun, provided the major portion of funds for the purchase of the first Synagogue for Russian Jews in America, known as "Beth Hamidrash."

And now, in the cycle of Jewish destiny, American Jews of East European origin or ancestry are extending the arm of support and the hand of fellowship to the twentieth century refugees from Nazi Germany.

Only in time will it be seen what special contribution this latest element will make to the life of American Israel and to the character of the American Jewish community. If precedents mean anything, there is reason to believe that American Jewry and American Judaism will emerge stronger and more vital as a result of its latest acquisitions.

In the meantime, one fact at least can be observed both as prognosis and as retrospect. The immigrants of today are finding a Jewish community not nearly as stratified into separate social and cultural layers as was the community of previous generations. Snobbishness dies hard, but it cannot thrive when some of the "best" Spanish and Portuguese families have been infiltrated by German Jewish stock while the latter have intermarried with East European stock.

It will take a long time before all the components of American Israel will become fused into an endemic type of Jew, but it is an eventuality which in the long range cannot be successfully resisted.

How Modern Are Modern
Bible Scholars?

An introductory chapter of a projected volume on "Medieval and Modern Commentators on the Book of Job."

How Modern Are Modern Bible Scholars?

B
IBLE EXEGESIS, THE art and science of Bible interpretation, is
virtually as old as the Book itself. Every verse, every word,
every letter of Scripture has been the subject of searching study
not only for the past twenty-two hundred years since the Bible
Canon was established but long before while the books were
still an oral tradition. Such painstaking devotion to the Word
was to have been expected of a people to whom the Book of the
Torah was the staff of life even before its land was invaded and
its political statehood destroyed.

The Torah was more than literature. It was also and more-
so, law. As the developing life of the Jewish people brought
inevitable changes in the laws governing its life, the words of
the Torah were invoked by the process of interpretation as the
ultimate sanction of the "Halakah" (legal code). It is a process
familiar to all students of law. The Constitution of the United
States is similarly invoked as the sanction for the growing legislation which keeps pace with developing American life.

At the same time the words of the Torah served as the basis
and springboard for the artistic, imaginative side of the folk
psychology, stimulating folk tale, fancy, and legend, the "Agga-
dah" portion of the Jewish tradition, which though not as practical as the "Halakah," was of vital importance to the survival
of the Jewish people.

When the Roman armies reduced Judaea and its Jews at first
to vassalage and subsequently to dispossession and dispersion,

the study of the Book became more than ever before the desperately needed outlet not only for the academically and juridically minded but also for the politically, historically, nationalistically and romantically minded. Legalism, mysticism, moralism, nationalism, Messianism, in addition to the academic quest for "peshat," the plain meaning of the text, all found expression and satisfaction in the study and interpretation of the Bible. The Talmud and the Midrash are the two main repositories of these expressions.

Bible exegesis has never been to the Jew merely an intellectual exercise. It was of the very essence of Jewish life. The process continued, through the centuries, absorbing the best influences of the environmental cultures. When Arabic culture made its impact upon Jewish scholars in the period beginning with the tenth century, its influence upon Bible exegesis reflected itself in a concern with the science of grammar and philology. Saadia Gaon was the first great Jewish scholar to reflect the Arabic influence. When Jewish philosophers fell under the influence of Greek philosophers, the new contact was also registered in Bible exegesis. Philo and Maimonides are the foremost examples of that influence.

The highest point of Bible exegesis was reached in the eleventh and twelfth centuries with Rashi, Abraham Ibn Ezra, and the Kimhis. Rashi was the exegete "par excellence."

In view of the historical background, it would be expected that Bible exegesis, at least as far as the Hebrew Scriptures are concerned, would remain a peculiarly Jewish art and science. Paradoxical as it may seem, it is nevertheless a fact that in modern times the lead has been taken by Christian scholars. While there have been noteworthy Jewish Bible exegetes such as Luzzato, Malbim, Ehrlich and Kahana, the outstanding scholars in the field for the past three hundred years from Schultens and Rosenmüller to Delitzsch and Dillman in Germany, Driver in England, and Toy in this country, have not been Jews.

What has brought about this situation? The reasons given

are twofold. Undoubtedly the Protestant Reformation has had much to do with it, focusing attention upon the Bible rather than upon the Church. It is also assumed that Jews, generally speaking, were psychologically less qualified than others to approach their Book, the word of God, objectively and critically, since Bible interpretation for the Jewish people had always meant more than an academic approach to the text. Higher Criticism therefore did not become a Jewish vocation.

The modern Higher Critics, particularly the German school, have been hailed for their scientific approach and thoroughgoing scholarship. Their equipment includes comparative philology, a wide knowledge of Semitic languages in addition to Hebrew, and familiarity with modern archaeological explorations in Bible lands which have thrown new light upon the religious and cultural institutions of the peoples who have dwelt in the Bible lands. These are tools which give the modern school an obvious advantage over the schools of the medieval Jewish commentators.

A careful comparison, however, would reveal that the advantage is far from being preponderantly on the side of the moderns. Their lack of reverence for the Bible text often proves to be their exegetical undoing. Straining for bold effects, they are often reckless in the alteration and transposition of words, sentences, paragraphs and chapters. Texts are reconstructed beyond recognition. That which should be employed, if at all, as a last resort, is eagerly proposed as a first resort. Zöckler, Buddhe and Duhm of the German school, or Cheyne, an American scholar, might have used a little reverence and self-restraint to exegetical advantage.

Many of the modern scholars lack a first hand acquaintance with and a sense of indebtedness to the great labors of the medieval Jewish commentators. Quotations from Jewish sources are often taken over bodily from older Christian scholars such as Schultens and Rosenmüller who did have first-hand knowledge of the Jewish sources. Perhaps if more of the moderns delved into the original Jewish sources they might gain both in scholarship and in modesty.

That the modern school of Bible exegesis owes a debt to the medieval Jewish commentators can be validated by a comparative study of any of the books of the Hebrew Scriptures. The Book of Job, which presents a formidable challenge to the powers of exegesis, may serve as a case study. The Jewish sources which have been used as the basis for the comparative study are Saadia, Rashi, Abraham ibn Ezra, Gersonides, Joseph, Moses and David Kimhi, and a number of less known scholars. Among the moderns on the Book of Job, those which have been studied are Ewald, Delitzch, Dillman, Davidson, Zöckler, Buddhe and Duhm.

As is to be expected, many of the Jewish interpretations are followed by the moderns. Some of these are acknowledged. In Dillman's work on Job, which is probably the best of the modern commentaries on that book, eighty quotations from the ancient Jewish commentaries are cited. Forty of these have been generally adopted and followed by other modern commentators. In these instances, the influence of the Jewish sources is specifically referred to. Many times that number, however, must be the instances of unconscious or of deliberately unacknowledged influence.

It would require more than the theory of coincidence to explain the hundreds of cases in the Book of Job, of interpretations offered by modern scholars which are found in the Jewish commentaries. The words "berir halamut" in Chapter VI verse 6, may serve as an illustration. Hitzig, Hengstenberg, Zöckler, Davidson, and others explain it as follows: "Halamut" is to be understood according to the Talmudic term "halmonah", which means "yolk". "Rir halamut" would be therefore the slime of the yolk, hence the white of an egg. This is identically the explanation offered by Ibn Ezra and Moses Kimhi. The likelihood is that Hitzig and the other commentators were not themselves conversant with the Talmudic sources, but followed the comments of their predecessors Rosenmüller and Schutens who had first-hand knowledge of the commentaries of Ibn Ezra and the Kimhis.

Chapter XXXIX verse 24 offers another illustration. The text describes a steed ready to enter the battle array. He digs his hoofs into the ground, exults in his strength, and is eager to clash with armor. The phrase under discussion is "v'lo ya-amin ki kol shofar." Some moderns translate the phrase as, "he does not stand still when he hears the sound of the trumpet." They give to the root "oman" a secondary meaning of "to be steady." Other scholars such as Henstenberg and Davidson, give an interpretation, followed by the King James Bible, which is to be found in Rashi, Ibn Ezra and David Kimhi. According to it, the word "ya-amin" is given its normal meaning "believe." So impatient is the steed for the signal of battle, that when it is sounded, he can scarcely believe it, as if it were too good to be true. This interpretation of the text is more vivid and fits into the context more aptly than the other. It is doubtful if a mere accidental coincidence would explain the identical interpretations offered by the modern exegetes and the medieval Jewish scholars.

The transmission line is not difficult to trace. The Reformation stirred many a Christian scholar to study not only the Bible in Hebrew but also the medieval Jewish commentaries, as soon as they became accessible. Their scholarly researches and findings, they in turn transmitted in Latin to their disciples. Thus the King James version of the translation of the Bible into English embodied much of the Jewish tradition of Bible exegesis and, in turn, it exercised a great influence upon succeeding generations of scholars.

It is not unlikely that another transmission line existed, not through the written word as much as through the spoken word. Jewish interpretations of special aptness and ingenuity may have found wide circulation by word of mouth, from one scholar to another as happens with the folk songs, folk tales and other oral traditions.

In evaluating the relative merits of the two schools, it must be admitted that the modern commentators are superior with regard to those passages where a knowledge of history and geography are called for or allusions to ancient mythology and ancient concepts of Nature and astronomy, are referred to. The Book of Job abounds in references to constellations, plant and animal life, and mythological concepts of antiquity. According to this cosmology, the earth is encircled by an ocean upon which is marked out the circle of the celestial hemisphere, along which the sun and stars run their course. The regions of the stars and of light lies inside the circle and the region of darkness begins outside of it. That would explain Chapter XXVI verse 10, "A circle has he drawn upon the face of the waters, up to the boundary between light and darkness." Such references can be understood better today when new material from uncovered ancient cultures has been brought to light. Thus many a cosmological allusion in the Book of Job is clarified.

Where, however, the understanding of the Hebrew language itself is at issue, the moderns, in spite of their knowledge of cognate languages, do not show any superiority over the Jewish scholars, many of whom were conversant with Arabic, and some of whom were among the founders of the science of Hebrew grammar. They had the advantage also that to them Hebrew was a living tongue, while to the modern scholar, it is, at best, an academic tongue.

The knowledge of post-Biblical Hebrew, the language of the Mishnah and the Talmud, possessed by the Jewish commentators, was of considerable help to them in identifying some of the expressions in the Book of Job which occur nowhere else in the Bible. Chapter XI, verse 20, may be cited as an illustration. "The eyes of the wicked shall fail, every refuge vanishes from them, and their hope is the breathing out of the soul." This is the rendition of the moderns. The concluding phrase is the difficult one, "Mapah nefesh," "the breathing out of the soul," is interpreted as referring to death as the only hope of the wicked. The Jewish commentators, however, translate "mapah nefesh" as "disappointment," so that the phrase reads, "their hope is a disappointment." This is the meaning of the expressions "mapah nefesh" and "pahe nefesh" occurring in the Mishna and Talmud. (See Tractate Rosh Hashanah, Chapter II, Mishna 6.) It is an idiomatic phrase to express grief, disappointment or despair. Only those who are familiar with Talmudic Hebrew would be likely to know it.

It should also be said for the Jewish exegetes that they were more open-minded and less pedantic than most of the moderns, frequently recognizing the possibility of more than one interpretation. Time and again Rashi or Ibn Ezra quotes impartially as on a basis of parity with their own comments, interpretations, suggested by others. If modesty is the trait of the modern scientific approach to problems of research, the Jewish commentators of eight hundred years ago possessed this modern trait to a remarkable degree. Where the text is difficult they are frank to acknowledge the difficulty, instead of trying to get around it. The pointing out of the difficulty, even if it cannot be solved, is itself a contribution to the ultimate solution. That too is a modern scientific approach, in which the medieval Jewish scholar excelled.

Modern exegetes resort too readily to the device of textual emendation. Many texts are amended beyond recognition. Among the commentators on the Book of Job, Hitzig, Buddhe and Duhm are among the most flagrant offenders. Some of the attempts are no doubt justified and helpful, but for the most part, they can be dispensed with. The emendations of individual scholars, except when they are based on ancient versions, rarely obtain general acceptance. It is too easy a way out of a difficulty. Not infrequently the author finds it necessary to retract his own emendations in the second edition of his work.

To use as a first aid a device which is justified only as a last resort, is to shirk the task of exegesis.

The Jewish scholars too had a sense for textual emendation and often hinted at it as a last resort, but reverence for the text restrained them from actually suggesting it. Modern exegesis would gain in soundness if it were recognized more generally that the text of the Bible is not like the proofsheet of a newspaper, to be edited and corrected with an easy going blue pencil.

Bible interpretation is therefore a uniquely Jewish vocation, in its origin and development. The earliest portions of the Midrash contain already a number of exegetical remarks, some of them far-fetched, others of scientific value. Of greater importance for the development of Bible exegesis is the Targum. It was really more than a translation of the Bible into Aramaic. It contains a number of interpretations, some of which have come down into the English Authorized Version.

Perhaps the greatest merit of the Jewish commentators consists in their keen sense of "peshat," the natural, plain meaning of the text and context.

Scientific exegesis must be concentrated on the intrinsic meaning of the text. When the interpretation is strongly colored by philosophical or mystical bias, its scientific value is weakened. Among the Jewish commentators on the Book of Job, Nahmanides and Gersonides suffer from philosophical bias, while Zerahyah ben Shealtiel incurs the mystical bias. Among moderns, the Christological prejudice spoils many an otherwise scientific approach. "Legt man nicht aus so legt man unter," is the German saying which is still a much needed caution in the field of Bible exegesis.

Saadia, the great Gaon of the tenth century, was a pioneer in the scientific exegesis of the Bible, because he was the first to emphasize the use of reason in arriving at the meaning of the text and also because he urged close attention to grammar and philology. His pioneer efforts were subsequently carried to fuller development by the school of Jewish grammarians and philologists, Menahem, Dunash, Hayyuj, Abulwalid, and Abraham ibn Ezra, in Spain, and by Rashi and the Kimhi family in France.

To the extent that scientific exegesis requires the understanding of grammar and comparative philology, familiarity with the local setting in terms of historical, geographical, natural, cosmological, mythological allusions, modern Biblical scholarship represents an inevitable advance. Philological and archaeological tools which are available to them were not available to the scholars of a thousand or eight hundred years ago. To the extent, however, that open-minded inquiry, common sense, feeling for the language, understanding of its grammar, and respect for the text, are the criteria of scientific exegesis, the Jewish commentators of eight hundred and a thousand years ago are still masters in their field. Indeed, in some important respects, as has been indicated, they were more modern than the moderns.

The debt which the modern Bible scholars owe to the medieval Jewish scholars is one which cannot be too much emphasized or too often acknowledged.

One supreme qualification the Jewish commentators possessed which is perhaps the core of the matter,—sympathy as the key to understanding. There is more than sentiment in the remark of the sainted Solomon Schechter, that "our grandmothers and grandfathers who read the Psalms and had a good cry over them understood them better than all the professors." The insight of the Jewish exegetes into the text, the sheer intuition with which they resolved many a textual difficulty, has no parallel among the modern school. It grew out of the special unparalleled relationship between the people and its Book.

Our Good Earth

Substance of addresses as President of the Jewish National Fund of America, delivered at the World Conference of the Jewish National Fund, Lucerne, Switzerland, August 13, 1935, and at the American Conference of the Jewish National Fund at Detroit, October 10, 1937, in celebration of its thirty-fifth anniversary.

Our Good Earth

WE ARE A people in whose psychology "Zechuth Aboth," the Merit of the Fathers, plays an important part. It has never been with us a worship of the past, a dead ancestor worship, but rather a vivid awareness of our past, a psychological orientation which by helping us understand our beginnings has helped us understand our goals. Invoking the memories of our beginnings as a people, we weave the thread of continuity across the centuries, and each generation thus identifies itself with the line of Jewish destiny. "Zechuth Aboth" has had a functional value in the life of the Jewish people.

As we meet at the terminal point of the thirty-five years which have spanned the history of the Jewish National Fund, Keren Kayemeth LeIsrael, what can we do more fittingly than dedicate our first thought to the "Aboth," the founding fathers of the Keren Kayemeth who have proclaimed its purpose and fashioned its pattern? By this act of retrospection, we too can benefit, strengthening our own sense of continuity with our forebears and clarifying for ourselves the direction and value of our effort.

The first name in our record is that of Professor Hermann Schapira.

It often happens that an idea germinates anonymously for a time, and then attaches itself to someone who adopts it, nurtures it and brings it boldly into the field of organized discussion. That is what Hermann Schapira did for the idea of Keren Kayemeth which had been germinating in a number of minds before the Lithuanian student, Rabbi, factory worker, merchant, wanderer in quest of Western culture, and finally Professor of Mathematics at the University of Heidelberg when Heidelberg was still a university, became its foster father. He will also be remembered for having been the first to foster the idea of a Hebrew University in Jerusalem.

Hermann Schapira belonged to the original company of "Hovevei Zion," who may be properly regarded as the vanguard of political Zionism before the days of Herzl. It was in 1883 that Hermann Schapira first made public reference to the idea of a Jewish National Fund. In 1884, in a telegram to the historic conference of the "Hovevei Zion" in Kattowitz, he advocated the establishment of such a fund. The idea remained, however, in the realm of ideas, for the Zionist movement as an organized world movement, was still in its elementary stage. The first Zionist Congress held at Basle in 1897, in which Professor Schapira played an important part as one of those who drew up the Basle program, gave him the opportunity to bring forward to an organized forum of world Jewry the idea of a Jewish National Fund. In introducing his proposal, he said:

"Let us suppose that our forefathers had placed any sum of money, however small, in trust for the benefit of future generations; we should now be able to acquire immense tracts of land. And what our ancestors failed to do, that it is incumbent upon us to do for ourselves and for those who shall come after us."

Then he went on to outline his project in detail. The following items of his outline are still of interest to us:

"1. Money is to be collected from the Jews of the whole world, insofar as the laws of the lands in which they live permit it, from rich and poor alike, as regular and periodic contributions toward the establishment of a General Fund.

"2. Two-thirds of this Fund are to be used as a Land

Fund, and may be expended only for the purpose of acquiring land for the Jews, while the remaining third is to be applied for the preservation and cultivation of the land, as well as for other Jewish public purposes that are of equal importance with these.

"3. The land thus acquired is never to pass out of the control of the Fund, and it shall not be permitted to sell it to individual Jews, but only to lease it, for a period not to exceed forty-nine years, and that, too, in accordance with the statutes and by-laws specially drawn up for the purpose."

The proposal was warmly applauded and the resolution was adopted by the delegates. No action was taken, as the Congress was preoccupied with the formulation of a Zionist program and the drawing up of a constitution for the Zionist Organization.

Little more than a year later, Professor Schapira died. For a time his proposals remained unrealized, due to legal difficulties in connection with the establishment of a legal body in Palestine with the right to own land. Thanks to the influence and persistence of Theodore Herzl there was finally adopted at the fifth Zionist Congress, in 1901, a resolution calling for the establishment of the "Keren Kayemeth LeIsrael." The legal difficulties were left to the lawyers to solve.

Thus, Hermann Schapira and Theodore Herzl fathered and launched the Keren Kayemeth LeIsrael as a functioning institution under the aegis of the World Zionist movement.

The first president of the newly organized institution was Johann Kremenetsky. Then there followed Dr. Max Bodenheimer and Nehemiah de Lieme, and, in 1921, Menahem Ussishkin. Under Ussishkin's powerful leadership, and aided by the general rise in Zionist sentiment and support, it grew unprecedentedly. Whereas in the early years the income of the Jewish National Fund had averaged fifty thousand dollars per annum, and its land holdings as late as 1920 amounted to no more than twenty thousand dunams, the income since that time has grown consistently, reaching a figure of more than two million dollars for the past year, and the land holdings of the Jewish National Fund today approximate four hundred thousand dunams. In the thirty-five years of its existence, the Jewish people has given to the Jewish National Fund a free-will offering of twenty-four million dollars.

Hermann Schapira, Theodore Herzl and their colleagues have built with wisdom and with faith. Thanks to the "Zechuth Aboth," we can celebrate this great milestone. All honor to the founding fathers!

The retrospect and the orientation are not complete without some consideration of the name, "Jewish National Fund, Keren Kayemeth LeIsrael."

The name "Jewish National Fund" is not a translation of the Hebrew name "Keren Kayemeth LeIsrael." Each of the two names represents a special emphasis, but both together are the necessary ingredients of the one identity. In the Hebrew name, the emphasis is on "Kayemeth," permanence. It was conceived as a project not for an age but for the ages. No institution in the "Galuth" was deemed worthy of such a title. Only in Eretz Israel could there be a "Keren Kayemeth." In the English name, the emphasis is on the word "National." The Fund was intended to be a fund of the people, by the people and for the people. Through it, the poorest Jew was to feel that he has a stake in Eretz Israel; and the land acquired by means of this Fund was to remain the inalienable property of the whole Jewish people. These are not homiletic interpretations but actual purposes which were in the minds of founders and which have played an important part in making the Jewish National Fund— Keren Kayemeth LeIsrael, the most popular Jewish fund in the world.

If, as its twin names indicate, this fund has sentimental values which have made it universally popular, it must also be recalled that the Keren Kayemeth has been invested from the beginning with practical values and that it has come to possess even greater practical values than the founders at first contemplated. In a sense they built better than they knew, but not better than they deserved.

The land fund was meant to bring the Jew back to the soil, thus curing the economic and psychological dislocations which had been visited upon him by centuries of landless existence. It was meant to give practical embodiment to the Mosaic ideals of social justice, counteracting the economic evils which so often attach themselves to the private ownership and exploitation of land. These purposes have been served, so that we have in Palestine upon Jewish National Fund land today a Jewish peasantry of 50,000 souls, and nearly as many on privately-owned land, the largest percentage of Jewish population to be found in agriculture anywhere in the world.

The principle that the land to be acquired by the Jewish National Fund was to be neither sold nor mortgaged and was to remain the inalienable property of the Jewish people was not only in keeping with the Mosaic law which provides for the reversion of the land to the original owners in the Jubilee year, but was also in accord with modern theories for avoiding abuses arising out of the private ownership of land. The settler on the land is assured that he and his family shall enjoy the fruit of their labor. The Jewish National Fund grants him a hereditary lease and building right on the land for forty-nine years, at a low rental (1% or 2% of the value on agricultural land, 3% on suburban land, 4% on urban land). At the end of ten or fifteen years or more, depending on whether it is urban or agricultural land, the rental is increased to correspond with the rise in land values so that any increment due to public investment may accrue to the community. Should a tenant for any reason desire to transfer his lease, he can do so only with the consent of the Jewish National Fund, which reserves the right to re-assign, thus preventing speculation. The rental is usually fixed for a certain portion of the lease, so as to protect the tenant from a sudden rise in rent, but at the same time the Jewish National Fund is protected by a provision for the revaluation and revision of rental every ten or fifteen years. A further provision is made with regard to the size of the property, enabling the Jewish National Fund to sub-divide any plot so as to accommodate new settlers if owing to intensive cultivation or any other factor, a smaller plot would be adequate for the lessee. He is reimbursed for any improvements effected by him at his own cost. Apart from certain minor points the aforegoing represents also the contract made between the Jewish National Fund and the numerous co-operative groups settled on its land. Its main features provide that a settler should have no more than sufficient land for himself and his family to cultivate thus obviating the necessity for hired labor.

Other purposes not envisaged by the founders have also been served. The principle of the national ownership of the land has proved to be of great economic advantage nationally. Only a large land-purchasing institution, in a position to spread its investments over large areas, can afford the expensive amelioration which most of Palestine land requires. Only an institution like the Keren Kayemeth can enable settlers without capital to survive the difficult early years of land cultivation. The principle of Jewish labor inherent in the Keren Kayemeth lease, creates maximum employment opportunities for Jews. Only on nationally owned land can close settlement be planned, so as to increase the absorptive capacity to a maximum.

To these economic advantages may be added political advantages of no mean import.

It is a grim reality in the affairs of nations as in the affairs of individuals, that possession is nine points of the law. The Jew, least of all, can expect consideration on the basis of the justice of his claims. Even in Palestine, it is sadly true that whatever the Jewish people has not bought and paid for dearly it does not today possess. Not even waste lands are given him by the government, though they have been given to Arabs, who sold much of them at high prices to the Jews as in the case of the Beisan lands. It is significant that the Royal Commission of

1936, having admitted the justice of the Jewish claim to the whole of Palestine west of the Jordan and having adorned the admission with elaborate documentation in support of the rightness of the Jewish claim, proceeded to propose a Jewish State limited to a small fraction of the area to which the Jewish people has a just claim, according to the previous admission. That meager area was, in the main, the area which Jews had bought, colonized and developed.

The conclusion to be drawn from the experience of the last twenty years is clear, that for Palestinian land to come into Jewish possession and to remain in Jewish possession, is a national political necessity of the first order. It is the Jewish National Fund which performs that necessary task.

The Jewish National Fund stands as the mother-fund of the Zionist movement, which has set the precedent for building the foundations of the Jewish Homeland with national funds. Private capital is of course indispensable for the economy of the Yishub. It has been poured into Palestine in much larger amounts than national funds. Yet it is the national funds, the Keren Kayemeth land fund and the Keren Hayesod colonization fund which have given our effort its unique character. It is the national funds which have brought to Palestine the man-power and the woman-power which is most depression-proof, most bomb-proof, most terror-proof and most pessimism-proof. No matter what happens, they stay.

"What's in a name?", may be a good rhetorical question. The fact is, however, that a name is often the key to the personality of an idea, an institution or a movement. The Jew has intuitively felt great respect for names and has given names with great care. The name of "Keren Kayemeth LeIsrael—Jewish National Fund," with all its implications, sentimental, economic and political, is the key to what it has been in effect, the most popular Jewish institution, the most idealistic and at the same time the most practically useful Jewish institution, the most characteristic and the most character-building Jewish institution.

True to its name, may it prove to be the most enduring institution of the Jewish people.

"Eretz" is the "aleph" in the alphabet of our program.

Land in Palestine is our real estate in the most literal sense, for without a substantial land foundation our estate in Palestine is not real. The present disparity between the proportion of Jewishly owned land in relation to the total land area west of the Jordan, which is seven per cent, and the proportion of the Jewish population in relation to the total population of that area, which is thirty per cent, carries its own commentary on past performance and on future needs and opportunities.

As we look back upon the three and a half decades of the Keren Kayemeth aim to make as much as possible of our "good earth" ours, we have reason to re-endorse the aim not only out of a sense of Jewish self-interest but also in the broadest human sense, bearing in mind the welfare of the Arab as well.

The alleged plight of the "landless Arab," on the face of it, makes an appeal to liberal-minded men and women who would not like to see native populations anywhere dispossessed and disinherited from the soil.

What are the facts of the situation in Palestine? The bare fact that after all these years of Jewish colonization in Palestine less than seven per cent of the land is in Jewish hands, speaks for itself. The Palestine Government has been challenged again and again in recent years to produce statistical evidence to substantiate its claims regarding the "landless Arabs." It has failed to do so.

The last available figures which go back to 1930, show that the total number of Arabs who have been removed from their land as a result of land transfers to Jews, was 688, less than one-tenth of one per cent of the total Arab population, in Palestine, and that 447 of these were resettled on other land, thus continuing their agricultural mode of life. The situation since 1930 is even less of an argument, because Jewish purchasers have gone out of their way to make provisions not only for tenants but even for squatters, so that they may be properly resettled. A responsibility which the government should bear is borne by the Jewish purchaser.

It is well to note that most of the land purchased by Jews is purchased from large absentee landlords who hold their Arab tenants in feudal subjection and in penury afflicting both the land and its people. In Jewish hands the same land flourishes and supports hundreds where formerly sparse scores could barely eke out a miserable existence. In other instances, small farmers sell a portion of their land, at prices far beyond its intrinsic worth which they can secure only from Jewish buyers, and thereupon use the proceeds from the sale of a part of their land, in order to improve the remainder, thus increasing their income and improving their livelihood.

Two-thirds of Palestine consisted of land which Arabs could not cultivate. At the same time Jews have, in the Valley of Jezreel and in other places, demonstrated by draining swamps and irrigating parched soil, that what the Arab could not cultivate they can cultivate and make fertile and flourishing, adding new acres to the soil of Palestine.

In the past twenty years, since the Balfour Declaration, the Arab population of Palestine, which has increased one hundred percent, has increased not only through birthrate but through the influx of Arabs from impoverished surrounding countries to those parts of Palestine particularly where Jews were settling, working and thriving.

Only the malarial mosquito would gain by the restriction of the right of Jews to purchase land.

As American Jews and Zionists, called together for the American observance of the thirty-fifth anniversary of the Jewish National Fund, it is for us to ask ourselves in this hour of retrospect, "What has been American Israel's contribution to that which the Keren Kayemeth has achieved?"

The Jewish National Fund Bureau in America, as a separate Bureau, came into existence in 1910. For a decade before that time, the work was carried on by the Federation of American Zionists and the Order Knights of Zion as a part of their general Zionist activity.

It did not take long for the Bureau to justify its existence. The total sum collected by the Keren Kayemeth in this country during these years amounts to six million dollars representing twenty-five per cent of the total sum raised throughout the world. With grateful remembrance the presidents of the Jewish National Fund of America who have headed its administrations from the beginning up to the present time are recalled, —David H. Lieberman, Senior Abel, Bernard A. Rosenblatt, Dr. Joseph Krimsky, Joseph Barondess, Emanuel Neumann, and Nelson Ruttenberg.

If the present administration has made any special contribution to the progress of the work in the United States, it has been perhaps in two main directions, that of raising the standard of the gifts and that of broadening the scope of the givers. For years, the Jewish National Fund has been looked upon as a small-coin collection. Its blue and white box, with all its beautiful sentiment, connoted, in the minds of many, a small-coin enterprise. Recognizing the injustice of identifying a great cause and a great need with small coin collections, we have been making the effort for the past several years to hew out a new and larger path for the Keren Kayemeth. The response of the American Jews has justified our policy.

The other direction in which progress has been made is the penetration of non-Zionist groups. In recent years, as Palestine has become the best available salvation for large numbers of the Jewish people in lands of oppression, and as it became accordingly the concern not only of the Zionist movement but of the whole Jewish people, the time was felt to be opportune to challenge and enlist the support of non-Zionist groups. Our efforts in this direction, too, have been rewarded, notably by the response of B'nai B'rith, the Labor ranks, and the Orthodox religious groups.

For Zionists themselves, the Keren Kayemeth, apart from its material contributions to "Geulath Ha-aretz," has served a useful purpose in providing them with an opportunity to exercise themselves in a day to day routine of practical accomplishment for the benefit of Eretz Israel. The varied and incessant calendar of the Keren Kayemeth activity is an endless spur. Men and women in their districts and chapters, young people in their clubs, children in their Hebrew schools, and family units in their homes, on occasions of joy and sorrow, punctuating the four seasons of the year, have been exposed to persistent reminders of Eretz Israel, via the inexhaustible gamut of Keren Kayemeth appeals.

On the whole, the record of the Keren Kayemeth in this country during these thirty-five years has been as strong or as weak as the American Zionist movement itself. After all, the Keren Kayemeth is primarily an arm of the Zionist movement, the only arm in the Zionist movement in the world which has remained uninterruptedly under exclusive Zionist control. For a time it seemed that the organization of the colonization fund, the Keren Hayesod, might divert some strength from the Keren Kayemeth. Actually, however, American Jews, for the most part, have fulfilled neither their duty to the Keren Hayesod nor to the Keren Kayemeth. To our shame, it must be confessed that our per capita contributions for Palestine through both funds have been lower than those of some of the impoverished Jewries of Europe. If we American Jews, blessed as we have been during these thirty-five years, with resources unparalleled by any other Jewish community in the world, had given what we should have given for land and colonization at a time when land could have been bought and colonized for a fraction of its present price, there would be a different story to tell today.

Nevertheless, with due contrition for our sins of neglect, we American Jews can still point, however modestly, to a measure of accomplishment. We can point to thousands of dunams which, because of our contributions, have been redeemed in every strategic area now owned by the Jewish people in Palestine.

We can point to scores of agricultural settlements which would not have been established, had it not been for our material aid. That is our share in the "Zechuth" of having provided the enduring foundation.

These results achieved by us of American Israel, satisfactory or unsatisfactory as these may be, would not have been possible, had it not been for the co-operation of all Zionist parties and groups. The Keren Kayemeth has been and continues to be their common denominator. Box collections and Golden Book inscriptions, Flag and Flower Day actions, bequests and living legacies, propaganda and money-raising, in clubs, in Synagogues, in workers' circles, in the home and on the street, on Purim and Tisha B'Ab, Chamisha Assar and Lag B'Omer, the army of Keren Kayemeth volunteers marches on,—an army recruited from the Zionist Organization of America, Hadassah, Poale Zion, Pioneer Women, Young Poale Zion, Habonim, Mizrachi, Mizrachi Women, Hapoel Hamizrachi, Hashomer Hatzair, Junior Hadassah, Avukah, Masada, Young Judaea. Each one feels that he belongs to the Keren Kayemeth and the Keren Kayemeth belongs to him.

To those who are skeptical on the subject of Jewish unity, it should be encouraging to see how in the Keren Kayemeth all the groups and parties meet and work together. Perhaps these exercises may prove to have been valuable rehearsals for that unity which we trust will one day command us in the service of a Jewish State.

The historical retrospect validates anew the fundamental character of the Keren Kayemeth. It is characteristic of a permanent ideal that at different times it assumes different aspects. The ideal is constant. Its value and meaning may change in accord with the needs of changing situations. Thus "Geulath Ha-aretz," the ideal of converting Palestine into Eretz Israel, has aspects as versatile and manifold as the changing kaleidoscope of world events and the manifold needs, problems and projects of our people. For every conjuncture of circumstances, the Jewish National Fund has demonstrated a special value.

There were times when the social idealism inherent in the concept of nationally owned land used to be stressed. There were other times when the emphasis had to be placed upon the return of Jews to a wholesome agricultural mode of living and upon agriculture as the indispensable balance in national economy. There are times when the land acquisition must serve as the token of our protest against the government's restrictions. To the government's order, "Diminish the place of thine abode," we reply with dunams of land, "Expand the place of thine abode, lengthen thy cords and strengthen thy stakes." In recent years land has come to mean footholds for refugees. There are times when land means primarily food, self-subsistence in the face of a situation which makes access to food supplies difficult or impossible. A new tractate, "Zeraim," may have to be written upon the soil of present-day Palestine. "Keren Kayemeth" has and will continue to have any and all of these meanings, values and functions.

Ussishkin once said: "When the Jewish people has redeemed the land of Israel, the land of Israel will redeem the Jewish people." That has been and remains the twin formula of our movement,—"Geulath Ha-aretz U-tehiyath Ha-am," the redemption of the land and renascence of the people.

Keren Kayemeth LeIsrael belongs to that category of which the Rabbis said: "We enjoy the fruits thereof for the present," "veha-keren kayemeth la-olam habbah," "and the foundation endures for the future." (Mishnah Peah Chap. I.)

Of necessity, this has been an historical review. Perhaps a little history once in thirty-five years can be endured. A nation, however, in the process of achieving nationhood or regaining nationhood, cannot afford to pause too long for retrospects. The past must serve as a spring-board for the future.

And now with three and a half decades behind us, we face the next step. What is the next step?

The next step is to do today that which can and needs be done, and by doing it as well and as quickly as possible, to strengthen our hold upon tomorrow.

How else shall we be worthy of kinship with the Yishub itself, which is defending every position with moral and physical heroism? The least that we can do to prove worthy of them, is to say with our funds that which they are ready to say with their lives, "We shall go forward!"

Modern Courts of Arbitration
and the Jewish
Historical Background

An introductory chapter of a projected
volume on the same subject. A summary
of the article is scheduled to appear in the
Universal Jewish Encyclopedia.

The material was used in part in an
address delivered as President of the Jewish Conciliation Court of America, at its
annual meeting, New York, January 11,
1938.

Modern Courts of Arbitration and the Jewish Historical Background

THE HISTORY OF law is the history of the progress of man."
In a telescopic review of the history of law by E. F. Hannan
("Docket," Vol. IV, No. 12), the theme is thus summarized at
the conclusion. While the summary is valid as a long range
observation, there are intermediate stages at which gaps appear
between law and progress. The problem of developing laws and
legal institutions to keep pace with change and progress in the
social order is a standing challenge.

One of the difficult problems is that of judicial procedure. The
need of reforming our judicial procedure has been long recognized by the legal profession as well as by the public.

Mr. Elihu Root, in a foreword to a book, "Justice and the
Poor", (R. H. Smith, Carnegie Foundation for the Advancement of Teaching, New York, 1919), expressed the opinion that
the obligation rests upon the government to secure justice for
those who, because they are poor and weak, find it difficult to
protect their rights.

Professor I. Maurice Wormser, recognized legal authority, in
an article in "The Nation" of February 24, 1934, takes our
judicial machinery severely to task. According to him, business
men are becoming increasingly dissatisfied with the juridical
process, its delays, the technicalities which result frequently in
a denial of justice. He deplores the fact that too often the law
itself, instead of being a part of life, is apart from life. Because

of this situation, he states, disrespect for the law and the courts is growing steadily.

Similarly critical views have been expressed by other eminent leaders in the legal profession. The Supreme Court of the United States, now vested with the power to modify judicial procedure in the lower courts, may be looked to for the introduction of necessary reforms, but it will probably be a slow process.

As the layman looks at our present legal machinery, he is impressed by the existing disparity between our social institutions which have progressed and our legal juridical institutions which have remained relatively stationary. Professor Wormser is skeptical regarding the possibility of changes by the legal fraternity, due to their professional engrossments with procedural precedents and technicalities. He says that it is a job for laymen.

In England, a lay approach to the problem has been tried with a fair degree of success. The effort should be made here too. A commission composed of business leaders, labor leaders, and sociologists, together with legal authorities, given the necessary authorization to conduct a survey and to present recommendations, might make an important contribution toward simplifying, modernizing, and humanizing our courts of justice.

Partly because of the imperfections of the juridical process and partly because of the feeling that problems in specialized fields can be best understood and adjudicated by those who are most familiar with them, arbitration tribunals in the fields of business and industry, have become increasingly popular. The attitude of bar associations toward these has been friendly. In many States, the law has recognized that arbitration agreements in writing are valid and are enforceable. New York, in 1920, was the first state to enforce an arbitration agreement. In 1925 a Federal Arbitration Act of restricted scope was adopted. The American Arbitration Association, in the commercial field, and the Arbitration Board of the Amalgamated Clothing Workers of America, comprised of appointees of employers and workers, in the industrial field, are among the outstanding institutions of their kind.

The inadequacies of our judicial procedures impose hardships particularly upon the poor. Although theoretically the poor have the same rights before the law as the rich, actually the poor man is at a disadvantage because he cannot afford the expense of engaging legal talent for the protection of his rights comparable to the talent which the rich can afford. Cost of litigation frequently bars the poor man from the court or else delays the processes of justice, to his serious detriment.

For the poor of the community, whose problems requiring adjudication do not fall into the category of labor disputes, there is hardly any recourse outside the courts to institutions of established character and reputation. "Radio courts" broadcasting private lives are calculated more for the purposes of entertainment than of social service. Yet it is a social service necessity to have such agencies under unquestionably communally-minded sponsorship where individuals and families assured of sympathetic private hearing may come for adjudication, conciliation, advice and guidance. In every large community, there should be such clinics in human relations. The administration of justice needs to be made more congenial in its method to the people for whom it is intended.

In relation to the Jewish community the matter is of more than ordinary significance. In addition to the factors which make arbitration and conciliation tribunals useful and even necessary for all the elements of a community there are special circumstances affecting Jewish life which give additional justification and value to Jewish tribunals.

Immigrant groups naturally require a certain lapse of time for adjustment to their new environment. This is true with regard to their use of courts of justice. In many European countries, justice is not as simple and democratic as it is in America. Paradoxical as it may seem, immigrants from such countries are terrified at the thought of seeking justice in courts. This applies to Jews no less than to Christians. Ideologically and spiritually many an immigrant is more American than some of the native-born. Because of his different background, he is in a special position to appreciate American democracy. Due to the strangeness of the language, manners and customs, however, the process of Americanization takes time. When the immigrant is beset by a problem requiring adjudication and conciliation, he can feel most at ease in the presence of members of his own group, preferring to discuss his problem in the Yiddish language with which he is most familiar and in which he can explain all the intimate nuances of the situation before those who are able to understand him.

Disputes sometimes arise in Jewish fraternal or religious organizations, or among Jewish families, which involve religious laws and customs of an indigenous character such as would not be thoroughly understood by a civil tribunal. Among many Jews who feel keenly the sense of Jewish honor, there is a sensitiveness with regard to airing Jewish disputes under civil auspices. Over and above these considerations, there is in many Jewish quarters a feeling of confidence in the unique quality of Jewish justice, validated by a two-thousand-year-old history of Jewish jurisprudence not encumbered to the same extent as general jurisprudence by accumulated formalities and rigid institutionalism.

A brief retrospect upon the way in which Jewish courts have functioned in lands where Jews dwelt as minorities would throw light upon the functional value of the institution not only for its intrinsic merits but also for its relation to the problem of Jewish self-preservation.

The history of juridical autonomy among Jews in the Diaspora is at least as old as the loss of Judaea. The Talmud, the source-book of Jewish laws, was developed, for the most part, outside of Palestine. Subsequent codifications of Jewish law, based upon it, governed Jewish life throughout the Diaspora. In many lands Jewish communities were granted a large measure of juridical autonomy. Under the rule of the Romans neither Jews nor Christians willingly resorted to pagan courts. The rule implied in the question of Paul of Tarsus to the Corinthians, "Dare any of you, having a matter against another go to law before the unjust, and not before the saints?" (I Corinthians, Chapter VI) was simply an application to the Christian community of the rule generally applied by contemporary Jews. The corruption of the Roman courts amply justified this attitude.

Jews who lived under Christian rule in the Middle Ages resorted to their own courts, not only because they had greater confidence in the well-developed system of Jewish jurisprudence stemming from the Talmud, but also beecause the secular courts and their procedures were based upon the assumption that the litigants were Christians. Moreover, the question of Jewish survival depended upon the maintenance of those Jewish institutions which helped toward continuing the identity of the Jews as a group. Among these the Jewish court was one of the most important. Jewish Rabbinic authority therefore condemned Jews who brought their disputes to non-Jewish courts. On the other hand, the Christian attitude segregated the Jews not only in communal matters but also in juridical matters. (H. J. Zimmels, "Beitraege zur Geschichte der Juden in Deutschland in Dreizehnten Jahrhundert," Vienna, 1926.)

Thus for inner and for outward reasons Jewish courts have played an important part in Jewish life throughout the centuries.

Even before the fall of Judaea, Jewish communities living outside of Palestine, particularly the communities in Egypt, enjoyed a large measure of self-government. (Erwin R. Goodenough, "The Jurisprudence of the Jewish Courts in Egypt," New Haven, 1929.) Josephus (Antiquities, xiv, 7) describing the organization of the large Jewish community in Alexandria, mentions that the head of the community, in addition to his other administrative functions, "held court, and took care that the laws and regulations of the community were carried out."

Generally the Roman Emperors were favorable to Jewish internal autonomy. Jewish courts were recognized and protected by the Roman Law. To the Jews themselves these rights meant more than political rights because they were concerned for the maintenance of their communal identity. The imperial protection continued even after the fall of Jerusalem, until the unsuccessful revolt against Rome brought a hostile reaction. After Hadrian, Jewish autonomy continued without interference. By the end of the fourth century Jewish courts were declared as having the status of courts of arbitration.

When Babylonia became the center of Jewish life, following the destruction of the Jewish State, Jewish communities under Persian rule were given wide legislative, judicial and administrative powers. The Exilarch, who was the Jewish representative before the Persian government, exercised judicial authority over his people.

Under Islam the toleration of Jewish autonomy exceeded even the Roman and Persian precedents. The Exilarchate and Gaonate became a powerful central institution having all the characteristics of a state within a state. (Salo W. Baron, "A Social and Religious History of the Jews," New York, 1937, vol. I, p. 376.) Obedience to the decisions of the courts was ensured by compulsions, ranging as far as excommunication.

The status of the Jewish community as a corporate body continued throughout the Middle Ages. By virtue of the authority entrusted to it by the state to collect taxes from the Jews on behalf of the state, the Jewish community exercised great influence upon its individual members. Outside the "ghetto," the individual Jew had only limited rights. His legal status was not that of a citizen. Inside the "ghetto," however, he was regarded as a full-fledged member who could rightfully claim equality before the Jewish law. Under such circumstances Jewish courts necessarily flourished. It was the most vital point of Jewish self-government.

The charter granted by King John to the Jews of England in

1199, may be cited as an illustration of similar dispensations received by some of the Jewish communities in Europe during the Middle Ages.

"Know that we have granted and by our present charter confirmed to our Jews in England that the breaches of right which shall occur among them, except such as pertain to our crown and service, as touching homicide, mayhem, deliberate assault, housebreaking, rape, larceny, arson and treasure trove, be examined and amended among themselves according to their law, so that they may administer their own justice among themselves." (Rigg, "Select Pleas," London, 1902, p. 2.)

In Jewish communities in Germany during the Middle Ages a system of higher and lower courts functioned. The usual number of judges was three, consisting of laymen in addition to Rabbis. Jewish tradition looked with disfavor upon counselors. Every Jew was expected to be able to present his own case. The authority of the Jewish community was firmly held. (David Shohet, "The Jewish Court in the Middle Ages," New York, 1931.)

In Italy the authority of Jewish communities weakened, as the hostility of the non-Jewish population increased, coming to a head with the Inquisition. A pronouncement of the Synod which met in Ferrara in 1554 declared that if a Jewish litigant had taken the case before a Gentile court, he could not afterward bring it back to the Jewish court without the consent of the other litigant. The leniency of the provision is significant, pointing to the fact that the Jewish communities of Italy were not strong enough to prohibit appeal to Gentile courts.

The Talmudic law prohibited the use of Gentile courts in any case (Gittin 84b). The first Synod at Troyes (1150), however, permitted it if mutually agreed upon in the presence of signed witnesses. The relaxation of the Talmudic prohibition may have been due to the greater feeling of tolerance on the part of the French Rabbis and also in recognition of the spirit of the time which was full of accusations against the Jews. (Louis Finkelstein, "Jewish Self-Government in the Middle Ages," New York, 1924, p. 156.) The Synod of 1603 at Frankfurt prohibited appeals to secular courts. It was an attempt to regain authority for the Synods which had been weakened since the persecutions attendant upon the Black Death.

A series of ordinances adopted by the Synod held at Valladolid (Castile) in 1432 attempted to regulate among other things, the jurisdiction and powers of the courts in the Jewish communities of Castile, as well as the manner of their election and the rules of procedure. Written briefs were provided for. A writ obtained from the Rabbi of the Court, in order to be valid, had to be presented to the opposing party or placed in front of his door in the presence of an adult member of his family within fifty days. Bodily apprehension was permissible only by written order of the judge, signed by himself and witnesses and stating the reason, except in a case of defamation or a capital crime. The preamble states that the assembly was convened at the invitation of the King. (Finkelstein, pp. 348-375.)

The forms of punishment employed by the Jewish courts in the Middle Ages included public reprimand, fines, flagellation, deprivation of certain rights, imprisonment, expulsion and varying degrees of excommunication. Where the right of capital punishment was granted to the Jewish courts by the State, as in Spain up to 1379, it was never exercised without the sanction of the government, and the execution of the sentence was left to non-Jewish bailiffs. (Israel Abrahams, "Jewish Life in the Middle Ages," p. 51.) Congregations had their own prisons or separate room in the official prisons set aside for Jewish offenders.

A curious item which throws light on the efficiency of the Jewish courts in Eastern Europe is a complaint by a Russian commissioned to investigate the conditions of the peasants in White Russia, that many Christian peasants turned to Jewish courts for the litigation of their cases. (Baron, Vol. II, p. 97.)

The highest point of Jewish autonomy was reached in Poland in the period 1650 to 1750. As far back as the fourteenth century, a charter of rights and privileges was granted to the Jews by King Baleslov of Kalish. It was later ratified and extended to all the provinces of Poland by Casimir the Great. The charter was renewed and amplified by Casimir IV (1453), guaranteeing the Jews liberty of residence and commerce, protection against attacks, and communal and judicial authority. It also freed them from the jurisdiction of the ecclesiastical law courts. Successive rulers believing that their fiscal interests would be most efficiently realized by concentrating power in the hands of Kahals, entrusted to them powers which grew to assume the proportions of self-government.

The Magna Charta of Jewish autonomy in Poland was the charter of Sigismund Augustus issued August 13, 1551. (S. Dubnow, "History of the Jews in Russia and Poland," Phila., 1916, Vol. I, p. 106.) Jews were granted the right to elect their own Rabbis and judges who were authorized to administer all matters of a religious and ritual nature, perform marriages and grant divorces, execute transfers of property and exercise other acts of civil character. They were authorized to settle disputes between Jews in accordance with the "Mosaic Law," and were given the right to impose punishments for refusal to submit to their authority. Local officials were instructed to assist the Jewish courts in carrying out the orders. If a Jew disregarded the sentence of the Jewish court his case could be brought before the King who could sentence him to death and confiscate his property.

A firmly knit organization of communal self-government accordingly developed among Polish Jewry.

From the middle of the sixteenth to the eighteenth century, the central body of Jewish autonomy in Poland was the Council of the Four Lands,—Great Poland (Posen), Little Poland (Cracow), Polish or Red Russia, that is, Podolia and Galicia (Lemberg), and Volhynia (Ostzog and Kremenetz). The Council was vested with wide powers, extending even to criminal cases. Locally, affairs were administered by the Kahal, the administrative body of the community. Two kinds of courts functioned, the lower communal court, and the higher court of appeal in litigation between two Kahals or between private individuals and a Kahal.

The Kahal had the power to apportion and collect taxes, punish individual Jews for unscrupulous acts which were likely to arouse Christians against Jews, give permission to own real estate, or lend money to a Gentile, try cases and inflict punishment, and mediate between Jews and the Polish government.

With the partitioning of Poland, the antagonism of the Church and the unfavorable attitude of the Russian government toward Jewish autonomy, the Council disappeared and the authority of the Kahal declined. By a Russian decree of 1844, the Kahals were abolished and their affairs were transferred to the city administrations except in Riga and some towns in Courland where they continued to exist until about 1893.

Although bereft of legal standing, Jewish communal authority continued to wield an influence upon Jewish life. The "Din-Torah," arbitration before a Rabbi or group of Rabbis, was the method of adjudication which public opinion sanctioned.

With the period of the Emancipation in Western Europe a new epoch in Jewish history began.

In the petition of the Jews of Paris to the National Convention on August 26, 1789, the petitioners though not without dissent by some communities, expressed their readiness in demanding equal rights for the Jews to surrender their privileges of juridical autonomy. The Emancipation Decree issued by the National Convention on September 28, 1791, conceded the request as formulated. The price of equality was the surrender of communal autonomy. Not only in France but wherever its influence reached, the Emancipation, while it improved the condition of Jews economically, socially and politically, created a problem for Jewish religious and cultural life. In Austria, Hungary and Galicia, the Edict of Toleration issued by Joseph II in 1872 brought about the dissolution of the Jewish courts and the weakening of Jewish communal organizations. His views on the Jewish question were conveyed in the following words addressed in 1788, "Nothing useful will derive from this carefully prepared charter of Jewish rights (Juden Patent) if the Jewish laws and customs . . . are recognized or in any way combined with the now operative government decrees."

When by the decree of Napoleon, an assembly of Jewish notables was called for July 15, 1806, a number of questions were put to them bearing on the character of the Jewish law. In their answers they stated that the Jews do not form a nation, that they abide by the Talmudic principle that "the law of the government is the law," and that they have abolished the Rabbinical court and have limited the functions of the Rabbinate to ecclesiastical matters. The call of the Grand Sanhedrin followed. It approved the answers given by the Assembly of notables. These answers became principles, having legal force for the Jews throughout the French empire.

By a special decree of the Emperor a system of Consistories was instituted, comprising both Rabbinical and lay elements. Every community of two thousand Jews was to form a Consistory. Paris was to be the seat of the central Consistory which was to have authority over the provincial organizations. The consistories were charged with seeing to it that no one evade military service, and that the principles incorporated in the resolutions adopted by the Sanhedrin be carried out. The status of Jewish communities throughout the lands of Europe which fell under Napoleon's sway were regulated by this decree.

Jewish efforts at maintaining and resorting to their own juridical institutions did not cease. Wherever large Jewish communities existed, Jewish courts continued in some form, though they lacked the compulsive sanction of the state. Wherever there was a recognized Rabbinical authority there was a "Beth-Din," a legal tribunal whose authority and binding power were recognized as a matter of Jewish self-discipline. The effort was all the more remarkable because it was purely voluntary. It was a crucial part of the Jewish struggle for survival. (S. Assaf "Botei ha-Din veSidreihen," Jerusalem, 1922.)

In the Russian areas, where Emancipation had not penetrated, Jewish autonomy declined because of the weakened conditions of Jewish communities following the partition of Poland, and because of local strife which further undermined the authority of the Kahals. Nevertheless it continued to enjoy a measure of recognition at the hands of the government. The jurisdiction of the Jewish court was limited to strictly religious matters, but included marriage and divorce. Well organized and extensive courts functioned there. Rabbinical commissions authorized to deal with these questions were officially recognized by the Russian Ministry of Interior. Jewish members of the community voluntarily brought to these courts for adjudication other matters involving controversies between individuals as well as congregations, family problems, money matters, and disputes between employers and employees.

With the advent of the Russian Revolution in 1917 and the establishment of the Communist regime, Jewish juridical autonomy in the traditional sense ceased though the principle of autonomy for separate cultural groups reflects itself in the official recognition of the Yiddish language and Jewish personnel in courts located in areas where Jews are the preponderant population.

The minority rights granted to Jews in Central and East European countries following the World War stimulated the extension of an additional measure of cultural and juridical autonomy to a number of Jewish communities. Unfortunately, the guarantees, for the most part, were short-lived.

The best functioning Jewish tribunal in Western Europe is the London Beth-Din. It is a voluntary court of arbitration and conciliation under the supervision of the Chief Rabbi and supported by the United Synagogue. Though it concerns itself chiefly with ecclesiastical matters such as "Shehitah" and "Kashrut," much of its time is given to civil and domestic problems. The judges are Rabbis. Parties to the controversy sign a legally enforceable agreement to accept the decision of the judges.

Among Jewish communities in Egypt and Turkey, before the World War, the old principle, to a great extent, continued, that religious law governs matters of personal status. Rabbinical courts have jurisdiction also in such matters as marriage and divorce as well as inheritance.

The highest point to which Jewish juridical autonomy has attained in modern times is in Palestine.

There are two types of courts functioning in Palestine, Rabbinical and secular. The secular courts of arbitration consist of Jewish Peace Tribunals (Mishpat Shalom Ibri), Labor Federation Courts, and Courts of Communal Committees in small rural settlements.

The history of these institutions throws light upon their character.

Under the Turkish government, Jews along with other national minorities enjoyed a great measure of freedom in their internal affairs. Every large community had its Chief Rabbi who was recognized by the government. There was no central authority. The first effort to organize Palestine Jewry as a whole was made in 1903 but it was unsuccessful. Another effort was made in 1909 seeking to establish a Palestinian Council. Weak and short-lived as it was, it had the distinction of having constituted a special committee of nine to function as a Jewish Board of Arbitration, thus creating the first organized Jewish court for the entire Jewish community of modern Palestine.

In 1918, after Palestine came under British control, Dr. Weizmann attempted to bring about a unified center of ecclesiastical authority, but was unsuccessful.

A Rabbinical Assembly summoned by a special committee acting on behalf of the High Commissioner, Sir Herbert Samuel, was convened in 1921. It elected two Chief Rabbis, Rabbi Kook for the Ashkenazic community and Rabbi Meir for the Sephardic community. They with six other Rabbis were to constitute the

Rabbinical Council. Subsequently, it was agreed, that three lay-men should be added as counselors to the Rabbinical Council. They were not to interfere in matters of law but were to be consulted "about matters of order and procedure and to assist the Rabbis with such information as is outside the domain of the laws of the Torah." The powers of the Rabbinical Council were expressly stated in the announcement by the government. "The government of Palestine will recognize the Council and any Beth Din sanctioned by it as the sole authorities in matters of Jewish Law. It will execute through the Civil Court judgments given by the Beth Din of the Council in first instance or in an appeal, as well as the judgments given by any Beth Din in Palestine sanctioned by the Council." (M. Burstein, "Self-Government of the Jews in Palestine since 1900," Tel Aviv, 1934, p. 176-177.) This was a wide definition of powers.

The powers of the Rabbinical courts as defined by article 53 of the Order in Council of 1922 are:

a) Exclusive jurisdiction in matters of marriage and divorce, alimony and confirmation of wills of members of their community, other than foreigners as defined in article 59;

b) Jurisdiction in any other matter of personal status of such persons, where all the parties to the action consent to their jurisdiction;

c) Exclusive jurisdiction over any case as to the constitution or internal administration of a Wakf or religious endowment constituted before the Rabbinical Courts according to Jewish Law. (Ibid., p. 177.)

The following powers were granted to the Rabbinical courts by the order in Council of 1922 and restated in the "Regulations."

The Rabbinical Council and officers are given the right to

a) draw wills according to Jewish law;

b) exercise control over such Jewish charitable endowments, the majority of whose managers or trustees invite or accept such control, and may for this purpose appoint committees which shall consist partly or wholly of persons who are not Rabbis;

c) Subject to the provisions of the following Regulations, appoint officials required for the execution of their duties, and discharge such officials;

d) Arbitrate, in accordance with the provisions of the Arbitration ordinance in force from time to time in any dispute arising between Jews where a written submission of the parties has been obtained. (Ibid., p. 180.)

The history of the Jewish secular courts likewise stems from the time when Palestine was under Turkish regime. Finding the Rabbinical courts too conservative and the Turkish courts too corrupt to their liking, many elements in the communities turned to the idea of establishing their own courts.

In 1909 the Palestinian Council selected a committee of nine to serve as a Board of Arbitration. The opposition of the Rabbinical Courts hampered the early attempts of these Peace Tribunals. Eventually, however, they succeeded in gaining public confidence. Their decisions are upheld by the Civil Courts, in accordance with the arbitration ordinances promulgated by the government. The provision in the "Regulations" issued by High Commissioner Lord Plumer on December 30, 1927, gives the right to each local community to appoint "a tribunal of arbitration to which members of the community may resort in accordance with the provisions of the arbitration ordinance in force from time to time, for the settlement of civil disputes." (Ibid., p. 253.)

Local tribunals handle civil cases involving sums not exceeding £100. There are three District or Circuit tribunals which handle cases involving sums over £100 and also serve as Court of Appeals from the lower tribunals. There is a Supreme Tribunal which is the highest Court of Appeal.

The judges are legally trained or laymen elected by committees of the local communities. They are guided in their decisions by considerations of Jewish law, equity, laws of the country, and former precedents of the Tribunals. From time to time the members of the tribunals meet to work out rules of procedure.

The constitution of the Labor Federation of Palestine (Histadruth) prescribes the establishment of courts for its members. It is obligatory for every member of the Histadruth to repair to these courts and to abide by their decisions. They deal with disputes affecting individual members, or organizational units, or between employers and employees, when the employer consents to bring the dispute to these courts. There are small local courts, large local courts and a Central High Court. (Paltiel Dickstein, "Takannoth of the Histadruth Courts," in ha-Mishpat, Jerusalem, 1927, p. 65.)

In small rural communities local committees still function as arbitration courts, set up by the litigants for each separate case as it arises.

It is altogether consistent that in Palestine where Jewish life is most vital and resourceful, Jewish juridical autonomy should be most in evidence.

The situation in American Jewry requires a special study. Undoubtedly the need of a medium for settling Jewish disputes internally was felt as early as the settlement of the earliest Jewish community upon this continent. The "Din-Torah" must have served as a recourse here as elsewhere and the Rabbis here as elsewhere must have exercised their traditional functions of urging the application of traditional principles of Jewish justice to specific controversies arising within the life of the Jewish community. It was a phase of human relations normal to every Jewish group.

If numbers are a determining factor, an American Jewry numbering nearly five millions today should have a substantial amount of judicial autonomy to show. The evidence, however, does not point that way. Fraternal organizations such as B'nai Brith and Brith Sholom lodges have set up similar tribunals. There is an arbitration committee attached to the Canadian-American Jewish Congress, but its activity is not extensive. In a number of communities in the United States, such as Baltimore, Cincinnati, Cleveland, Detroit, Harrisburg and St. Louis, the effort has been made under the aegis of the Community Council to establish a committee or an institution for the purpose of arbitration and concentrating Jewish disputes.

An interesting instance is the situation in Detroit. The Jewish Arbitration and Conciliation Court organized there in 1937 is a function of the Community Council which was organized two years earlier. It was established to meet a problem which involved the honor of the Jewish name in the community. A committee of fifteen members appointed by the head of the Jewish Council is charged with the supervision of the Court. The fact that it operates under the Community Council makes it difficult for the defendant to ignore the summons of the Court for fear lest his standing in the community be impaired.

These have been secular institutions. Rabbis have given cooperation and have participated in their administration, but the tribunals had no ecclesiastical authority. The "Beth Din," dealing with religious matters, functions wherever a Rabbi of recognized standing sponsors it. They are not, however, community-sponsored efforts.

The outstanding examples of Jewish courts may be expected to be found in New York, the scene of the greatest Jewish community in America. Unfortunately, the disorganized state of the Jewish community in New York reflects itself in the sporadic establishment and unorganized functioning of institutions not all of which deserve the name of "Jewish court."

The pioneer effort in New York was made in 1920 when the Jewish Court of Arbitration was organized. The best part of its sponsorship constituted the Board of the Jewish Conciliation Court of America, chartered in 1930.

Administered by a Board of Directors comprising leaders in the Rabbinate, the professions and business, the Jewish Conciliation Court of America has developed techniques of procedure which have served as precedents for the establishment of similar institutions in other cities.

A wide variety of cases comes before this tribunal. Aged

parents claiming support at the hands of their children, husbands and wives whose relations are strained because of economic or temperamental difficulties, members of fraternal and benevolent societies claiming "sick benefits," "death benefits," or cemetery privileges, disputes arising in Congregations, religious schools and other types of Jewish organizations, sometimes involving breach of contract between an employee of the organization, claims of marriage brokers for fees which had been promised, are a few of the gamut of cases which occupy the attention of the Jewish Conciliation Court of America.

Some of these cases would seem strange, bizarre or incomprehensible to a Gentile judge. The litigants would feel ill at ease in his presence. Their problems would not be likely to receive the sympathetic, intimate understanding which may be expected of a Jewish tribunal. Some disputes are of such nature as would not furnish legal grounds to be brought before civil courts, yet require some form of solution. Often the problems call for conciliation more than adjudication. Frequently the expression of appreciation is heard from one or the other of the litigants that such disputes can be tried under Jewish auspices. The honor of the Jewish name is served thereby. It is a secular court without any claims to ecclesiastical authority.

There are three judges at every session, a Rabbi, a lawyer, and a layman. Thus every case receives consideration from several angles. The judges are selected from a list comprising personalities of recognized standing in the community. The procedure is simple, direct, informal and free from technicalities. Litigants are not permitted to have lawyers argue their cases. They present their cases themselves, in English or in Yiddish, whichever is most convenient. There is no fee or charge of any kind. The effort is directed toward conciliation even more than adjudication. Many cases are settled amicably "in camera" before they reach an official hearing.

Attached to this court is a Social Service worker who carries the influence of the court into homes where it may be needed, brings to bear the help of other social agencies wherever required, and offers material assistance wherever a situation requires temporary relief which cannot be obtained otherwise. The cost of administration including the Social Service department is met by voluntary contributions.

The authority of the court has been tested and sustained in the Supreme Court of the State of New York, on the basis of the Arbitration Law adopted in 1920. Sometimes, judges of the civil courts refer cases to this tribunal which in their opinion involve a peculiarly Jewish situation. A case referred by a United States District Court involved the reorganization of a Hebrew School under section 77-B of the Federal Bankruptcy Laws. Another case, referred by the Supreme Court of the State of New York, involved an important Synagogue dispute and the rights of members to own and dispose of Synagogue pews.

The value of an institution of this type would be increased manifold if it were to function as an official arm of the Jewish community organization. A Jewish medium for adjudication and conciliation is indispensable to every well-organized Jewish community, supplementing educational, philanthropic, religious and other institutions for the strengthening of the Jewish consciousness, inculcation of Jewish content, cultivation of Jewish spiritual quality and defense of Jewish rights.

If every substantial Jewish community in America would have its tribunal for the adjudication and conciliation of Jewish disputes, it would be a step forward in enhancing not only the dignity of Jewish life but also the cause of unencumbered justice for a large segment of the general community.

IN MEMORIAM

ADOLPH S. OCHS—PHILANTHROPIST
> Delivered at a Memorial Meeting at the
> Jacob H. Schiff Center, New York, May
> 12, 1935.

WILLIAM M. LEWIS—COMMUNAL LEADER
> Delivered at a Memorial Meeting, Phila-
> delphia, February 13, 1940.

JOSEF ROSENBLATT—CANTOR
> Delivered at a Memorial Meeting, at Car-
> negie Hall, New York, June 27, 1933.

DAVID FINKELGREEN—ARTIST
> Delivered at the Funeral Service, Phila-
> delphia, August 12, 1931.
>
> The titles of Finkelgreen's best-known
> paintings, "Wohin," "Twilight," "At the
> Wailing Wall" and "The Scholar," were
> woven into the theme of the eulogy.

SAMUEL LEVINGER—SOLDIER OF DEMOCRACY
> Delivered at a Memorial Meeting, New
> York, February 27, 1938.

In selecting the memorial tributes which follow, consideration was given to the inclusion of personalities which comprised a representative cross-section of various fields of endeavor, and were at the same time relevant to the main themes of the volume as a whole.

Adolph S. Ochs–Philanthropist

THIS MEMORIAL SERVICE is not so much to render a tribute to the dead, as it is to draw a lesson for the living. The spirit of Adolph Ochs might feel uneasy in this atmosphere of eulogy, were it not that the main purpose of this hour is not so much to glorify him as to ennoble ourselves, to ennoble ourselves by fixing our minds upon the traits, principles and ideals, which he personified. By such memorials we make the dead to live again. They offer us an object lesson in the art of living.

The theme of Adolph Ochs as citizen and publisher has been dealt with by Dr. Finley, himself a distinguished citizen and publicist. Let it be my province to speak as a Jew touching the Jewish values in the career we are here memorializing.

Ten years ago, when my Congregation celebrated its one hundredth anniversary, Mr. Ochs participated in our Jubilee. His presence with us on that historic occasion was more than a casual courtesy. The words he uttered that evening deserve to be remembered. Unfortunately, it is impossible to recapture for this hour the ring of sincerity in his voice and the grace and majesty of his person, as he appeared that night. It is possible, fortunately, to recall the substance of his address. What better content can we give to this memorial hour than his own living words?

"Think what has come to the Jews within a hundred years, particularly in America. 1825! Six months after that date, in 1826, my father was born in the town of Furth, in Bavaria. In the city of Furth, as many of you know, there was one of the most intellectual Jewish communities.

"My father, or any Jew living in the city of Furth, was not permitted to stay over night in Nuremburg, five miles away from there, because he was a Jew. At the age of nineteen he was in Frankfurt on the Main. He wanted to get married, and he made an application for a license to marry, but it was denied because the quota of Jews that were permitted to be married at that time was filled and he would have to wait. After this experience, he wisely concluded that Germany was no country for him, and he came to this country in 1844, and here he partook and had the advantage of a freedom and liberty that was accorded to the man of any race.

"Now we are here in this great country, participating in everything on terms of equality, with no restrictions as to our best efforts and purposes. It is to this great country, the United States, that we are indebted. We ought to be very thankful, on this Thanksgiving night, for the rights and privileges that we enjoy. We should sound Hosannahs and cry aloud, 'Sound the loud timbrels o'er Egypt's dark sea, Jehovah has triumphed and Israel is free.'

"To my mind, there is nothing that is as sweet as the memory of my Jewish home, where there was piety, reverence, love and affection in the family. When I gaze into some of the homes that I have entered here in New York, where they say they haven't any religion, my heart wrings for those children that are brought up in that kind of an atmosphere. What kind of a memory will they have of home when they grow up to manhood and womanhood?

"The religious spirit in the old Jewish home, as every one of you knows who has had that kind of a home, is the most delightful, pleasant memory of your life. This Jewish spirit should be awakened and encouraged. It should be made known to these young people that their failure to have it is the loss of what is the sweetest memory that can come to them later in life.

"Every Jew has reason to stand up, unafraid, and assert the fact that he is a Jew, that he has given to the world the Bible, the Commandments, the Prophets, the Proverbs and the Psalms. It is the heritage of civilization. It spells humanity, it spells civilization, it spells everything that makes life worth living.

"We Jews are the shuttle that is weaving the fabric of a religion of reason for the whole enlightened world. And we should continue doing so."

In these words we have the text on which the life of Adolph Ochs was the commentary. He was a Jew who never forgot the rock from which he had been hewn. The memory of his sweet Jewish home never left him. To the memory of his parents, he built a memorial shrine in the city in which his earlier career was fashioned. Others of his generation who rose to success, soon succumbed to the temptation of self-made men to worship their makers. Others removed themselves from contact with their Jewish brothers. Adolph Ochs resisted the centrifugal forces. He sought to enrich the birthright which was his heritage.

He was a Jew without pretense and without apologies. Keenly aware of the social and political disabilities from which his fellow-Jews suffered and still suffer in many parts of the world, he regarded these disqualifications not as a badge of inferiority upon the victim, but as a brand of shame upon the oppressor.

The picture he drew of Germany in his father's day is mild in comparison with the Germany of today. No Jew worthy of his name will permit his self-respect to suffer under the stress of hounding. To be a Suffering Servant, to receive bruises at the hands of a contumelious adversary, is testimony not to one's own unworthiness, but to the adversary's evil guilt and shame. Persecution may wrack Israel's body. It must never sear his soul.

Adolph Ochs was a Jew who was mindful of the Divine injunction to Israel, "Holy shall ye be." Modest gentleman, he was incapable of a "holier than thou" attitude toward his fellowmen.

Unctuousness was alien to his nature. Yet in the dichotomy between the sacred and the profane, between the pure and the unholy, he was to be found on the side of righteousness, spirituality, and ethical idealism. These were not his Sabbath code but his week-a-day routine. He was the builder of a Temple in the city of his early career as a memorial to his parents, but the noblest sanctuary he builded was his own character, in which dwelt the sanctities of life.

Let other Jews take note that worldly success at the expense of personal righteousness is not the Jewish way and that the Jew is summoned to sanctify God's Name in his week-a-day life. There are too many who arrange their life plan into water-tight compartments, one labeled "Religion," restricted to Sabbaths and devoted to piety,—the other labeled "business," for weekdays, and often devoted to piracy. The interpenetration of religion and life is a Jewish concept and a Jewish imperative.

Personal righteousness, however, is not enough in a world where social injustice is rampant and human need and suffering are widespread. Adolph Ochs was a Jew who followed the ancient precept of Rabbi Hillel. "Do not stand apart from the community." Avoiding public office and eschewing public acclaim, he sought the welfare of his brethren, Jew and Gentile alike. He was a philanthropist in the literal sense, a lover of his fellow men. The love of his fellow men was in his pulse-beat. "Love thy neighbor as thyself," was his social dynamic. His philanthropies were as broad as his human contacts. If significant causes such as Zionism were omitted from his scope, the omission was due not to a lack of feeling, but to a lack of conviction. Would that every one of us might catch something of his humanitarian passion.

Adolph Ochs was a Jew who loved America with all his heart, with all his soul and with all his might. Here he found an abundance of those opportunities which elsewhere were denied the Jew. He took this gift, wrought it into a splendid career and gave to this land which he loved, a reciprocation manifold.

America is richer for his having lived in it. Both for himself and for the Jew as such, he regarded the opportunities which this blessed land offered not as a warrant of privilege but as a charter of responsibility. May such sense of responsibility never cease to move us.

The still small voice of a man's exemplary living goes farther than stormy protestations and fiery affirmations. There is not one of us who cannot afford to take a page out of the book of life of Adolph Ochs, to let our actions speak louder than words, to preach by example more than by precept, to demonstrate by our daily conduct that our Judaism, whatever else it include, counts as its broadest exhortation the ageless prescription of the prophet Micah, which is the essence of all religions, "What doth the Lord require of Thee, O Man, but to do Justice, to love Mercy and to walk humbly with Thy God."

Judge William M. Lewis–Communal Leader

I wish i might be able to shed the official labels and nomenclatures and speak to you tonight as a fellow-Philadelphian and friend of Judge William Lewis. It was so difficult to be formal and official with him and in his presence, that at this memorial meeting in his honor it would seem that the quality of solemnity should not be strained. At the same time, it is also to be borne in mind that this meeting derives its purpose and value from the extent to which it will deal with the things that mattered most in his life.

His personal warmth and geniality were so disarming that one who did not know him well would not have felt that he was in the presence of a man of efficiency and capacity for carrying responsibilities such as are rarely matched. So easy was his manner, so unhurried his approach to people, so inclusive his scope of friendships.

Just as in the work of a great artist the technical efficiency and design are hidden beneath the flow of line and the warmth of color, so in the personality of William M. Lewis the efficiency and the workmanship which were there in abundant measure were not conspicuous because they were overlaid by the grace and colorfulness of the human texture of the man.

I served with him on innumerable occasions and innumerable committees,—from the Executive Committee of the Zionist Organization of America, where, for a time, he was the Acting President, to the large deliberative assemblies of the organization where he knew how to wield the gavel with unmatched dignity and charm, to the great conferences of the United Palestine Appeal whose peripatetic campaigner he was, a familiar, popular figure from coast to coast. He worked as hard as any of us, rendered services as manifold as any of ours, yet he never appeared harried or hurried. His geniality never capitulated to the stern pressure of duty. Therein he was unique as a man.

In searching for a text which should adequately fix our attention upon the more important aspects of Judge Lewis' life, one could not find a text more suitable than the one from the Ethics of the Fathers cited in the name of Rabban Simon Ben Gamliel, —"By virtue of three values the world exists, Truth, Justice and Peace."

Truth is a broad term. It implies the absence of false notes, of pretense and ostentation. William Lewis was without pose, or guile or ostentation. Truth implies sincerity, constancy and vitality. These qualities William Lewis possessed in high degree. The verse of Lowell describes him well.

> *"His magic was not far to seek,*
> *He was so human!. Whether strong or weak*
> *Far from his kind he neither sank nor soared,*
> *But sate an equal at every board;*
> *No beggar ever felt him condescend,*
> *No prince presume; for still himself he bare*
> *At manhood's simple level; and where'er*
> *He met a stranger, there he left a friend.*
> *His look, where'er its good fortune fell,*
> *Doubled the feast without a miracle."*

Justice was not only his vocation, but his disposition. It was not the stark, mechanical ruthless justice of mathematics, astronomy or physics. It was human justice, the kind described in the Rabbinic legend that when the Creator of the universe contemplated the principle of justice as the ruling principle for mankind, the angels pleaded that it should not be a strict, unmitigated rule of justice but it must be justice tempered with mercy, else human life would be impossible. Judge Lewis tempered his sense of justice with his human understanding and his compassion. He was a student of law, but more than that he was a student of mankind.

The word, "Peace," does not quite convey all the connotations of the Hebrew word, "Shalom," one of those idioms which cannot be translated adequately. "Shalom" means well-being of body, mind and spirit. It means wholesomeness and harmony; it means a well-integrated program of life. William Lewis was one of the fortunate company blessed by the divine gift, "Behold I give him my covenant of peace." As conciliator of differences and controversies, he brought peace between man and man, as well as between group and group. He fostered the proper integration of the Jew within his group believing that goodwill, like charity, begins at home. Hence, his deep devotion to the Brith Sholom fraternal order. He believed in a complete Jewish community life that should include not only philanthropy but education, especially at a time when the catastrophes befalling centers of Jewish culture abroad impose upon American Jewry an added obligation to keep the torch of the Torah burning here. Hence his service to the cause of Jewish education in this community.

In his philosophy of life, Zionism was the spiritual dynamic. It was the proper formula for a well-integrated Jewish personality. He understood that Zionism was the force that has driven out the "Dybbuk" from the soul of the Jew and has cured him of his inferiority complexes and "ghetto" phobias.

Carlyle once said, "Alas, how many causes there are that can plead well for themselves in the courts of Westminster, and yet in the free soul of man have no free word to utter." In the soul of William M. Lewis many causes pleaded successfully and harmoniously. It was amazing to the many who knew him that this man could have done so many things so well. He wore himself out in the service of his people because he was permitted, nay, driven to spend himself with prodigal recklessness.

Judge Lewis has been taken hence while the sun was still at the height of the day. In a measure, we are to blame, those of us who could have put our shoulders to the task but failed to do it, those of us who had talents and resources but hugged complacently our leisure, taking shelter behind the anonymity of the multitude. Because too many of us take their Jewishness vicariously, leaders become worn out prematurely.

It is too late to spare him, but it is not too late to carry on the work which was the content and the motivation of his life.

We Zionists believe that if Judge Lewis were here tonight, he would bid us go forward. He would take stock of contemporary Jewish life and of the past two decades which separate us from the last war, and he would note that while the inventory shows deficits and minus signs in other parts of the world, including even our own America where the Jewish position today is not as firm or as secure as it was a generation ago, the one place which shows a plus sign of constructive achievement and gain is Palestine. He would challenge us to continue to strengthen the Jewish National Home.

He would then turn our vision to the future, to the time when an Allied victory would be followed by the Peace Conference to discuss the fate of nations great and small, and he would arouse our hopes that at the peace table there would be discussed a sequel to the Balfour Declaration which would unequivocally establish our rights in Palestine. He would charge us to use every opportunity in the meantime to increase immigration, enlarge our land possessions and strengthen our industrial positions, so that when the time comes to present our case before the nations we may be able not to plead for charity but to insist upon justice validated by our own achievement.

You have done well to perpetuate his name in the land of his hopes and labors, by undertaking to plant the Judge William M. Lewis Memorial Park in Palestine on Jewish National Fund soil. What can more beautifully preserve his memory than these trees which you are planting. They will be the silent sentinels to keep watch that his memory shall remain ever green in the land of his fathers.

There is another Jewish national fund, an "Otzar Israel," the spiritual treasure house where are enshrined the memories of Israel's valiant sons. The memory of William M. Lewis will there abide.

Josef Rosenblatt—Cantor

THE VOICE OF one of the great Cantors in Israel has been stilled. It has been stilled at the height of its glory. Its last tones were saved for Zion.

More than once Cantor Rosenblatt told me of his longing to be in the hills of Judaea and in the streets of Jerusalem." A thousand times he must have intoned the prayer, "Bring us unto Zion, Thy city, with song." His prayer was granted. He died in the arms of Mother Zion.

I have stood upon the hills of Judaea, which echoed with the last notes of Josef Rosenblatt's majestic voice. From those hills, I gazed upon the Jordan which he visited on the day before his life ended, and upon the Dead Sea, a silver streak in the distance, where he bathed. It was a fitting close, a "Neilah" to his life.

Josef Rosenblatt embodied within himself the highest traditions of his calling. It is a calling whose precedents go back to the Paitanim of the Middle Ages, to the Levites who sang in the Temple of Jerusalem, and to King David himself, the sweet singer of Israel, whose harpstrings and heartstrings were moved by the Divine Spirit.

The Hazan (Cantor) has held a unique place in Jewish life. For centuries, the Jew, shut off from the musical development of the Western world, found in the chant of the Synagogue the nourishment for his musical cravings. Someone has said that "a people is its most natural self in its prayer and in song." In the Synagogue and in the art of the Cantor, song and prayer, "rinah" and "tefillah" were combined. In the Synagogue, which was the Jewish refuge from a bitterly hostile world, the Jew could at last be himself. The chant of the Hazan was his musical nourishment from Sabbath to Sabbath. The Cantor's merits or demerits formed the topic of conversation for the entire week. The congregants prided themselves on their appreciation of the cantorial art. An "u-mipne hato-enu" or a "tikanto shabbos" held as important a place in the musical education of that Jew, as the Bell Song from "Lakme" or the famous tenor solo from "La Juive" holds in the life of the music lover of today. Within the circumscribed life of the Jewish community in the old homesteads, the Cantor held a unique place in the affections of his people. To the names of their most beloved Cantors, the people affixed the affectionate diminutive suffix, "Dovidel, Leibele," "Nissele."

"Yosele" Rosenblatt belongs to that line of affectionate tradition.

Even today, when the Synagogue has lost much of its hold, when Jewish life is no longer circumscribed, and music lovers among our people flock instead to the opera houses and concert halls, the song of the Synagogue still finds a responsive chord. I have met young men who have drifted far away, yet in whom the chant of the Synagogue fans a dormant spark of Jewish emotion and loyalty. I have seen Jewish Bolsheviks in Russia who scoffed at religion with their mouths, slyly entering into the Synagogue to hear the ancient chants.

It is difficult to classify Cantor Rosenblatt as belonging to any one school of the Cantorial art. Though he understood and followed the dignified tradition of musicianship established by Sulzer, Naumburg and Lewandowsky, and was himself the author of scores of musical compositions, yet he also excelled in the art of improvisation, an art which depends primarily upon feeling rather than upon training. In that art, he inherited the mantle of Nissa Belzer and of Alter Bauman who was his teacher. His gift for improvising Jewish chants was rooted in deep

Jewish piety and fervent Jewish emotion. He did not have to resort to "bel canto" to stir the Jewish heart. His mere articulation of the Hebrew prayer was enough to warm the Jewish soul because in his own voice were vocalized the pulsebeats of his people.

Well versed in Hebrew law and lore, Cantor Rosenblatt understood not only the "perush ha-miloth," the meaning of the lines, but he also understood the story between the lines, the story of Jewish achievement and of Jewish martyrdom and of Jewish hope, the story of Jewish sighs and of Jewish tears and of Jewish joys. He translated that story into a language which is the universal language of our people, Hebrew tinged with melody, a language understood alike in Warsaw and New York, in Jerusalem and Buenos Ayres.

To the non-Jew as well as to the Jew in this country, he was the interpreter-in-chief of the song of the Synagogue. He interpreted that song with dignity, with piety, with incorruptible beauty. There have been Cantors whose vocal pyrotechnics have been described as "pilpul" set to music. Rosenblatt avoided the extremes. He sang with simple dignity and sincere feeling. In him the art of "rinah and tefillah," song and prayer, were exquisitely combined. The Synagogue Jew will remember him as unique in his generation. His voice could be tremulous with Jewish tears and it could also be thunderous with Jewish triumphs. His voice could cry out with Jewish pain and it could also ring forth with the song of Zion rebuilt.

Thus he sang himself into the hearts of his people.

Cantor Rosenblatt was first a noble Jew and then a noble artist. That is as it should be. Jewish tradition always demanded of the "sheliach tzibur," the emissary of the Congregation, character as well as talent. Rosenblatt graced and honored his calling because of his character, as much as because of his talent. Acclaimed by hundreds of thousands as the greatest Cantor of his generation, he never lost his genial modesty and his democratic good fellowship. While others, with a fraction of his talent assumed the poses and the idiosyncrasies of "prima donnas," he never lost his balance as a human being.

Every Jewish and humanitarian endeavor found him willing to contribute his golden voice. If one could compute the actual sums which his golden voice has helped to raise, without any compensation to himself,—for America's Liberty Bond campaign during the World War, for the relief of European Jewry, for the Palestine funds, for orphan asylums, hospitals, homes for the aged, and for the relief of his fellow Cantors in distress, the sum would run into hundreds of thousands of dollars. True to his name, Josef, he had as his guiding motto, "I seek my brethren." His golden voice was matched by his golden heart. I knew something of his personal philanthropies, of his open house to which all were welcome, of his generous hospitality, of his aid to musicians in distress, even when he himself was laboring under heavy burdens.

I knew something of his ambitions for his children, ambitions worthy of a noble Jewish father. He wanted his children to be well educated, to be good Jews and to shed honor upon the Jewish name. These things to him meant more than wealth. I knew how happy it made him to see one of his sons attain distinction in the field of Hebrew scholarship and another in the field of Jewish music.

Thus, he was first a noble Jew and then a great artist. The honor of the Jewish name was dear to him. People often protest that they are good Jews at heart, but it would take a heart specialist to discover it. Cantor Rosenblatt's Jewishness was not difficult to discern. He made sacrifices for the honor of the Jewish name, refusing to touch a hair of his beard for all the money which the operatic stage could offer. Gentile America respected him for it. They respected him as a Jew who held principle higher than purse. And the Jewish people loved him for it.

When Solomon Sulzer, the most distinguished Cantor of his day and the father of the modern Cantorate died in Vienna in

1890, Dr. Jellinek, who pronounced the eulogy, used for his closing text the verse, "He was a priest of God on High." That text may well be spoken of Josef Rosenblatt, the most distinguished Cantor of this day.

If his life has ended prematurely, let us remember that it ended at the top note, at the climax of his career as an artist, before the ravages of age could dim the luster of his tone, and at the climax of his career as a Jew, who had the privilege to end his days in the land where the oldest prayers of the Synagogue had been cradled, where the Temple had stood, and where the Levites had sung.

The Torah ordains for the Levites as follows: "At the age of fifty, his service shall cease." It was to cease before he passed the zenith of his powers. Josef Rosenblatt, having passed his fiftieth year, and still at the zenith of his powers, was by the Almighty decree summoned hence from the Service of the Synagogue.

The music of his golden voice and of his golden heart will long be recalled.

David Finkelgreen–Artist

S OONER OR LATER every mortal upon earth must experience alone and for himself the answer to the ultimate question, "Wohin—Whither." The rich man with all his worldly goods and the beggar with his bundle of rags, are equals in the face of that impenetrable mystery, "Wohin."

Now David Finkelgreen has joined that innumerable caravan.

Our hearts are heavy with grief that such a life should have been cut down like a stalwart tree in the prime of its growth. I loved him as a brother. Life seemed less sordid when he was present. With aught that was base or unworthy, he would never barter. He was as pure and as guileless as a child, trusting to the point of naïveté, and gentle to the point of self-immolation.

He was your son, your brother, your kinsman. It is not for me to touch upon these home and family ties, for they are your holy of holies into which strangers' lips must not venture. But he belonged also to a larger family. He was wedded to his art. He was a citizen of his community of Philadelphia. He felt an abiding kinship with his Jewish people.

One would hardly have suspected from his modest speech, which was free from the slightest trace of pride or conceit, that he was an artist of outstanding reputation, to whom portrait commissions were entrusted by leaders in civic and industrial affairs, and whose paintings important communal institutions were proud to have upon their walls. Young as he was, he had behind him a generation of achievement, both as student and teacher of his art. Many a young talent ripened under his tutelage in the Graphic Sketch Club of this city, which he headed for a number of years. During the World War, a foreign government paid him the homage of recognition. Yet success had no effect in destroying those qualities of sincerity and genuineness which distinguished his art even as they distinguished his character.

David Finkelgreen was above all, honest. He was the soul of honor in his personal life. He was honest in his art. How could a true artist be otherwise? One of our contemporary philosophers has said that Beauty is the apotheosis of Truth. David Finkelgreen was a lover and creator of beauty and truth. He found his materials in nature inanimate, more than that in nature animate, and most of all, in human nature. "Materiam superabit opus." With workmanship which exalted his material, he wrought upon the canvas, things of enduring beauty, and of enduring truth.

I never knew what was his religious credo. It did not matter, for it was apparent to anyone who knew him at all that he was a deeply religious soul. Goethe once said, "Art is based on a strong sentiment of Religion,—on a profound and mighty earnestness; hence it is so prone to co-operate with Religion." David Finkelgreen fulfilled that definition.

I said before that he felt a kinship with the Jewish people. It was more than a sense of kinship. He felt the Jewish "Weltschmerz" which he expressed in "Wohin." He appreciated keenly Israel's place as the People of the Book, which he expressed in "The Scholar." He saw beneath the outward uncomeliness of the hounded Jew, the imperturbable beauty and dignity of the spirit which was immune to hardship, persecution and exile. His Jewish faces are majestic. It was something of the dignity and beauty of his own spirit which he poured into his subjects.

He felt the romance of Palestine in Jewish life. The Wailing Wall held a fascination for him. Yet he sought beyond the weepers of Zion,—the builders of Zion. Therefore, he went again to Palestine to find the "Halutz" who tilled his soil, and made its deserts blossom. But he came to Palestine at a time of trouble, when the Jewish pioneer was battling in defense of his very life against wanton attacks. He saw with what Maccabean valor the new generation in Palestine, risen from "Emek Ha-bakha," the vale of tears, to the heights of self-respecting man-hood, defended its honor and its life. It was his last vision. Alas, he was not spared to put that vision upon the canvas.

The last experience thrilled him, but the sight of trouble pained and shocked his sensitive nature.

Then came the twilight, a twilight so sudden, so untimely, so unlike the "Twilight" which he had painted.

It had been my privilege to see him and to be with him many hours during his heyday, when the sun was at noon-day's height. It was my sad privilege to be with him also one hour of his twilight. It was the hour when his workshop was to be dismantled because he had not the strength any more to work. His health was shattered obviously beyond repair. There he stood in his workshop, surrounded by his paintings. His physical world had crumbled, but all around him were the creations of his spiritual life, and they were as beautiful as ever. Illness had ravaged his erstwhile splendid physique until he was a mere shell of his former self, but nothing could ravage the beauty of his artistic creations.

Years will go by. Men famed for their wealth and power will die and be forgotten, but in many a home and in many a Synagogue and communal institution, there will be men and women who will gaze upon David Finkelgreen's art, and thank him.

Samuel Levinger—Soldier of Democracy

THERE MAY BE some issues where it is difficult to make a choice, where the right and the wrong are separated by a hair's breadth. There are situations where the choice, once made, leaves one without the enthusiasm of certainty. In the Spanish struggle, however, the choice is not difficult and can be made unhesitatingly. We choose to say with the democratic forces in Spain, as Samuel Levinger chose to say with his life, "The foreign invaders shall not pass."

I do not consider myself qualified to speak of Samuel Levinger in a personal vein, because it was not my privilege to know him. One who was closer to him than any, his father, will speak. Nor am I qualified to say anything first-hand regarding the land and the people for whom he gave his life. That first-hand report you will hear from one who had the opportunity to observe the scene with his own eyes only a few weeks ago.

The limitations, however, are at the same time credentials to speak what is felt or should be felt by the public at large, who, like myself, had no personal relationship to this boy and have no first-hand knowledge of Spain or its people. It should be enough to know on what side Hitler and Mussolini are. Every instinct of decency and civilization would prompt us to support the other side.

When a youth leaves his home, his friends, his country, not for the sake of adventure, but in order to throw his life into the scale on the side of justice and democracy, in order to help a

343

people that is a total stranger to him racially, culturally, geographically, but with whom he feels the kinship of a universal ideal, as hundreds of American boys like Samuel Levinger have done, it is a manifestation which merits something deeper than applause. It merits a deep respect for the American youth which can produce such young people. It merits also a profound self-prodding and contrition by the elders, who can remain complacent in the face of happenings which stir their sons to offer their lives. It merits that we should shake ourselves out of our indifference, and that we should resolve to make such contribution as we can make, moral and material, to the cause which is bound up with universal issues.

Levinger and the American boys who went to Spain with him believed that they were going into an arena where not merely the fate of that little peninsula was being fought out, but the fate of European civilization. They believed that if the Fascist forces could be stopped in Spain, they would be less likely to pursue their aggression elsewhere, and every nation over which their shadow is now hovering would be more likely to breathe freely. We Americans can afford to stake much on the right choice.

I do not know whether Samuel Levinger deliberated on the Jewish stake in the struggle. There is reason, however, to believe that reared in a home where Jews and Judaism were a daily concern, he had occasion more than once to relate this question to his entire "Weltanschauung." Surely, for us who are gathered here as a Jewish audience, it needs only to be stated in order to be recognized that the fate of the Jew in the modern world is bound up with the fate of democracy. We have seen enough of Fascism and its workings to know that in Fascism lies our peril, and that in democracy lies our salvation.

1917 to 1937—these dates span the life-time of the Jewish youth whose memory we honor tonight. In the year of his birth, millions of American youth were called to a war to save democracy, and tens of thousands of them died in that war. That war, it appears, did not accomplish its purpose, if the saving of democracy ever was its genuine purpose. The aftermath has been a generation of disillusionment.

Fortunately for the race, however, it possesses the gift of starting afresh, unmortgaged by the psychological encumbrances of past mistakes. The present struggle which has its spearhead in Spain is fraught with issues affecting the future of democracy.

Perhaps it was insight more than fantasy which prompted the Hebrew prophet to picture a youth at the head of the Messianic procession. It may be a psychologic law that the world must be saved by its youth, for having no past to look upon, youth can only look forward, and having no experience to daunt it, youth goes forth unafraid.

The presence of Samuel Levinger's father on this platform, prompts me to say a word of personal condolence as a colleague in the Rabbinate, and as a parent of a son nearly the age of his Samuel. I restrain myself, however, realizing that this is more than a condolence meeting. We have come here not to condole but to take heart and inspiration from a young life which has been spent in a noble cause.

In Jewish tradition, there is a phrase which expresses the noblest type of living, and the noblest type of dying. It is the phrase, "Kiddush Hashem," "the sanctification of God's Name." I believe it is not taking God's Name in vain to say that Samuel Levinger died "Al Kiddush Hashem." His memory is already a blessing, for in honoring him we also honor and espouse the ideal for which he died.